أخبار الدجال

# Reports on the Dajjāl

A TRANSLATION OF

**Akhbār al-Dajjāl**

COMPILED BY

**Imam ʿAbd al-Ghanī al-Maqdisī**

TRANSLATED BY

**Talut Dawood**

Imam Ghazali
PUBLISHING

# Contents

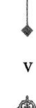

# Translator's Preface

All praise is due to the revealer of the truth, Allah ﷻ, Who said: "Say: The truth has come and falsehood has perished. Indeed, falsehood is ever bound to perish."[1] He ﷻ has also said, "Nay, We launch the truth at falsehood and it defeats it, thus it departs."[2] We praise Him despite our tongues which are incapable of rendering the praise that He deserves, and we acknowledge and thank Him for all His favours – apparent and hidden.

Among those favours is that He revealed for us a complete religion that addresses every situation that we may face, among which are the signs and portents of the end times. Since we are the last *ummah* of the last Prophet ﷺ, it is inevitable that it will be members of our nation who will face and endure the trials of such times. Thus, having sufficient knowledge of these events is necessary.

We send prayers and peace upon His final Messenger ﷺ, the one to whom full knowledge of the signs of the end times was revealed, who then presented a detailed account of everything that would pass from his time until the Day of Judgement. In the famous hadith, he ﷺ said in answer to Jibrīl ؑ when questioned regarding the signs of the Hour, "That the slave girl would give birth to her mistress, and that barefoot, naked,

1 *Al-Isrā'*, 81.
2 *Al-Anbiyā'*, 18.

and destitute shepherds would compe
buildings."[3] May Allah send continu
and peace upon him for all eternity, ar
among his followers and those who v
lake. *Āmīn*!

Knowing the signs of the Hour, what they entail, and understanding how to react in such times is one of the dimensions of Islam. In the hadith of Jibrīl عليه السلام, Jibrīl asked the Prophet ﷺ four questions: What is Islam? What is *īmān*? What is *iḥsān*? When is the Hour?

Commenting on the final question, the Prophet ﷺ remarked that he only had as much knowledge of its exact time as Jibrīl did. So, Jibrīl asked him about its signs, to which the Messenger of Allah ﷺ gave a succinct answer that presented some major signs from which to be on guard. 'Umar رضي الله عنه was not aware of the questioner, and the Prophet ﷺ informed him that it was indeed Jibrīl. More importantly, he told him that he had come "to teach you your religion".[4]

Thus, the end times were established as part of the dimensions of our religion concerning which it is necessary to have knowledge and understanding. However, what does such knowledge entail? There are a number of sects of different religions that have apocalyptic myths. Furthermore, just as many reactions to these myths, predictions, and prophecies exist. Some people are paralysed by the thought of the end times. Others believe that they must take an active role in both

3 *Ṣaḥīḥ Muslim*, hadith no. 8.
4 Ibid.

bringing them about as well as managing them. Some believe that they will occur, but take a more passive role, perhaps even denying that apparent signs are indeed signs. Yet, others believe that they are "tales of the ancients".

Despite the fact that we as Muslims are to be the "intermediate nation"[5], we find all these various groups present within our ranks. There are those who obsess, night and day, about the signs of the Hour. There are others who treat the signs as some sort of Bible code, attempting to interpret modern politics in accordance with them. There are those who position themselves as the primary adversaries of the antagonist in the story. Others seem to believe that the signs are part of the hidden matters; thus, we cannot know if what we are seeing are truly signs of the end times. Considering all this, what exactly is the correct framework for a Muslim dealing with these matters? We will attempt to solve this question in this introduction.

We have divided this introduction into three sections:

Section 1: A succinct account of some of the major signs.
Section 2: The proper way to respond to the appearance of the signs.
Section 3: Correcting misconceptions about the Dajjāl.

**Section 1: A Succinct Account of Some of the Major Signs**

Among the signs about which the Prophet ﷺ informed us is that the slave girl would give birth to her master. The scholars

5 *Al-Baqarah*, 143.

have provided a number of interpretations for this statement. One interpretation is that it referred to the proliferation of *umm walads*[6], specifically those who bore children to Arab fathers. Other interpretations include children coming to own or sell their mothers, either out of ignorance or due to circumstances borne of the proliferation of slavery. However, another interpretation – which is perhaps more apt for our time – is that it refers to widespread abuse of parents and neglect of their rights.

Among the signs is also that naked, barefoot, and destitute shepherds will compete in the construction of tall buildings.

Sheikh al-Ḥabīb Abū Bakr al-Mashhūr has stated that these above-mentioned two signs form the two pillars of the knowledge of the end times. These two pillars are in turn the archetypes for two principles: the destabilization of governance and general order, and the weakening of knowledge and belief.

Examples of the former are the hadiths that indicate that close to the end times, trustworthiness and fidelity (to oaths, pacts, and contracts) would be lifted. In that time the liar will be deemed truthful, the truthful will be regarded as a liar, the trustworthy person will be suspected of treachery, and the treacherous person will be trusted.[7] In another narration, the Prophet ﷺ said that in such a time, authority would be given to those least deserving of it, such that the rulers would be the worst and most treacherous of the people.

6 *Umm walad* is a slave girl who bears her master's child.

7 *Sunan Ibn Mājah* , hadith no. 4036.

An example of the latter (the weakening of knowledge) is the disappearance of knowledge by the passing away of scholars. The Prophet ﷺ said, "From among the signs of the Hour is that knowledge will be lifted, ignorance will become widespread, drinking wine will be prevalent, and fornication and adultery will be committed openly."[8] The lifting of knowledge has been explained in another hadith, where he ﷺ says, "Indeed, Allah ﷻ does not lift knowledge by snatching away from His servants. Rather, He lifts knowledge by causing the scholars to die."[9] In another narration, he ﷺ said that people would then turn to the ignorant in order to seek legal verdicts, who would then give verdicts without knowledge – being in misguidance themselves and misguiding others.

Subsequently, the signs are divided into major and minor signs. Among the minor signs are:

- The appearance of false teachers.
- The prevalence of reciters and scarcity of *fuqahā'*.
- The selling of authority.
- The disappearance of knowledge by the death of the scholars.
- Bearing false witness.
- Mistrusting the trustworthy and trusting the treacherous.
- The dreams of the believer becoming true.
- Cutting of family ties and violation of the rights of parents.
- The appearance of reciters whose recitation does not pass their throats.
- The destruction of the Ka'bah.

8 *Ṣaḥīḥ al-Bukhārī*, hadith no. 80.

9 *Ṣaḥīḥ al-Bukhārī*, hadith no. 100.

- The lifting of the Qur'an.
- The cold that will take the life of every believer.

General turmoil in which the one sitting is better than the one standing, and the one standing is better than the one walking.

Among the major signs are:

- The appearance of the Mahdi.
- The appearance of the Dajjāl.
- The appearance of 'Īsā .
- The appearance of Ya'jūj and Ma'jūj, their spreading corruption to every part of the Earth, and their eventual death at the hands of a parasite.
- The appearance of the smoke.
- The sinking of the Earth in three regions.
- The fire that will usher people to their place of reckoning.
- The beast of the Earth.
- The rising of the Sun from the West.
- The blowing of the Trumpet.

Among these signs is also the prevalence of afflictions. In some hadiths, they are described as "coming like the waves of the ocean".[10] In another hadith, the Prophet ﷺ compared them to darkness that blots out any light, saying, "Before the Hour, there will be trials and afflictions like portions of a dark night."[11]

The Prophet ﷺ has also given a rough timeline for many of these signs. In a number of hadiths found in *Ṣaḥīḥ al-Bukhārī*

---

10  *Ṣaḥīḥ Muslim*, hadith no. 144. The wording, "waves of the ocean" is mawqūf upon 'Umar.
11  *Sunan Abī Dāwūd*, Mu'assasah al-Risālah, hadith no. 4281.

and *Ṣaḥīḥ Muslim*, he mentions that the first of the major signs to appear will be the Mahdi, who will signal the return of the Islamic *khilāfah*. Prior to his emergence, there will be years of turmoil, injustice, and inversion of the general order of things. Wine will be drunk, fornication and adultery committed, and homosexuality will be prevalent. All of this will be open and public. In addition, men will imitate women and women will imitate men. *Al-harj* (indiscriminate and widespread killing) will also appear.

Then, the Mahdi will emerge. The believers will swear allegiance to him. At that time, the Sufyānī will send an army against him. They will be swallowed altogether by the Earth. Then, the Mahdi will set about filling the Earth with justice, just as it had been prior filled with injustice. At some point, a mutual enemy will appear and the Muslims will make a peace treaty with the Christians. The Christians will betray that peace treaty and there shall be a great battle in which one-third of the Muslim army will desert, one-third will be killed, and one-third will be victorious. The Muslims will then liberate Constantinople, and while distributing the spoils they will hear that the Dajjāl has emerged and is among their women and children. They will turn away from the spoils and return. While they are returning, the Dajjāl will truly emerge.

The Dajjāl will then spread corruption in every part of the land, claiming at first to be a messenger, and then God Himself. He will remain on Earth for as long as Allah wills, with the only people opposing him being the followers of the Mahdi. Then, at the height of his corruption and evil, Allah will send ʿĪsā ibn Maryam from Heaven. He will kill the Dajjāl, abolish the *jizyah*, and quash all other religions. He will then receive inspiration that Allah has released the Ya'jūj and Ma'jūj. They will emerge from the East, covering every slope and consuming all the resources in the land. They will kill, pillage, and besiege 'Īsā and his followers. Then, Allah will send a parasite that will kill them all at once.

When 'Īsā and his followers descend, the entire Earth will be covered with the rotting corpses of the Ya'jūj and Ma'jūj. So, they will pray to Allah, Who will send a type of bird to pick up the corpses and drop them wherever Allah wills. Then, they will pray to Allah again and He will cause it to rain until the entire Earth is purified and the land bears food in excess of people's needs. After this, Allah will cause 'Īsā  to pass away.

After that, people will remain for some years. Then, Allah will cause a beast to emerge from the Earth. He will mark the noses of the disbelievers until everyone can recognize who the believers are and who the disbelievers are. While in that state, Allah will send a cold current that will cause all the believers on Earth to die. All that will remain will be the worst of people who will commit indecencies openly. It is upon these people that the final major signs will occur: the Sun rising from the West – signalling the closing of the door to repentance, the smoke, the three earthquakes, and the fire that will usher people to their place of assembly.

We have synthesized and summarized this account from several hadiths in the Six Books, *al-Muwaṭṭa'*, and *Musnad al-Imām Aḥmad*. We ask Allah for protection of our faith and our lives, and to fortify us in the presence of these signs. *Āmīn!*

## Section 2: The Proper Way to Respond to the Signs

There are two considerations regarding how a Muslim should respond to the signs of the end times. The first deals with a Muslim's faith in the signs. The second deals with his reaction and situation in the midst of the signs occurring around him. As for the first, Allah says about the successful god-fearing people who are upon guidance from their Lord,[12] "(They are) those who believe in the unseen."[13] The signs of the end times comprise unseen realities that Allah has informed us about upon the tongue of His final Prophet and Messenger ﷺ. Upon hearing these reports, our response is, "We believe in it. All of it is from our Lord."[14] Thus, whatever has been narrated authentically from the Prophet ﷺ regarding these matters is to be believed and confirmed.

Part of our belief in these matters is our method of interpreting these signs. Unfortunately, there is a tendency among people who lack knowledge of trying to interpret the signs figuratively in order to fit a particular political ideology. Their goal is to convince Muslims that they are living out the signs in their time. This approach is both uncalled for and mistaken.

The correct approach is that these signs should be interpreted with their apparent meaning, as long as there is no reason to interpret them figuratively. This is a well-known *uṣūlī* principle – Texts are interpreted according to their apparent meaning unless there is circumstantial evidence (a *qarīnah*) indicating

12 *Al-Baqarah*, 5.

13 *Al-Baqarah*, 3.

14 *Āl ʿImrān*, 7.

the contrary. Such evidence should show the impossibility, or high improbability, of the apparent meaning being applied due to textual evidence from revelation, or due to it being rationally impossible.

As an example, when Allah says in the Qur'an that He did *istiwā'* on the *'arsh* – the literal meaning of *istiwā'* being to rise over or to sit – we know that it is textually impossible due to Allah's saying, "And there is nothing whatsoever like Him".[15] It is also rationally impossible because it implies that Allah's Essence inhabits space, moves around in that space, and contacts created objects, etc. Allah ﷻ is far above such a lowly description. Consequently, since the apparent meaning is textually and rationally impossible for Allah ﷻ, the text is either left without interpretation, or, when needed, interpreted according to the principles of the sacred law and the rules of the Arabic language.

However, if a description is neither textually nor rationally impossible, such as Allah's being Merciful, Forgiving, Kind, Generous, Just, etc., then it is left as it is without any interpretation. In a similar manner, if there are signs that are textually or rationally impossible when interpreted according to their apparent meaning, then they would be interpreted figuratively. Nevertheless, since the overwhelming majority – if not the entirety – of these signs are both textually and rationally possible, they are interpreted according to their apparent meaning. As such, interpreting the Ya'jūj and Ma'jūj as a world system, or interpreting the Beast of the Earth as

15 *Al-Shūrā*, 11.

anything other than a beast that emerges from the Earth would be invalid. This is because not only are they not textually or rationally impossible, but we have textual evidence of their occurrence as well as both being rationally possible. As for the Dajjāl and the different interpretations regarding him, this will be covered in Section 3 of this introduction.

Concerning the Muslim's attitude to the signs of the end times, just as in all things, Allah has revealed to us the moderate way. Such matters should not paralyze us. Nor should we take an active role, attempting to save the world and its people as a hero. Rather, our reaction is governed, firstly, by the fact that Allah has obligated us to act as a Muslim at all times and in all circumstances. Verses of the Qur'an such as, "Whoever fears Allah, He will make for him a way out (of every difficulty), and will provide for him from where he had not expected",[16] and hadiths such as, "Be mindful of Allah and you will find Him in front of you" apply to all times and situations. They are not suspended due to the occurrence of the signs. Rather, they are even more important and become similar to a lifeline for anyone who wishes to weather the end times successfully.

A Muslim is to be always upright and righteous. Performing prayers on time and with perfect reverence and attention is the start of this. A Muslim is to avoid getting involved in what does not concern him. The latter is a way to avoid the majority of trials and tribulations. If one minds his own business, then he will avoid every tribulation except those that show up on his doorstep.

16 *Al-Ṭalāq*, 2-3.

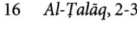

Finally, a Muslim is required to believe in, accept, and be satisfied with the decree and predestination of Allah ﷻ. This includes believing that the world, at every instant, is exactly as Allah has willed it. Anything of the signs that are occurring in front of us is happening exactly how Allah has willed it and erected it. There is no way to change it and it could never have existed in any other way. In that way, a believer is relieved of the stress and anxiety of what is happening around him. He is then free to focus on what is important: what Allah has demanded of him. He should always remember that Allah has not made him responsible for the running, preservation, or correction of the world order at large. Rather, He has made him responsible for fulfilling the personal and communal obligations with which He has made him liable for.

It is also imperative that the believer keep in mind that whatever is occurring around him is a glad tiding. The Prophet ﷺ said, "Amazing is the affair of the believer. In all of his situations, there is good. If he is blessed, he is thankful and rewarded. And if he is afflicted, he is patient and rewarded."[17] It is also a glad tiding from the point of view that it confirms the veracity of the Prophet ﷺ and increases our belief and certainty in him ﷺ and his message.

In his book, *al-Nubdhah al-Ṣughrā*, which has been translated as *The Concise Article*, Sheikh al-Ḥabīb Abū Bakr al-Mashhūr gives a concise account of how the believer responds to the end times. Rather, we should be patient with what is happening, insulate ourselves as much as possible, and know that they

17 *Ṣaḥīḥ Muslim*, hadith no. 27.

are events about which we have been informed. Two hadiths demonstrate this attitude. The first is the hadith, "I fear for you some things more than the Dajjāl."[18] In some narrations, one of those things is each person's temptation.

Another very important hadith is the saying of the Messenger of Allah ﷺ, "If the Hour occurs and a man is planting a tree, he should continue to plant the tree."[19] This hadith brings to the forefront that the responsibility of the human being is to do good work, whether that is worship or that which benefits other people. His responsibility is not the governing of the world or changing its course, unless he has been given authority. His duty is to either benefit himself and those around him through worship, or to benefit them through the beneficial acts that he is able to perform. If he sees the signs exhibiting around him, then his recognition of them should encourage him to become eager for good works and to be busy with what concerns him in terms of his relationship with Allah and the matter of his Hereafter.

In addition, it is imperative for a Muslim to seek refuge in Allah the Almighty ﷻ from the evil of the trials and tribulations that occur, either through means of supplication, or through means of acts. As for supplication, there are authentically narrated supplications in which the Prophet ﷺ would seek refuge in Allah from the trial of the Dajjāl, poverty, debt, and from being dominated by other people. One should learn these supplications and others and put them into consistent practice. Specifically, regarding the Dajjāl, one should memorize the

18 *Sunan al-Tirmidhī*, Dār al-Risālah al-ʿĀlamiyyah, hadith no. 2390.

19 *Musnad al-Imām Aḥmad*, Mu'assasah al-Risālah, hadith no. 12902.

first ten and last ten verses of Sūrah al-Kahf and recite them as a protection. As for actions, then they are maintaining the five prayers in congregation as much as possible, as there are narrations which mention that this is a protection.

Seeking out and attending the gatherings of remembrance – whether they are gatherings of knowledge or gatherings for the specific purpose of invoking Allah and sending prayers upon the Prophet ﷺ – is also a protection as the scholars have said. And, finally, avoiding the places where the tribulations are occurring is highly recommended. This may lead to having to follow the prophetic advice of staying in your home in order to avoid it. All of these practices will provide a Muslim an ample amount of protection from the majority of the trials and tribulations. However, one should realize that the Prophet ﷺ described some of these tribulations as entering every home. So, we should be under no impression that we will avoid all of it. Rather, we should be certain that we will be affected in some way by them and stand firm with certainty in the decree of Allah and observe enduring perseverance for His sake.

To summarize, there are three aspects to a Muslim's reaction to the signs of the end times. The first is to confirm the veracity of all that the Prophet ﷺ is reported to have informed us, believe in these authentic reports firmly, and not interpret them in a way that contradicts established Islamic principles. The second is to be an upright god-fearing Muslim at all times, regardless of what is going on around us. And the third is to seek refuge in Allah ﷻ from the trials and tribulations that will occur and that are occurring.

## Section 3: Correcting Misconceptions About the Dajjāl

"Say: O mankind, the truth has come from your Lord, so whoever is guided is only guided for his own benefit."[20]

"The truth has come and the command of Allah has been established, though they dislike it."[21]

It has become common practice to subsume Muslim beliefs in the Dajjāl, the Mahdi, and other beliefs relating to the end times into the modern conspiracy theorist dynamic. This takes many forms. However, the basic formula is interpreting the Dajjāl both figuratively as a world system and literally as the man that would lead that world system, and attempting to fit each of the characteristics of the signs into the current geopolitical landscape. Such approaches inevitably fall into using Judeo-Christian scriptures, interpreting Islamic texts according to those scriptures, and misinterpreting or bending Islamic texts to fit their interpretations. In addition, people who involve themselves with these matters, in this way, treat the Islamic texts as some code that needs to be solved. They regard the signs as obscure and hidden, needing to be discovered. They find the identity of the Dajjāl to be the single most pressing issue of the people of the end times. All of this is misplaced and should be avoided.

Such misconceptions, though widespread, can be corrected in just a few steps. The first is to remind Muslims that our stance towards previous scriptures, as they exist in the hands of their

20 *Yūnus*, 108.
21 *Al-Tawbah*, 48.

communities now, has one of three possibilities. Firstly, they may be reporting what our revelation has confirmed – In that case, we confirm it and believe in it. Or, it may be that they are reporting what our revelation has proven false – In that case, we deny it and affirm its falsehood. It could also be that they are reporting what our revelation has not addressed; thus, we neither confirm nor deny it though we may still report it or relate it. However, it should not affect our practice of Islam or our belief system in any consequential way.

For example, we do not adopt any attribute or name of Allah, as part of our obligatory doctrine, that is not reported in Islamic texts. Similarly, the signs of the end times form part of our doctrine. As such, we should only form a belief about the end times from our texts. This is a well-known principle. If, as is recommended, we inculcate and repeat the Prophetic supplication,

رَضِيتُ بِاللهِ رَبًا وَبِالإِسْلَامِ دِينًا وَبِمُحَمَّدٍ صَلَّى اللهُ عَلَيْهِ وَسَلَّمَ نَبِيًّا

"I am satisfied with Allah as (my) Lord, with Islam as (my) religion, and with Muhammad ﷺ as (my) Prophet", then what follows is that Allah, His Prophet ﷺ, and His revelation will be sufficient for us. We need not look elsewhere to explain our scripture. Everything that we must necessarily know about the end times has been revealed by Allah ﷻ on the tongue of our Prophet ﷺ. To go looking elsewhere is folly. Thus, while we do not deny what has neither been confirmed nor falsified in our revelation, we still do not confirm it. Nor do we make it a part of our belief or an important piece of some cosmic puzzle. They are simply reports from previous communities that may or may not be true, the consequential meanings of which are already contained within the revelation that we have received. We are satisfied with our Prophet ﷺ and with all that he has brought – believing in it, confirming it, and exalting it over all other scriptures.

Regarding the misconceptions about the Dajjāl himself, they are first resolved by applying the principle mentioned before. Are the characteristics of the Dajjāl that are mentioned rationally or textually impossible? If not, then why are they being interpreted figuratively? It can also be resolved through the description of the Dajjāl himself, as the narrative is neither rationally nor textually impossible to begin with. In various hadiths, it is mentioned that he is one-eyed, with one eye being blind or defective. In some narrations, it is mentioned that it has a film or mucus over it, and that the other eye bulges like a grape. He is also short, stocky with pale skin, and has curly hair. The attribute that has drawn the most speculation here is that he is one-eyed, as the rest of the description is that of a normal person. So, we should first determine what it means to be one-eyed here. It does not mean that he is a cyclops, or that he is missing an eye as some have assumed. Rather, *aʿwar* means to be blind or have a defect in one eye, or to have one eye that has a permanent squint. These meanings are covered by the English word one-eyed. All of these attributes are those that occur normally in the world, either through birth defects or through injuries that occur. Thus, none of these attributes are rationally impossible. Consequently, there is no need to decode this description according to pop culture fads, images on money, or anything else.

As for textual impossibility, then the texts themselves belie such interpretations. It is clear from the texts of the different hadiths that the Dajjāl is a human being, mortal, and does not possess any power beyond what an ordinary human being may be able to accomplish. The fact that he is a human being is established by the various hadiths in many different collections, all of which describe the Prophet's ﷺ investigation of Ṣāf ibn Ṣā'id (Ibn Ṣayyād). The Prophet ﷺ attempted on several occasions to determine whether Ibn Ṣā'id was indeed the Dajjāl. This one fact alone belies other interpretations. However, in the description of the Dajjāl, the fact that he is visible, has eyes, will be limited as to who he can kill, and that he will melt in front of 'Īsā ibn Maryam and be killed by him all point to the fact that a real person is being described and not some abstract system.

A person may ask, "Can it not be both literal and figurative?" In principle, texts may have literal and figurative aspects at the same time. However, for a tribulation that the Prophet ﷺ referred to as the greatest to befall mankind from the time of the creation of Adam until the blowing of the Trumpet, to be ambiguous or unclear would be unlike the Prophet ﷺ. In matters of utmost importance, he spoke clearly and directly. For him to speak in riddles about the greatest threat to his followers would be averse to his noble character. So, while it is indeed possible, such a reading would put the Prophet's ﷺ deliverance of the message in doubt, which is inconceivable.

**A Final Note**

There are two general principles to keep in mind. The first is that the major signs that occur, such as the Mahdi, the Dajjāl, the descent of 'Īsā ibn Maryam, etc. must be apparent for all to see. They cannot be ambiguous signs that only an elite few would understand. The Prophet ﷺ said that the Dajjāl will have the word *kāfir* or the letters *kāf-fā'-rā'* written on his forehead and that every believer would be able to read it, whether he was literate or illiterate. This implies that his emergence will be apparent for all to see, and not be some hidden agenda. Similarly, other signs such as the descent of 'Īsā are apparent. The Prophet ﷺ said that his breath will kill any disbeliever it falls upon, and that it will reach as far as he can see. This means that all people will see and recognize 'Īsā ibn Maryam ﷺ.

The second is that there is an order to the major signs. In the various hadiths, it is clear that the Mahdi will appear before the Dajjāl. He will accomplish many of his goals, eventually defeating the forces of the Christian world in a decisive battle. It is after these events that the Dajjāl will emerge. Since the world is still filled with injustice and the Mahdi has not yet arrived, it follows that whatever system is running the world right now cannot be the Dajjāl. Nor is it "his" system. It can be termed "Dajjālic", as the Dajjāl is also an archetype. So, any system that is adept at deception to an unprecedented level, deceiving even good people, can be termed "Dajjālic". However, it is not his system.

اَللَّهُمَّ إِنَّا نَعُوذُ بِكَ مِنْ فِتْنَةِ المَسِيحِ الدَّجَّالِ

اَللَّهُمَّ صَلِّ عَلَى سَيِّدِنَا مُحَمَّدٍ الفَاتِحِ لِمَا أُغْلِقَ
وَالخَاتِمِ لِمَا سَبَقَ نَاصِرِ الحَقِّ بِالحَقِّ
وَالهَادِي إِلَى صِرَاطِكَ المُسْتَقِيمِ
وَعَلَى آلِهِ حَقَّ قَدْرِهِ وَمِقْدَارِهِ العَظِيمِ

# Foreword

With the Name of Allah, the Merciful Benefactor, the Merciful Redeemer. All praise and thanks belong to Allah, and may prayers and peace be upon our master Muhammad the seal of the prophets, and upon his family, righteous companions and whoever follows them in excellence until the Day of Judgment, and what follows.

Islamic eschatology as it relates to the signs of the end of time is an important aspect of theology. The Qur'an relays clear signs for believers that there will inevitable be an end to the existence of this temporary world followed by the Day of Resurrection in which people will be brought back to life to answer for their faith and every deed performed. In addition to signs of the last days given in the Qur'an, Prophetic narrations also convey signs about different events that will signal the conclusion of all worldly matters. Within these narrations, a central sign of the end of time is the appearance of the Dajjāl. Moreover, the Dajjāl will sow the greatest seeds of discord in the history of humankind.[1]

According to the famed Arabic linguist al-Farāhidī[2], the etymological meaning of Dajjāl is "the prolific con-artist and

1 Al-Safarīnī, *Al-Buhūr al-Zakhīrah fi 'Ulūm al-Ākhīrah*, p. 344 (Beirut: Dar al-Kutub al-'Ilmiyyah, 2022)

2 Al-Khalīl bin Aḥmad al-Farāhadī was an 8th century CE Arabic language scholar who produced one of the earliest texts of etymology in Arabic. He is one of the teachers of 'Amr bin 'Uthmān Sibawayh who wrote the first text on Arabic grammar written by a non-Arab. Al-Farāhadī like Sibawayh was Persian in lineage.

false anointer whose fraud is deceptive [like magic]; his lies bring in what is bogus into what is legitimate which causes confusion."[3] Allah ﷻ says in Surah Ghāfir, Ayah 6:

> *Indeed, those who dispute concerning the signs of Allah without [any] authority having come to them – there is not within their breasts except arrogance, [the extent of] which they cannot reach. So, seek refuge in Allah. Indeed, it is He who is the Hearing, the Seeing.*

Several commentators of the Qur'an including al-Alūsī[4] (may Allah have mercy upon him) said in relation to this ayah that no prophet was sent to his community except that he warned them about the Dajjāl.[5] Hence the spiritual disease of arrogance afflicts the one who rejects the Qur'an and vigorously authenticated and widely transmitted narrations of Prophet Muhammad ﷺ. And among those narrations that have been vigorously authenticated pertain to the appearance of the Dajjāl. Allah ﷻ also says in Surah al-Baqarah, Ayah 42:

> *Do not dress up the truth with falsehood, nor conceal what you know.*

Al-Ṭustarī[6] (may Allah have mercy upon him) said that this ayah carries the meaning "which is to not dress up a matter of the worldly life (*Dunya*) with a matter of the latter-life (*Ākhirah*)."[7] Thus a trait of those persons who will be with the Dajjāl is that they will do the opposite of this Divine command

3 Al-Farāhadī, *Kitāb al-'Ayn*, v. 2, p. 9 (Beirut: Dar al-Kutub al-'Ilmiyyah, 2003)

4 Sayyīd Maḥmud bin Abdillah al-Husaynī al-Alūsī was a 19th century CE scholar in Iraq and a Hanafi mufti who lived in the last century of Ottoman rule.

5 Al-Alūsī, *Ruh al-Ma'ānī*, v. 24, p. 79 (Cairo: Idarah al-Taba'ah al-Muniriyyah, 2008)

6 Saḥl al-Ṭustarī was a 9th century CE Persian ascetic.

7 Al-Ṭustarī, *Tafsīr al-Ṭustarī*, p. 31 (Beirut: Dar al-Kutub al-'Ilmiyyah, 2007)

by methodically confusing people through religion to promote worldly corruption. We seek refuge with Allah ﷻ from that.

There are numerous signs of the end of times which are manifesting before our eyes that reflect the approach of the epoch of the Dajjāl. Fornication has become popular to the extent that the taboo which used to surround it has been virtually lost in the West and has begun to rapidly erode in the East. The consumption of intoxicants is widespread to the extent that not only are television commercials promoting alcohol on a global level, but there is even open drinking of alcohol in many Muslim majority countries – it is becoming commonplace. Males now openly imitate females and vice versa not only in dress but also in traditional gender roles; the corruption has spread to the extent that there is a phenomenon of individuals who claim that they are not even fully human, such as being trans-wolves or trans-felines. All of these signs and more reflect the ushering in the epoch of the Dajjāl.

Among the prophecies of the appearance of the Dajjāl include the advent of Imam al-Mahdī who will be a descendant of Fātimah al-Zahrā (may Allah be pleased with her) and the return of 'Isa bin Maryam (peace be upon them). The coming of these two, the former being a saint and the latter being a prophet and messenger, are narrated in widely transmitted reports that are beyond doubt. Those who are upon truth and are alive will give spiritual allegiance to them following the sacred law given to Prophet Muhammad ﷺ in fighting the Dajjāl, his minions, and acolytes. Hence, each generation of Muslims is duty bound to remind the Ummah about the traits of the Dajjāl and the signs that will be in existence when he appears so that they and their successive generations do not get easily confused, nor lose their faith when deception spreads and evil gets redefined as good.

To this end, Ustadh Talut Dawood (may Allah preserve him and elevate his station) translated *Akhbār al-Dajjāl* (Reports on the Dajjāl) by the illustrious Hanbali scholar Taqī al-Dīn Abū Muhammad ʿAbd al-Ghanī ibn ʿAbd al-Wāḥid ibn ʿAlī ibn Surūr ibn Rāfiʿ ibn Ḥasan ibn Jaʿfar al-Ḥanbalī (may Allah have mercy upon him.) The translation of this essential text serves the valuable purposes of both keeping the generational obligation of reminding Muslims about the Dajjāl as well as giving clarity in this present era of growing confusion which is rapidly increasing by the day.

We ask Allah ﷻ to grant us refuge from the Dajjāl, to have us safeguard the first ten and last ten ayat of Surah al-Kahf, and to place us in the company of righteous teachers who connect us to sound spiritual chains of transmission that assist in guarding from falsehood and confusion.

[Imam] Dawud Walid

Canton, Michigan, USA

6 Sha'ban 1444 AH

# The Imam

GLIMPSES INTO THE LIFE OF

**Imam ʿAbd al-Ghanī al-Maqdisī**

He is the Imam, the ʿĀlim, the great Ḥāfiẓ, the truthful one, the exemplar, the worshipper whose example is followed, Taqī al-Dīn Abū Muhammad ʿAbd al-Ghanī ibn ʿAbd al-Wāḥid ibn ʿAlī ibn Surūr ibn Rāfiʿ ibn Ḥasan ibn Jaʿfar al-Ḥanbalī, who was originally from the Jammāʾīl district of Nablus. His origin (al-Maqdisī) is ascribed to Jerusalem, as Nablus and all its districts are considered part of the jurisdiction of Jerusalem. He was most likely born in the month of Rabīʿ al-Ākhir in the year 541 AH/1146 CE. He was four months older than Muwaffaq al-Dīn Ibn Qudāmah, who was born in Shaʿbān of the same year.

At an early age, his family moved from Jerusalem to the area of the Abū Ṣāliḥ Mosque just outside the eastern gate of Damascus. Then, they moved again to the foot of Mount Qasioun. There, they built an estate, calling it Dār al-Ḥanābilah (the Abode of the Ḥanbalīs). They then began building the first school at Mount Qasioun, known as al-Madrasah al-ʿUmariyyah. The neighbourhood in which they lived came to be known as al-Ṣāliḥiyyah due to its association with them, since they were among the people of knowledge and piety (*ṣalāḥ*). He had a pious upbringing in Damascus. He is the author of *al-Aḥkām al-Kubrā* and *al-Aḥkām al-Ṣughrā*.

The Ḥāfiẓ Ḍiyāʾ al-Dīn Abū Abdullah al-Maqdisī said, "He was not pale. Rather, he tended towards being brown-skinned.

He had beautiful hair, a bushy beard, a wide brow, and a large build. He was perfectly formed and it was as if light emanated from his face. His vision weakened as he aged due to crying, reading, and copying texts."

He heard hadiths as well as most of the books from the majority of scholars in Damascus, Alexandria, Jerusalem, Egypt, Baghdad, Harran, Mosul, Isfahan, and Hamadan. He heard from Abū al-Fatḥ ibn al-Baṭṭī, Abū al-Ḥasan ʿAlī ibn Rabāḥ al-Farrāʾ, Hibat Allāh ibn Hilāl al-Daqqāq, Abū Zurʿah al-Maqdisī, Muʿammar ibn al-Fākhir, Aḥmad ibn al-Muqarrab, Yaḥyā ibn Thābit, Abū Bakr ibn al-Naqqūr, Aḥmad ibn ʿAbd al-Ghanī al-Bājisrāʾī and a number of others in Baghdad. He also heard from al-Ḥāfiẓ Abū Ṭāhir al-Silafī and wrote around one thousand small books from him. In Damascus, he heard from Abū al-Makārim ibn Hilāl, Sulaymān ibn ʿAlī al-Raḥabī, Abū al-Maʿālī ibn Ṣābir, and a number of other scholars. In Egypt, he heard from Muhammad ibn ʿAlī al-Raḥabī, ʿAbdullāh ibn Barrī, and a group of scholars. In Isfahan, he heard from Abū Mūsā al-Madīnī, Abū al-Wafāʾ Maḥmūd ibn Ḥamakā, Abū al-Fatḥ al-Kharqī, Ibn Yanāl al-Turk, Muhammad ibn ʿAbd al-Wāḥid al-Ṣāʾigh, and Ḥabīb ibn Ibrāhīm al-Ṣūfī. In Mosul, he heard from Abū al-Faḍl al-Ṭūsī and others.

He travelled to Baghdad twice (in search of knowledge). In the year 566 AH, he travelled to Baghdad with his maternal cousin, Sheikh Ibn Qudāmah. They would always leave their homes and go everywhere together, accompanying one another to their lessons and hadith gatherings. They were two well-organized young men, which caused some of the people of Baghdad to fear them. The Ḥāfiẓ's inclination was towards hadith while Ibn Qudāmah was more inclined towards jurisprudence (*fiqh*). Thus, the Ḥāfiẓ learned *fiqh* alongside Ibn Qudāmah, and Ibn Qudāmah heard many hadiths with the Ḥafiẓ as well.

When the people saw that they were intelligent, chaste, and rarely associated with people unnecessarily, they began to love them and treat them charitably. They then obtained an ample portion of knowledge after staying in Baghdad for around four years. They arrived first in the presence of Sheikh ʿAbd al-Qādir[1]. He treated them excellently, but he passed away around fifty days after they arrived. Then, they both busied themselves studying *fiqh* and disagreements at the hand of Ibn al-Munā.

The Ḥāfiẓ (al-Maqdisī) travelled to (study from) al-Silafī in the year 566 AH. He stayed for a short time. He also travelled to study from him in the year seventy. A few years after 570 AH, he travelled to Isfahan. He stayed there for some time and studied a good number of books.

The Ḥāfiẓ ʿAbd al-Ghanī was an Atharī Ḥanbalī in *ʿaqīdah*, yet many of the lands that he visited, studied, and taught in were dominated by Ashʿarī scholars. This caused a lot of controversy, especially given his criticism of the Ashʿarīs and his harsh and abrasive manner of dispute. This was exacerbated by the rise to power of the Seljuk minister Niẓām al-Mulk, who was partial to the Ashʿarīs and opened a number of schools for them in Baghdad and other parts of Iraq. This situation caused the Sheikh a lot of hardship.

1 Al-Jīlānī.

During one of his stays in Isfahan, where the Sheikh had often visited, he read the book Asmā' *al-Ṣaḥābah* (*The Names of the Companions*) of Abū Nu'aym, who was one of the greatest Ash'arī scholars. He corrected him in 290 places. This greatly angered the Ash'arī scholars in Isfahan. They brought him before the leader of Isfahan, al-Ṣadr al-Khujandī, who intended to kill him. However, a group of his students snuck him out of Isfahan.

He was also driven out of Mosul for reading the book *al-Ḍu'afā'* of al-'Uqaylī, when he read what al-'Uqaylī said about Abū Ḥanīfah, namely that the latter had a weak memory. He was imprisoned and the people intended to kill him, but his friend al-Wā'iẓ ibn al-Barnas saved him with his intellectual prowess. Consequently, they released him.

Back in Damascus, he began to teach hadith. His gatherings were filled to the brim with people and had a great effect on them. Due to this, it is said that his opponents became jealous of him and challenged him to a debate in front of the ruler of the land, Burghush. He was harsh and stern after presenting his proof against their evidence. So, Burghush banished him from Damascus, after which he went to Baalbek. In Baalbek, the people supported him and offered to defend him against the people that opposed him. However, he refused because he did not want to cause any sedition between the Muslims.

He then went to Egypt and began narrating hadiths and teaching in the year 595 AH. However, his opponents in Damascus were not pleased with this. So, they sent a number of different fatwas to Prince 'Imād al-Dīn ibn Ṣalāḥ al-Dīn, maligning the Ḥanbalīs and Ḥāfiẓ 'Abd al-Ghanī in particular.

They accused them of anthropomorphism, likening Allah to His creation, and apostasy. It reached the extent that 'Imād al-Dīn intended to banish all the Ḥanbalīs from every region of Egypt. However, he died before he could enact his plan. After that, the Ḥanbalīs became great in the estimation of people. However, the Ḥāfiẓ's opponents again turned King al-ʿĀdil ('Imād al-Dīn's successor) and his son Prince al-Kāmil Muhammad against him. Some of them went as far as anathematizing him, considering him outside the fold of Islam, and regarding his blood as lawful. The matter reached such a stage that every day the Sheikh would receive word of another accuser or critic. It worried him excessively until he passed away in Cairo in the month of Rabīʿ al-Awwal in the year 600 AH. He was just under sixty years old.

The Sheikh was known for his worship and his generosity. He would pray 300 cycles of prayer every night. He would seek out the widows and orphans to give to them generously. He was also generous and kind to the students of knowledge. He was of keen intellect and insight and had a light on his face. Some of the scholars said, "No one among Ahl al-Sunnah saw him except that he fell in love with him." He used all his time in beneficial matters and did not waste a moment. He used to frequently perform ablution at night. He would say, "I like to pray while my limbs are still wet."

A group of scholars narrated from him, including Sheikh Muwaffaq al-Dīn Ibn Qudāmah, al-Ḥāfiẓ 'Izz al-Dīn Muhammad, al-Ḥāfiẓ Abū Mūsā 'Abdullāh, the jurist Abū Sulaymān and his children, al-Ḥāfiẓ Ḍiyā' al-Dīn, al-Khaṭīb Sulaymān ibn Rahmah al-Asʿardī, al-Bahā' 'Abd al-Raḥmān, the Sheikh and jurist Muhammad al-Yūnīnī, al-Zayn ibn ʿAbd al-Dāʾim, Abū al-Ḥajjāj ibn Khalīl, al-Taqī al-Yaldānī, al-Shihāb al-Qūsī, ʿAbd al-ʿAzīz ibn ʿAbd al-Jabbār al-Qalānisī, al-Wāʿiẓ ʿUthmān ibn Makkī al-Shāriʿī, Aḥmad ibn Ḥāmid al-Urtāḥī, Ismāʿīl ibn ʿAbd al-Qawī ibn ʿAzzūn, Abū ʿĪsā Abdullāh ibn ʿAllāq al-Razzāz, and a great number of other scholars.

Among the texts that he wrote are:

1. *Al-Miṣbāḥ fī ʿUyūn al-Aḥādīth al-Ṣiḥāḥ* – a text in which he narrated the hadiths of *Ṣaḥīḥ al-Bukhārī* and *Ṣaḥīḥ Muslim* with his own chains of narration.
2. *Nihāyah al-Murād min Kalām Khayr al-ʿIbād.*
3. *Tuḥfah al-Ṭālibīn fī al-Jihād wa al-Mujāhidīn.*
4. *Al-Ṣifāt.*
5. *Miḥnah al-Imām Aḥmad.*
6. *Faḍāʾil Makkah.*
7. *Iʿtiqād al-Imām al-Shāfiʿī.*
8. *Manāqib al-Ṣaḥābah.*

He was buried in the Qarafah graveyard in Egypt.

# 1 HADITH ONE

أَخْبَرَنَا أَبُو الْقَاسِمِ يَحْيَى بْنُ ثَابِتِ بْنِ بُنْدَارَ بْنِ إِبْرَاهِيمَ الْبَغْدَادِيُّ بِهَا أَنْبَا أَبُو الْمَعَالِيِّ ثَابِتُ بْنُ بُنْدَارَ أَنْبَا أَبُو بَكْرٍ أَحْمَدُ بْنُ مُحَمَّدِ بْنِ غَالِبٍ الْبَرْقَانِيُّ الْخَوَارِزْمِيُّ أَنْبَا أَبُو بَكْرٍ أَحْمَدُ بْنُ إِبْرَاهِيمَ بْنِ إِسْمَاعِيلَ الْجُرْجَانِيُّ الْإِسْمَاعِيلِيُّ أَنْبَا الْقَاسِمُ الْمَقْدَمِيُّ ثَنَا فَرَاجُ أَحْمَدُ بْنُ مَنْصُورٍ ثَنَا عَبْدُ اللّٰهِ بْنُ عُثْمَانَ أَنْبَا عَبْدُ اللّٰهِ عَنْ يُونُسَ عَنِ الزُّهْرِيِّ أَخْبَرَنِي سَالِمُ بْنُ عَبْدِ اللّٰهِ بْنِ عُمَرَ عَنْ أَبِيهِ أَخْبَرَه أَنَّ عُمَرَ بْنَ الْخَطَّابِ رَضِيَ اللَّهُ عَنْهُ انْطَلَقَ مَعَ رَسُولِ اللَّهِ صَلَّى اللّٰهُ عَلَيْهِ وَسَلَّمَ فِيْ رَهْطٍ قِبَلَ ابْنَ صَائِدٍ حَتّٰى وَجَدُوْهُ يَلْعَبُ مَعَ الْغِلْمَانِ عِنْدَ أُطُمِّ بَنِيْ مُغَالَةَ وَقَدْ قَارَبَ ابْنُ صَيَّادٍ يَوْمَئِذٍ الْحُلُمَ فَلَمْ يَشْعُرْ حَتّٰى ضَرَبَ رَسُوْلُ اللّٰهِ صَلَّى اللّٰهُ عَلَيْهِ وَسَلَّمَ ظَهْرَهُ بِيَدِهِ ثُمَّ قَالَ رَسُوْلُ اللّٰهِ صَلَّى اللّٰهُ عَلَيْهِ وَسَلَّمَ لِابْنِ صَائِدٍ أَتَشْهَدُ أَنِّيْ رَسُولُ اللّٰهِ فَنَظَرَ ابْنُ صَائِدٍ إِلَيْهِ فَقَالَ أَشْهَدُ أَنَّكَ رَسُولُ الْأُمِّيِّيْنَ فَقَالَ ابْنُ صَائِدٍ لِرَسُوْلِ اللّٰهِ صَلَّى اللّٰهُ عَلَيْهِ وَسَلَّمَ أَتَشْهَدُ أَنِّيْ رَسُولُ اللّٰهِ فَرَفَضَهُ رَسُوْلُ اللّٰهِ ﷺ فَقَالَ آمَنْتُ بِاللّٰهِ وَبِرُسُلِهِ ثُمَّ قَالَ لَهُ رَسُوْلُ اللّٰهِ صَلَّى اللّٰهُ عَلَيْهِ وَسَلَّمَ مَاذَا تَرٰى قَالَ ابْنُ صَائِدٍ يَأْتِيْنِيْ صَادِقٌ وَكَاذِبٌ فَقَالَ لَهُ رَسُولُ اللّٰهِ صَلَّى اللّٰهُ عَلَيْهِ وَسَلَّمَ خُلِّطَ عَلَيْكَ الْأَمْرُ ثُمَّ قَالَ لَهُ رَسُوْلُ اللّٰهِ صَلَّى اللّٰهُ عَلَيْهِ وَسَلَّمَ إِنِّيْ قَدْ خَبَأْتُ لَكَ خَبِيْئًا فَقَالَ ابْنُ صَائِدٍ هُوَ الدُّخُّ فَقَالَ لَهُ رَسُوْلُ اللّٰهِ صَلَّى اللّٰهُ عَلَيْهِ وَسَلَّمَ اخْسَأْ فَلَنْ أَوْ فَلَمْ تَعْدُوَ قَدَرَكَ فَقَالَ لَهُ عُمَرُ بْنُ الْخَطَّابِ ذَرْنِيْ يَا رَسُوْلَ اللّٰهِ أَضْرِبْ عُنُقَهُ فَقَالَ رَسُولُ اللّٰهِ صَلَّى اللّٰهُ

# 1 HADITH ONE

عَلَيْهِ وَسَلَّمَ إِنْ يَكُنْ هُوَ لَنْ تُسَلَّطَ عَلَيْهِ وَإِنْ لَمْ يَكُنْ هُوَ فَلَا خَيْرَ لَكَ فِي قَتْلِهِ. وَقَالَ سَالِمٌ سَمِعْتُ ابْنَ عُمَرَ يَقُولُ انْطَلَقَ بَعْدَ ذَلِكَ رَسُولُ اللهِ صَلَّى اللَّهُ عَلَيْهِ وَسَلَّمَ وَأُبَيُّ بْنُ كَعْبٍ الْأَنْصَارِيُّ إِلَى النَّخْلِ الَّتِي فِيهَا ابْنُ صَيَّادٍ حَتَّى إِذَا دَخَلَ رَسُولُ اللهِ صَلَّى اللَّهُ عَلَيْهِ وَسَلَّمَ طَفِقَ يَتَّقِي بِجُذُوعِ النَّخْلِ وَهُوَ يَخْتَالُ أَنْ يَسْمَعَ عَنِ ابْنِ صَيَّادٍ شَيْئًا قَبْلَ أَنْ يَرَاهُ ابْنُ صَيَّادٍ فَرَآهُ رَسُولُ اللهِ ﷺ وَهُوَ مُضْطَجِعٌ عَلَى فِرَاشٍ فِي قَطِيفَةٍ لَهُ فِي زَهْزَهَةٍ وَرَأَتْ أُمُّ ابْنِ صَيَّادٍ رَسُولَ اللهِ ﷺ وَهُوَ يَتَّقِي بِجُذُوعِ النَّخْلِ فَقَالَتْ لِابْنِ صَيَّادٍ يَا صَافِ وَهُوَ اسْمُ ابْنِ صَيَّادٍ هَذَا مُحَمَّدٌ فَقَامَ ابْنُ صَيَّادٍ فَقَالَ رَسُولُ اللهِ صَلَّى اللَّهُ عَلَيْهِ وَسَلَّمَ لَوْ تَرَكَتْهُ بَيَّنَ. قَالَ سَالِمٌ قَالَ عَبْدُ اللهِ بْنُ عُمَرَ فَقَامَ رَسُولُ اللهِ صَلَّى اللَّهُ عَلَيْهِ وَسَلَّمَ لِلنَّاسِ فَأَثْنَى عَلَى اللهِ بِمَا هُوَ أَهْلُهُ ثُمَّ ذَكَرَ الدَّجَّالَ فَقَالَ إِنِّي لَأُنْذِرُكُمُوهُ وَمَا مِنْ نَبِيٍّ إِلَّا وَقَدْ أَنْذَرَهُ قَوْمَهُ وَلَكِنْ أَقُولُ لَكُمْ فِيهِ قَوْلًا لَمْ يَقُلْهُ نَبِيٌّ لِقَوْمِهِ تَعْلَمُونَ أَنَّهُ أَعْوَرُ وَأَنَّ اللَّهَ لَيْسَ بِأَعْوَرَ. أَخْبَرَنَاهُ عِدَّةٌ عَنِ ابْنِ الزُّبَيْرِ عَنْ أَبِي الْوَقْتِ عَنِ الدَّاوُدِيِّ عَنِ ابْنِ حَمَوَيْهِ عَنْ عَبْدِ الْعَزِيزِ أَنْبَا مُحَمَّدُ بْنُ إِسْمَاعِيلَ ثَنَا عَبْدُ اللهِ بْنُ عُثْمَانَ فَذَكَرَ نَحْوَهُ. صَحِيحٌ مُتَّفَقٌ عَلَيْهِ رَوَاهُ الْبُخَارِيُّ عَنْ عَبْدِ اللهِ بْنِ عُثْمَانَ كَذَلِكَ وَرَوَاهُ مُسْلِمٌ عَنْ حَرْمَلَةَ عَنْ يُونُسَ عَنِ ابْنِ وَهْبٍ وَلَهُ طُرُقٌ وَرَوَاهُ أَبُو دَاوُدَ عَنْ خُشَيْشِ بْنِ أَصْرَمَ عَنْ عَبْدِ الرَّزَّاقِ عَنْ مَعْمَرٍ عَنِ الزُّهْرِيِّ. قُلْتُ كَانَ ابْنُ صَائِدٍ دَجَّالٌ صَغِيرُ السِّنِّ غَيْرَ الدَّجَّالِ الْأَكْبَرِ

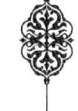

# 1 HADITH ONE

لِأَنَّ ذَاكَ أَعْوَرُ ضَخْمٌ وَابْنُ صَائِدٍ لَيْسَ بِأَعْوَرَ ثُمَّ إِنَّ ابْنَ صَائِدٍ قَدْ أَسْلَمَ وَشَاخَ وَمَاتَ وَقَدْ حَدَّثَ النَّبِيُّ ﷺ بَعْدُ عَنْ تَمِيمٍ الدَّارِيِّ بِأَنَّ الدَّجَّالَ مَغْلُولٌ فِي جَزِيرَةٍ مِنْ جَزَائِرِ الْبَحْرِ كَمَا سَيَأْتِي وَاللهُ أَعْلَمُ.

Abū al-Qāsim Yaḥyā ibn Thābit ibn Bundār ibn Ibrāhīm al-Baghdādī informed us: Abū al-Maʿālī Thābit ibn Bundār related: Abū Bakr Aḥmad ibn Muhammad Ghālib al-Burqānī al-Khwārizmī related: Abū Bakr Aḥmad ibn Ibrāhīm ibn Ismāʿīl al-Jurjānī al-Ismāʿīlī related: al-Qāsim al-Muqaddamī: Farrāj Aḥmad ibn Manṣūr related to us: ʿAbdullāh ibn ʿUthmān ibn ʿAbdullāh narrated to us from Yūnus from al-Zuhrī: Sālim ibn ʿAbdullāh ibn ʿUmar informed us that his father informed him:

ʿUmar ibn al-Khaṭṭāb ﷺ went with the Messenger of Allah ﷺ in a small group towards Ibn Ṣayyād[1]. They found him playing with some children near the fortress of Banū Maghālah. At that time, Ibn Ṣayyād was approaching puberty. Before he noticed him, the Messenger of Allah ﷺ patted him on the back. The Messenger of Allah ﷺ then said to Ibn Ṣayyād, "Do you testify that I am the Messenger

1 In the Arabic text, the name is spelled "Ibn Ṣā'id". Later on, it is spelled as "Ibn Ṣayyād". We have maintained the spelling of Ibn Ṣayyād throughout to correspond to the rendering found in the narrations of al-Bukhārī. The discrepancy, according to some commentators, occurs because Ibn Ṣā'id was later known as ʿAbdullāh ibn Ṣayyād.

of Allah?" Ibn Ṣayyād looked at him and said, "I bear witness that you are the messenger of the unlettered." Then Ibn Ṣayyād said to the Messenger of Allah, "Do you bear witness that I am the Messenger of Allah?" The Messenger of Allah ﷺ repudiated him and said, "I believe in Allah and in His Messengers." The Messenger of Allah ﷺ then said, "What do you see?" Ibn Ṣayyād said, "Both that which is true and false come to me." The Messenger of Allah ﷺ said, "You are confused." Then the Messenger of Allah ﷺ said, "I have concealed something from you." Ibn Ṣayyād said, "It is *dukhkh*[2]." The Messenger of Allah ﷺ said, "Away with you. You will not exceed your rank."[3] 'Umar ibn al-Khaṭṭāb then said to him, "O Messenger of Allah, permit me to strike his neck." The Messenger of Allah ﷺ replied, "If he is him (the Dajjāl), you will not overpower him. And should he not be

2 "*Dukhkh* – or *dakhkh* – is smoke (*dukhān*). He (the poet al-'Ajjāj) said, 'Near the corridor of the house, the smoke descends.' The hadith has been interpreted as referring to the verse, 'On the day that the heaven will bring forth an evident smoke' (*al-Dukhān*, 10). It has also been said that the Dajjāl will be killed by 'Īsā ﷺ near the mountain al-Dukhān. So, it is possible that he intended to allude to his being killed because Ibn Ṣayyād used to believe that he was the Dajjāl" (Ibn Athīr, *al-Nihāyah fī Gharīb al-Ḥadīth wa al-Athar*, Dār Ibn al-Jawzī, p. 300).

3 "Imam al-Nawawī said in *Sharḥ Ṣaḥīḥ Muslim*, 'The correct and most adopted opinion (regarding this hadith) is that the Prophet ﷺ had hidden in his hand the tenth verse of *al-Dukhān*. Qāḍī 'Iyāḍ said, "The most correct opinion is that Ibn Ṣayyād could not produce the verse which the Prophet ﷺ had hidden, except that particular part of the word. This is like the case of the soothsayers, to whom they (the jinn) transmit incomplete information that they are able to eavesdrop before they are struck by a meteor"'" ('Alī al-Qārī, *Mirqāt al-Mafātīḥ Sharḥ Mishkāt al-Maṣābīḥ*, Dār al-Kutub al-'Ilmiyyah, vol. 10, p. 151).

him, then there is no good in you killing him."[4] Sālim said, "I heard Ibn 'Umar say, 'After that, the Messenger ﷺ went with Ubayy ibn Ka'b al-Anṣārī to the date orchard in which Ibn Ṣayyād was found. When the Messenger ﷺ entered he began to hide himself behind the stumps of the date trees. It was a trick so that he could hear something from Ibn Ṣayyād before the latter saw him. The Messenger of Allah ﷺ saw him resting upon a silk cloth on his bed while he was lying on his side. He was mumbling softly. Ibn Ṣayyād's mother then saw the Messenger of Allah ﷺ while he was hiding himself behind the date palm stumps. Consequently, she said to Ibn Ṣayyād, "O Ṣāf – which was his name, here is Muhammad." So, Ibn Ṣayyād got up and the Messenger of Allah ﷺ said, "If she had left him, it would have been clarified.""'"[5] [6]

Sālim said, "'Abdullāh ibn 'Umar said, 'The Messenger of Allah ﷺ stood up before the people and praised Allah ﷻ in an appropriate way. Thenceforth, he mentioned the Dajjāl and said, "I warn you of him. And there is no Prophet except that he has warned his people of him. However, I will tell you something that no other Prophet told his people. You

4 *Ṣaḥīḥ al-Bukhārī*, hadith no. 3055 and 6173; *Ṣaḥīḥ Muslim*, hadith nos. 2930-2931.

5 In *Sharḥ al-Sunnah*, al-Baghawī said, "It means that his interior state would have been revealed." Imam al-Nawawī ؒ said, "His speech, contradicting itself, would clarify things for you until his affair becomes insignificant for you" ('Alī al-Qārī, *Mirqāt al-Mafātīḥ Sharḥ Mishkāt al-Maṣābīḥ*, Dār al-Kutub al-'Ilmiyyah, vol. 10, p. 151).

6 *Ṣaḥīḥ al-Bukhārī*, hadith no. 6174; *Ṣaḥīḥ Muslim*, hadith nos. 2930-2931.

should know that he is *a'war* (one-eyed)[7], and Allah is not one-eyed[8].""[9]

A number of people informed us of this hadith on the authority of Ibn al-Zubayr from Abī al-Waqt from al-Dāwūdi from Ibn Ḥamawayh from 'Abd al-'Azīz that Muhammad ibn Ismā'īl related: 'Abdullāh ibn 'Uthmān narrated to us. And he mentioned a similar hadith.

This hadith is authentic and agreed upon. Al-Bukhārī narrated it from 'Abdullāh ibn 'Uthmān, and Muslim narrated it from Ḥarmalah from Yūnus from Ibn Wahb. And it has a number of different chains of transmission. Abū Dāwūd narrated it from Khushaysh ibn Aṣram from 'Abd al-Razzāq from Ma'mar from al-Zuhrī.

I (al-Maqdisī) say: Ibn Ṣā'id (Ibn Ṣayyād) was a *dajjāl* in his young age, but different to the greatest Dajjāl because the latter is one-eyed and corpulent while Ibn Ṣā'id was not

7 The word *a'war*, according to *Lisān al-'Arab*, refers to a person who is blind in one eye. In *Sharḥ Ṣaḥīḥ Muslim* and *Fatḥ al-Bārī*, the authors describe it as a defect of the eye, with one explanation combining it with another narration – that his right eye will have a squint or have a protruding piece of flesh that will impair his vision (*mamsūḥah al-'ayn*).
Given this, he will be one-eyed in the figurative sense of the English term: lacking vision in one eye, lacking breadth of vision, or having a defect in the vision of one eye. It is not literal as some people have understood.

8 Mullā 'Alī al-Qārī, Imam al-Nawawī, and Imam Ibn Ḥajar all transmit that this is a figurative statement that is an eloquent way of affirming Allah's transcendence and does not attribute to Allah a physical eye. Rather, it is a phrase used because the defect in his eyes is a clear evidence, both for scholars and laymen, that the Dajjāl is a created, contingent being. See *Fatḥ al-Bārī*, *Sharḥ al-Nawawī*, and *Mirqāt al-Mafātīḥ – Kitāb al-Fitan* in all three.

9 *Ṣaḥīḥ al-Bukhārī*, hadith no. 6175; *Ṣaḥīḥ Muslim*, hadith nos. 2930-2931.

one-eyed. Additionally, Ibn Ṣā'id entered Islam, reached old age, and died. Furthermore, the Prophet ﷺ said in a hadith on the authority of Tamīm al-Dārī that the Dajjāl is chained up in a peninsula in the sea, as will come. And Allah knows best.

# HADITH TWO 2

أ - مُحَمَّدُ بْنُ سَلَمَةَ عَنِ ابْنِ إِسْحَاقَ عَنْ أَيُّوبَ عَنْ نَافِعٍ عَنِ ابْنِ عُمَرَ عَنْ حَفْصَةَ عَنِ النَّبِيِّ ﷺ قَالَ يَخْرُجُ الدَّجَّالُ مِنْ غَضْبَةٍ يَغْضَبُهَا.

إِسْنَادُهُ حَسَنٌ وَسَيَأْتِي.

ب - هَوْذَةُ بْنُ خَلِيفَةَ ثَنَا عَوْفٌ عَنْ أَبِي الْمُغِيرَةِ عَنْ عَبْدِ اللهِ بْنِ عَمْرٍو قَالَ أَوَّلُ مِصْرٍ مِنْ أَمْصَارِ الْعَرَبِ يَدْخُلُهُ الدَّجَّالُ الْبَصْرَةُ.

إِسْنَادُهُ قَوِيٌّ.

A) Muhammad ibn Salamah informed us on the authority of Isḥāq from Ayyūb from Nāfiʿ from Ibn ʿUmar from Ḥafṣah that the Prophet ﷺ said, "Extreme anger is that which will cause the Dajjāl to emerge."[10] Its chain is sound, as will come.

B) Hawdhah ibn Khalīfah related that ʿAwf narrated from Abū al-Mughīrah that ʿAbdullāh ibn ʿAmr said, "The first of the Arab cities into which the Dajjāl will enter is Basra." Its chain is strong.

10 *Ṣaḥīḥ Muslim*, hadith no. 2932.

# 3 HADITH THREE

مُسْلِمٌ نَا قُتَيْبَةُ نَا عَبْدُ الْعَزِيزِ عَنْ ثَوْرِ بْنِ زَيْدٍ عَنْ أَبِي الْغَيْثِ عَنْ أَبِي هُرَيْرَةَ أَنَّ النَّبِيَّ صَلَّى اللهُ عَلَيْهِ وَسَلَّمَ قَالَ سَمِعْتُمْ بِمَدِينَةٍ جَانِبٌ مِنْهَا فِي الْبَرِّ وَجَانِبٌ فِي الْبَحْرِ قَالُوْا نَعَمْ قَالَ لَا تَقُومُ السَّاعَةُ حَتَّى يَغْزُوهَا سَبْعُونَ أَلْفًا مِنْ بَنِي إِسْمَاعِيلَ فَإِذَا جَاءُوهَا نَزَلُوْا فَلَمْ يُقَاتِلُوْا بِسِلَاحٍ قَالُوْا لَا إِلَهَ إِلَّا اللهُ وَاللهُ أَكْبَرُ فَيَسْقُطُ أَحَدُ جَانِبَيْهَا ثُمَّ تَقُوْلُ الثَّانِيَةَ لَا إِلَهَ إِلَّا اللهُ وَاللهُ أَكْبَرُ فَيَسْقُطُ جَانِبُهَا الْآخَرُ ثُمَّ تَقُوْلُ الثَّالِثَةَ لَا إِلَهَ إِلَّا اللهُ وَاللهُ أَكْبَرُ فَتُفَرَّجُ لَهُمْ فَيَدْخُلُوْنَهَا فَبَيْنَمَا هُمْ يَقْتَسِمُوْنَ الْغَنَائِمَ إِذْ جَاءَهُمُ الصَّرِيخُ أَنَّ الدَّجَّالَ قَدْ خَرَجَ فَيَتْرُكُوْنَ كُلَّ شَيْءٍ وَيَرْجِعُوْنَ. رَوَاهُ ابْنُ عَسَاكِرٍ عَنِ الْمُؤَيَّدِ.

Muslim narrated: Qutaybah narrated to us: ʿAbd al-ʿAzīz narrated to us from Thawr ibn Zayd from Abū al-Ghayth from Abū Hurayrah that the Prophet ﷺ said, "Have you heard of the city of which one side is on land while the other is over the sea?" The people replied, "Yes." He said, "The Hour will not begin until seventy thousand people belonging to the descendants of Ismāʿīl lay siege to it. When they come to it, they will dismount. However, they will not fight with swords. They will say, 'La ilāha illa Allāh wa Allāhu Akbar' and one side's defenses will fall. They will say it a second time and the other side's defenses will fall. They will say it a third time, and it will be opened for them and they will enter it. While they distribute the spoils, a loud caller will come to them (informing them) that the Dajjāl has emerged. Consequently, they will leave everything and return."[11] It was narrated by Ibn ʿAsākir from al-Muʾayyid.

11 *Ṣaḥīḥ Muslim*, hadith no. 2920.

# 4 HADITH FOUR

أَحْمَدُ بْنُ حَنْبَلٍ ثَنَا مُحَمَّدُ بْنُ جَعْفَرٍ نَا شُعْبَةُ عَنْ قَتَادَةَ سَمِعْتُ أَبَا الطُّفَيْلِ قَالَ مَرَرْتُ عَلَى حُذَيْفَةَ بْنِ أُسَيْدٍ فَقُلْتُ مَا يُقْعِدُكَ وَقَدْ خَرَجَ الدَّجَّالُ قَالَ اُقْعُدْ فَذَكَرَ الْحَدِيْثَ وَقَالَ فِيهِ ثَلَاثُ عَلَامَاتٍ أَنَّهُ أَعْوَرُ وَرَبُّكُمْ لَيْسَ بِأَعْوَرَ وَلَا يَسْخَرُ لَهُ مِنَ الدَّوَابِّ إِلَّا حِمَارٌ رِجْسٌ عَلَى رِجْسٍ مَكْتُوبٌ بَيْنَ عَيْنَيْهِ كَافِرٌ يَقْرَأُهُ كُلُّ مُؤْمِنٍ كَاتِبٌ أَوْ غَيْرُ كَاتِبٍ. صَحِيحٌ.

Muhammad ibn Ja'far narrated to us: Shu'bah narrated to us that Qatādah said, "I heard Abū al-Ṭufayl say, 'I passed by Ḥudhayfah ibn Usayd and said, "What could make you sit while the Dajjāl has emerged?" He replied, "Sit." He mentioned a hadith and said, "He has three signs: he is one-eyed and your Lord is not one-eyed. No animal besides a donkey will be subjugated to him. He will be an impurity upon another impurity. Between his eyes is written *'kāfir* (disbeliever)'. Every literate and illiterate will be able to read it."'"[12] This hadith is authentic.

12 'Abdullāh ibn Aḥmad ibn Ḥanbal, *al-Sunnah*, hadith no. 833.

# HADITH FIVE 5

أَحْمَدُ بْنُ حَنْبَلٍ ثَنَا حَيْوَةُ بْنُ شُرَيْحٍ ثَنَا بَقِيَّةُ حَدَّثَنِي يَحْيَى بْنُ سَعْدٍ عَنْ خَالِدِ بْنِ مَعْدَانَ عَنْ عَمْرِو بْنِ الأَسْوَدِ عَنْ جُنَادَةَ بْنِ أَبِي أُمَيَّةَ حَدَّثَهُمْ عَنْ عُبَادَةَ بْنِ الصَّامِتِ قَالَ إِنَّ رَسُولَ اللهِ صَلَّى اللَّهُ عَلَيْهِ وَسَلَّمَ قَالَ إِنِّي قَدْ حَدَّثْتُكُمْ عَنِ الدَّجَّالِ حَتَّى خَشِيتُ أَنْ لَا تَعْقِلُوا جَعْدًا أَعْوَرَ فَاعْلَمُوا أَنَّ رَبَّكُمْ لَيْسَ بِأَعْوَرَ وَأَنَّكُمْ لَنْ تَرَوْا رَبَّكُمْ حَتَّى تَمُوتُوا. هٰذَا حَدِيثٌ حَسَنٌ مُتَّصِلٌ.

Aḥmad ibn Ḥanbal narrated: Ḥaywah ibn Shurayḥ narrated to us: Baqiyyah narrated to us: Yaḥyā ibn Sa'd narrated to me from Sa'd ibn Khālid ibn Ma'dan from 'Amr ibn al-Aswad that Junādah ibn Abī Umayyah narrated to them that 'Ubādah ibn al-Ṣāmit said, "The Messenger of Allah ﷺ said, 'I have narrated to you about the Dajjāl to the point that I fear that you will not understand. He has kinky hair and is one-eyed. Know that your Lord is not one-eyed, and that you will not see him until after you die.'"[13] This is a sound hadith with a contiguous chain.

13 *Sunan Abī Dāwūd*, hadith no. 4320; *Musnad al-Imām Aḥmad*, hadith nos. 19850 and 19967; *Musnad al-Bazzār*, hadith no. 3590.

# 6 HADITH SIX

أَحْمَدُ بْنُ حَنْبَلٍ نَا إِسْمَاعِيلُ بْنُ إِبْرَاهِيمَ أَنَا ابْنُ عَوْنٍ عَنْ مُجَاهِدٍ قَالَ كَانَ جُنَادَةُ بْنُ أَبِي أُمَيَّةَ أَمِيرًا عَلَيْنَا فِي الْبَحْرِ سِتَّ سِنِينَ فَخَطَبَنَا ذَاتَ يَوْمٍ فَقَالَ دَخَلْنَا عَلَى رَجُلٍ مِنْ أَصْحَابِ النَّبِيِّ صَلَّى اللَّهُ عَلَيْهِ وَسَلَّمَ فَقُلْنَا حَدِّثْنَا مَا سَمِعْتَ مِنْ رَسُولِ اللهِ صَلَّى اللَّهُ عَلَيْهِ وَسَلَّمَ فَقَالَ قَامَ فِينَا رَسُولُ اللهِ صَلَّى اللَّهُ عَلَيْهِ وَسَلَّمَ فَقَالَ أُنْذِرُكُمُ الْمَسِيحَ الدَّجَّالَ هُوَ رَجُلٌ مَمْسُوحُ الْعَيْنِ فَاعْلَمُوا أَنَّ اللَّهَ لَيْسَ بِأَعْوَرَ. وَهٰذَا صَحِيحُ الْإِسْنَادِ وَمَا خَرَّجَهُ السِّتَّةُ.

Aḥmad ibn Ḥanbal narrated: Ismāʿīl ibn Ibrāhīm narrated to us: Ibn ʿAwn narrated to us that Mujāhid said, "Junādah ibn Abī Umayyah was our commander at sea for six years. One day, he gave us a sermon saying, 'We entered upon a man from the Companions of the Prophet ﷺ. We said to him, "Narrate to us something you heard from the Messenger of Allah ﷺ." He said, "The Messenger of Allah ﷺ stood up in our gathering and said, 'I warn you of the disfigured one. He is a man that is disfigured. Know that Allah is not one-eyed.'"'"[14] The chain of transmission for this hadith is authentic, even if the authors of the Six Books did not narrate it.

14 *Musnad Aḥmad*, hadith nos. 23090 and 23683 with slight variation in the wording.

# 7 HADITH SEVEN

أَخْبَرَنَا مُحَمَّدُ بْنُ أَبِي الْفَتْحِ بِطَرَابُلُس أَنَا عَبْدُ الْوَهَّابِ بْنِ مُحَمَّدٍ أَنَا مُسَدَّدُ بْنُ الْخَصِيبِ أَنَا عَلِيُّ بْنُ الْمُسْلِمِ أَنَا أَحْمَدُ بْنُ عَبْدِ الْوَاحِدِ أَنَا خَلَفُ بْنُ مُحَمَّدِ بْنِ أَحْمَدَ بْنِ عُثْمَانَ أَنَا أَحْمَدُ بْنُ هِلَالٍ ثَنَا مُوسَى بْنُ عَامِرٍ نَا الْوَلِيدُ أَخْبَرَنِي شَيْبَانُ عَنْ لَيْثٍ عَنْ بِشْرٍ عَنْ أَنَسِ بْنِ مَالِكٍ قَالَ سَمِعْتُ رَسُولَ اللَّهِ صَلَّى اللَّهُ عَلَيْهِ وَسَلَّمَ يَقُولُ بَيْنَ يَدَيِ الدَّجَّالِ نَيِّفٌ وَسَبْعُونَ دَجَّالًا.

قُلْتُ إِسْنَادُهُ ضَعِيفٌ.

Muhammad ibn Abī al-Fatḥ informed us in Tripoli: ʿAbd al-Wahhāb ibn Muhammad informed us: Musaddad ibn al-Khuṣayb informed us: ʿAlī ibn al-Muslim informed us: Aḥmad ibn ʿAbd al-Wāḥid informed us: Khalaf ibn Muhammad ibn Aḥmad ibn ʿUthmān informed us: Aḥmad ibn Hilāl narrated to us: Mūsā ibn ʿĀmir narrated to us: al-Walīd narrated to us: Shaybān informed me on the authority of Layth from Bishr that Anas ibn Mālik said, "I heard the Messenger of Allah ﷺ say, 'Just before the Dajjāl, there will be seventy-something *dajjāls*.'"[15]

15 *Kanz al-ʿUmmāl*, 38379.

# 8 HADITH EIGHT

أَخْبَرَنَا إِسْمَاعِيلُ بْنُ عَبْدِ الرَّحْمَٰنِ بْنِ الْفَرَّاءِ أَنَا الْإِمَامُ أَبُو مُحَمَّدٍ عَبْدُ اللهِ بْنُ قُدَامَةَ أَخْبَرَنَا مُحَمَّدُ بْنُ عَبْدِ الْبَاقِيِّ بْنِ أَحْمَدَ بْنِ سَلْمَانَ أَنَا أَبُو الْفَضْلِ أَحْمَدُ بْنُ الْحُسَيْنِ بْنِ خَيْرُونَ قَالَ وَأَنْبَا يَحْيَى بْنُ ثَابِتٍ أَنْبَا أَبِي قَالَ أَنْبَا أَحْمَدُ بْنُ مُحَمَّدِ بْنِ غَالِبٍ قَالَ قَرَأْتُ عَلَى أَبِي الْعَبَّاسِ بْنِ حَمْدَانَ حَدَّثَكُمْ مُحَمَّدُ بْنُ أَيُّوبَ أَنْبَا عُبَيْدُ اللهِ بْنِ مُعَاذٍ ثَنَا أَبِي ثَنَا شُعْبَةُ عَنْ سَعْدِ بْنِ إِبْرَاهِيمَ عَنْ مُحَمَّدِ بْنِ الْمُنْكَدِرِ قَالَ رَأَيْتُ جَابِرَ بْنَ عَبْدِ اللهِ يَحْلِفُ أَنَّ ابْنَ صَائِدٍ الدَّجَّالُ قَالَ فَقُلْتُ تَحْلِفُ بِاللهِ قَالَ سَمِعْتُ عُمَرَ بْنَ الْخَطَّابِ يَحْلِفُ عِنْدَ النَّبِيِّ ﷺ فَلَمْ يُنْكِرْهُ النَّبِيُّ ﷺ قُلْتُ لَمْ يَكُنْ ﷺ جَزَمَ بِالنَّفْيِ. صَحِيحٌ مُتَّفَقٌ عَلَيْهِ رَوَاهُ مُسْلِمٌ عَنْ عُبَيْدِ اللهِ بْنِ مُعَاذٍ وَالْبُخَارِيُّ عَنْ حَمَّادِ بْنِ إِسْمَاعِيلَ عَنْ عُبَيْدِ اللهِ بْنِ مُعَاذٍ. قُلْتُ فِيهِ دَلِيلٌ عَلَى جَوَازِ الْحَلْفِ عَلَى غَلَبَةِ الظَّنِّ وَقَدْ نَهَى النَّبِيُّ ﷺ عُمَرَ بْنَ الْخَطَّابِ عَنْ قَتْلِهِ وَقَالَ:

Ismāʿīl ibn ʿAbd al-Raḥmān al-Farrā' informed us: Imam Muhammad ʿAbdullāh ibn Qudāmah narrated to us: Muhammad ibn ʿAbd al-Bāqī ibn Aḥmad ibn Salmān informed us: Abū al-Faḍl Aḥmad ibn al-Ḥusayn ibn Khayrūn informed us saying: Yaḥyā ibn Thābit related: My father related saying: Aḥmad ibn Muhammad ibn Ghālib related: I recited to Abū al-ʿAbbās ibn Ḥamdān: Muhammad ibn Ayyūb narrated to you all: ʿUbayd Allāh ibn Muʿādh related:

my father related that Shuʿbah narrated to us from Saʿīd ibn Ibrāhīm that Muhammad ibn Munkadir said, "I saw Jābir ibn ʿAbdullāh swear that Ibn Ṣā'id (Ibn Ṣayyād) was the Dajjāl. I said to him, 'Do you swear by Allah?' He replied, 'I heard ʿUmar ibn al-Khaṭṭāb swear to that in the presence of the Prophet ﷺ, and the Prophet ﷺ did not censure him.'"[16] I say (al-Maqdisī): He ﷺ was not sure about it being false. This hadith is authentic and agreed upon. Muslim narrated it from ʿUbayd Allāh ibn Muʿādh and al-Bukhārī narrated it from Ḥamdān ibn Ismāʿīl from ʿUbayd Allāh ibn Muʿādh.

I (al-Maqdisī) say: There is also evidence (in this hadith) of the permissibility of swearing an oath based on high probability.

The Prophet ﷺ prohibited ʿUmar ibn al-Khaṭṭāb from killing him by saying:

16 *Ṣaḥīḥ al-Bukhārī*, hadith no. 7355; *Ṣaḥīḥ Muslim*, hadith no. 2929.

# 9 HADITH NINE

إِنْ لَّمْ يَكُنْ هُوَ فَلَا خَيْرَ لَكَ فِيْ قَتْلِهِ. وَهٰذَا تَوَقُّفٌ فِيْ مِنْهُ فِيْ أَمْرِهِ.

"If he is not him (the Dajjāl), then there is no good in you killing him."[17]

This represented a suspension of judgement from him ﷺ regarding his (Ibn Ṣayyād's) affair.



17 Its source was mentioned in the sourcing of hadith no. 1.

# HADITH TEN 10

أَخْبَرَنَا يَحْيَ بْنُ ثَابِتٍ أَنْبَا أَبِيْ أَنْبَا الْبَرْقَانِيُّ أَنْبَا الْإِسْمَاعِيلِيُّ نَا يَحْيَى بْنُ صَاعِدٍ نَا يُوْسُفُ بْنُ سَعِيْدٍ ثَنَا حَجَّاجُ عَنِ [ابْنِ] جُرَيْجٍ أَخْبَرَنِيْ مُوْسَى بْنُ عُقْبَةَ عَنْ نَافِعٍ عَنِ ابْنِ عُمَرَ قَالَ ذَكَرَ رَسُولُ اللهِ صَلَّى اللهُ عَلَيْهِ وَسَلَّمَ يَوْمًا بَيْنَ ظَهْرَيِ النَّاسِ الْمَسِيحَ الدَّجَّالَ فَقَالَ إِنَّ اللهَ لَيْسَ بِأَعْوَرَ إِلَّا أَنَّ الدَّجَّالَ أَعْوَرُ الْعَيْنِ الْيُمْنَى كَأَنَّهَا عِنَبَةٌ طَافِيَةٌ وَقَالَ رَسُولُ اللهِ صَلَّى اللهُ عَلَيْهِ وَسَلَّمَ أَرَانِيَ اللَّيْلَةَ فِي الْمَنَامِ عِنْدَ الْكَعْبَةِ فَإِذَا رَجُلٌ كَأَحْسَنِ مَا يُرَى مِنَ الرِّجَالِ يَضْرِبُ لِمَّتَهُ بَيْنَ مَنْكِبَيْهِ رَجِلُ الشَّعْرِ يَقْطُرُ رَأْسُهُ وَاضِعًا يَدَهُ عَلَى مَنْكِبَيْ رَجُلَيْهِ فَهُوَ بَيْنَهُمَا يَطُوْفُ بِالْبَيْتِ فَقُلْتُ مَنْ هٰذَا قَالُوْا الْمَسِيْحُ ابْنُ مَرْيَمَ وَرَأَيْتُ رَجُلًا وَرَاءَهُ جَعْدًا قَطَطًا أَعْوَرَ الْعَيْنِ كَأَشْبَهِ مَنْ رَأَيْتُهُ مِنَ النَّاسِ بِابْنِ قَطَنٍ وَاضِعًا يَدَهُ عَلَى مَنْكِبَيْ رَجُلَيْنِ فَقُلْتُ مَنْ هَذَا فَقَالَ الْمَسِيْحُ الدَّجَّالُ. قَالَ فَقَالَ نَافِعٌ كَانَ عَبْدُ اللهِ بْنُ عُمَرَ يَقُوْلُ وَاللهِ مَا أَشُكُّ أَنَّ الْمَسِيْخَ الدَّجَّالَ ابْنُ صَيَّادٍ. صَحِيْحٌ مُتَّفَقٌ عَلَيْهِ رَوَاهُ الْبُخَارِيُّ عَنْ إِبْرَاهِيمَ بْنِ الْمُنْذِرِ وَمُسْلِمٌ عَنْ مُحَمَّدِ بْنِ إِسْحَاقَ الْمُسَيْبِيِّ كِلَاهُمَا عَنْ أَبِيْ ضَمْرَةَ أَنَسِ بْنِ عِيَاضٍ. وَرَوَاهُ مُسْلِمٌ أَيْضًا عَنْ مُحَمَّدِ بْنِ عَبَّادٍ الْمَكِّيِّ عَنْ حَاتِمِ بْنِ إِسْمَاعِيلَ كِلَاهُمَا. عَنْ مُوْسَى بْنِ عُقْبَةَ سَمِعْنَاهُ فِيْ الصَّحِيْحِ.

Yaḥyā ibn Thābit narrated to us: My father related: al-Burqānī narrated: al-Ismāʿīlī related: Yaḥyā ibn Ṣāʾid informed us: Yūsuf ibn Saʿīd informed us: Ḥajjāj narrated to us from[18] Jurayj: Mūsā ibn ʿUqbah informed me from Nāfiʿ that Ibn ʿUmar said, "One day, between the two afternoon prayers, the Messenger of Allah ﷺ mentioned al-Masīḥ al-Dajjāl. He said, 'Allah is not one-eyed. Indeed, the Dajjāl has a defective right eye, as if it were a floating grape.' The Messenger of Allah ﷺ also said, 'One night, in a dream, I was shown myself near the Kaʿbah when there appeared a brown-skinned man of the most beautiful of men that are seen among the brown-skinned[19]. His locks reached his two shoulders. His hair was curly and his head was dripping with water. He was placing his hand upon the shoulders of two men. He was walking between them and circumambulating the House. I said, "Who is this?" They responded, "ʿĪsā ibn Maryam." I also saw another man behind him. He had kinky hair, was of short height, and was one-eyed. The most similar of people to him in appearance was Ibn Qaṭan. He was placing his hands on the shoulders of two men. I said, "Who is this?" They said, "Al-Masīḥ al-Dajjāl."'"[20] The narrator commented, "Nāfiʿ said, 'ʿAbdullāh ibn ʿUmar used

18 Footnote from the original Arabic text: There is a missing word here. The narrator's name is Ibn Jurayj who is known to have narrated from Ḥajjāj, that is, Ḥajjāj ibn al-Aʿwar.

19 In the original Arabic text, the author omits the words "ādam" (brown-skinned) and "udm" (brownness). We have included it to correspond with the most authentic text in Ṣaḥīḥ al-Bukhārī.

20 *Ṣaḥīḥ al-Bukhārī*, hadith nos. 3439 and 3440; *Ṣaḥīḥ Muslim*, hadith no. 169.

to say, 'By Allah, I do not doubt that al-Masīḥ al-Dajjāl is Ibn Ṣayyād.'"[21]

This Hadith is authentic. Al-Bukhārī narrated it from Ibrāhīm ibn al-Mundhir and Muslim from Muhammad ibn Isḥāq al-Musayyibī, both by way of Abū Ḍamrah Anas ibn 'Iyāḍ. Muslim also narrated it from Muhammad ibn 'Ibād al-Makkī from Ḥātim ibn Ismā'īl, each from Mūsā ibn 'Uqbah. We heard it in "al-Ṣaḥīḥ".

21 *Sunan Abī Dāwūd*, hadith no. 4330.

# 11 HADITH ELEVEN

أَخْبَرَنَا يَحْيَى بْنُ ثَابِتٍ أَنْبَا أَبِي أَنَا أَحْمَدُ بْنُ مُحَمَّدٍ أَنْبَا أَحْمَدُ بْنُ إِبْرَاهِيمَ أَخْبَرَنَا مُحَمَّدُ بْنُ يَحْيَى بْنِ سُلَيْمَانَ ثَنَا عَاصِمُ بْنُ عَلِيٍّ ثَنَا إِبْرَاهِيمُ بْنُ سَعْدٍ ح وَأَخْبَرَنِي الْحَسَنُ ثَنَا مَنْصُورُ بْنُ مَزَاحِمٍ ثَنَا إِبْرَاهِيمُ يَعْنِي ابْنَ سَعْدٍ قَالَ وَنَا مُحَمَّدُ بْنُ خُلْدٍ ثَنَا إِبْرَاهِيمُ بْنُ سَعْدٍ. وَأَخْبَرَنَا أَبُو يَعْلَى ثَنَا أَبُو خَيْثَمَةَ نَا يَعْقُوبُ ثَنَا أَبِي عَنِ ابْنِ شِهَابٍ أَخْبَرَنِي سَالِمٌ سَمِعَ عَبْدَ اللهِ بْنَ عُمَرَ يَقُولُ لَا وَاللهِ مَا قَالَ رَسُولُ اللهِ ﷺ لِعِيسَى أَحْمَرَ وَلَكِنَّ رَسُولَ اللهِ ﷺ قَالَ بَيْنَا أَنَا نَائِمٌ أَرَانِي أَطُوفُ بِالْكَعْبَةِ فَإِذَا رَجُلٌ آدَمُ سِبْطُ الشَّعْرِ يُهَادِي بَيْنَ رَجُلَيْنِ يَنْطِفُ رَأْسُهُ دَمًا أَوْ يُهَرَاقُ رَأْسُهُ فَقُلْتُ مَنْ هٰذَا قَالُوا هٰذَا ابْنُ مَرْيَمَ فَذَهَبْتُ أَلْتَفِتُ فَإِذَا رَجُلٌ أَحْمَرُ جَسِيمٌ جَعْدُ الرَّأْسِ أَعْوَرُ الْعَيْنِ الْيُمْنَى كَأَنَّ عَيْنَهُ عِنَبَةٌ طَافِيَةٌ فَقُلْتُ مَنْ هٰذَا فَقَالُوا هٰذَا الدَّجَّالُ أَقْرَبُ النَّاسِ بِهِ شِبْهًا رَجُلٌ مِنْ خُزَاعَةَ يُقَالُ لَهُ ابْنُ قَطَنٍ. قَالَ مُحَمَّدٌ الزُّهْرِيُّ وَكَانَ ابْنُ قَطَنٍ رَجُلًا مِنْ خُزَاعَةَ وَهُوَ مِنْ بَنِي الْمُصْطَلَقِ وَهَلَكَ فِي الْجَاهِلِيَّةِ.

قَالَ مَنْصُورٌ عِنَبَةٌ طَافِيَةٌ أَوْ طَايِفِيَّةٌ شَكَّ مَنْصُورٌ. حَدِيثُهُمْ مُتَقَارِبٌ. صَحِيحٌ مُتَّفَقٌ عَلَيْهِ رَوَاهُ الْبُخَارِيُّ عَنْ أَحْمَدَ بْنِ مُحَمَّدٍ الْمَكِّيِّ عَنْ إِبْرَاهِيمَ بْنِ سَعْدٍ وَعَنْ أَبِي الْيَمَانِ عَنْ شُعَيْبٍ وَعَنْ سَعِيدِ بْنِ عُفَيْرٍ عَنِ اللَّيْثِ عَنْ عُقَيْلٍ وَمُسْلِمٌ عَنْ حَرْمَلَةَ عَنِ ابْنِ وَهْبٍ عَنْ يُونُسَ كُلُّهُمْ عَنِ الزُّهْرِيِّ وَابْنُ قَطَنٍ اسْمُهُ عَبْدُ الْعُزَّى بْنُ قَطَنٍ وَتَهَادَى بَيْنَ اثْنَيْنِ أَيْ يَعْتَمِدُ عَلَيْهِمَا

# HADITH ELEVEN 11

وَيَدُورُ مِنْ جَانِبَيْهِ وَيُوَحِّدُ بِعَضُدَيْهِ وَيَنْطِفُ رَأْسُهُ أَيْ يَقْطُرُ. أَخْبَرَنَاهُ جَمَاعَةٌ عَنِ ابْنِ الرُّتَيْلِ مِنْ مُسْنَدِهِ.

Yaḥyā ibn Thābit informed us: My father informed us: Aḥmad ibn Muhammad related: Aḥmad ibn Ibrāhīm informed us: Muhammad ibn Yaḥyā ibn Sulaymān informed us: ʿĀṣim ibn ʿAlī narrated to us: Ibrāhīm ibn Saʿd narrated to us: al-Ḥasan informed me: Manṣūr ibn Muzāḥim narrated to us: Ibrāhīm – meaning Ibn Saʿd – narrated to us, saying: Muhammad ibn Khuld informed us: Ibrāhīm ibn Ṣāʿd narrated to us.

And Abū Yaʿlā informed me: Abū Khaytham narrated to us: Yaʿqūb informed us: My father narrated to us from Ibn Shihāb: Sālim informed me that he heard ʿAbdullāh ibn ʿUmar say, "No. By Allah! The Messenger of Allah ﷺ did not say that ʿĪsā was of white complexion. Rather, the Messenger of Allah ﷺ said, 'While I was asleep, I was shown myself circumambulating the Kaʿbah. Suddenly a brown-skinned man appeared. He had lanky hair, and was walking between two men. His head dripped blood – or his head dripped sweat. I said, "Who is this?" They said, "This is ʿĪsā ibn Maryam."

I continued my path, looking around, and I saw a white complected man who was corpulent and had thick, curly hair. He was blind in the right eye. It was as if it was a floating grape. I said, "Who is this?" They said, "That is the Dajjāl." The closest of people in resemblance to him is a man from Khuzā'ah named Ibn Qaṭan.'"[22] Muhammad al-Zuhrī said, "Ibn Qaṭan was a man of Khuzā'ah from the clan of Banū al-Muṣṭaliq. He died during the period of Jāhiliyyah."

Manṣūr said (regarding "a floating grape"), "The word is either *'inab ṭāfiyah or 'inab ṭāyifah*." He was unsure, but their hadiths are very similar.

This hadith is *ṣaḥīḥ* and agreed upon. Al-Bukhārī narrated it from Aḥmad ibn Muhammad al-Makkī from Ibrāhīm ibn Sa'd, from Abū al-Yamān from Shu'ayb and from Sa'īd ibn 'Ufayr from al-Layth from 'Aqīl. Muslim narrated it from Ḥarmalah from Ibn Wahb from Yūnus. All of the previous narrations are through al-Zuhrī. Ibn Qaṭan's name is 'Abd al-'Uzzā ibn Qaṭan. "He was walking between two men" means that he was leaning upon them, turning from side to side, and uniting their two sides. "*Yanṭifu ra'suhū*" means to drip. A group informed us of this from Ibn al-Ratīl from his *Musnad*.

22 *Ṣaḥīḥ al-Bukhārī*, hadith no. 3441.

HADITH TWELVE 12

أَخْبَرَنَا يَحْيَى بْنُ ثَابِتٍ أَنبَا أَبِيْ أَنْبَا الْبَرْقَانِيُّ أَنْبَا الْإِسْمَاعِيلِيُّ أَخْبَرَنِيْ الْهَسَنْجَانِيُّ نَا مُحَمَّدُ بْنُ مُسْلِمٍ ثَنَا أَبُو الْيَمَانِ ثَنَا شُعَيْبٌ عَنِ الزُّهْرِيِّ قَالَ سَالِمٌ سَمِعْتُ عَبْدَ اللهِ ابْنَ عُمَرَ يَقُوْلُ انْطَلَقَ رَسُولُ اللهِ صَلَّى اللَّهُ عَلَيْهِ وَسَلَّمَ بَعْدَ ذٰلِكَ وَأُبَيُّ بْنُ كَعْبٍ قِبَلَ اِبْنِ صَيَّادٍ حَدَثَ فِيْ نَخْلٍ فَلَمَا دَخَلَ رَسُولُ اللهِ صَلَّى اللَّهُ عَلَيْهِ وَسَلَّمَ طَفِقَ يَتَّقِي بِجُذُوعِ النَّخْلِ وَابْنُ صَيَّادٍ فِيْ قَطِيفَةٍ لَهُ فِيْهَا زَهْزَهَةٌ فَرَأَتْ أُمُّ ابْنُ صَيَّادٍ رَسُوْلَ اللهِ ﷺ فَقَالَتْ يَا صَافِ هَذَا مُحَمَّدٌ فَوَثَبَ ابْنُ صَيَّادٍ فَقَالَ رَسُولُ اللهِ صَلَّى اللَّهُ عَلَيْهِ وَسَلَّمَ لَوْ تَرَكَتْهُ بَيَّنَ لَوْ تَرَكَتْهُ بَيَّنَ لَفْظُ حَمِيْدٌ وَقَالَ الْهَسَنْجَانِيُّ فَطَفِقَ يَتَّقِي بِجُذُوْعِ النَّخْلِ وَهُوَ يَحْتَالُ أَنْ يَّسْمَعَ مِنِ ابْنِ صَيّادٍ شَيْئًا قَبْلَ أَنْ يَّرَاهُ وَابْنُ صَيَّادٍ فِيْ قَطِيفَةٍ لَهُ فِيْهَا زَهْزَهَةٌ فَرَأَتْ أُمُّ ابْنُ صَيَّادٍ النَّبِيَّ ﷺ فَقَالَتْ يَا صَافِ هَذَا مُحَمَّدٌ يعني فَثَارَ أَوْ كَلِمَةٌ أُخْرٰى فَقَالَ رَسُوْلُ اللهِ ﷺ لَوْ تَرَكَتْهُ بَيَّنَ.

صَحِيْحٌ رَوَاهُ الْبُخَارِيُّ عَنْ أَبِي الْيَمَانِ كَذٰلِكَ أَخبَرنَاهُ أَقْوَامٌ وَجَمَاعَةٌ بِإِسْنَادٍ إِلَى الْبُخَارِيِّ فَوَقَعَ عَالِيًا بِدَرَجَةٍ

Yaḥyā ibn Thābit informed us: My father informed us: al-Burqānī informed us: al-Ismā'īlī informed us: al-Hisinjānī informed me: Muhammad ibn Muslim related: Abū al-Yamān narrated to us: Shu'ayb narrated to us that al-Zuhrī said, "I heard 'Abdullāh ibn 'Umar say, 'After that, the Messenger of Allah ﷺ went with Ubayy ibn Ka'b to Ibn Ṣayyād. He was speaking in a date grove. When the Messenger ﷺ entered, he ducked and hid himself with the stump of a date palm. Ibn Ṣayyād was on a bed mumbling something. Afterwards, the mother of Ibn Ṣayyād saw the Messenger of Allah ﷺ and said, "O Ṣāf, here is Muhammad." So, Ibn Ṣayyād jumped up. The Messenger of Allah ﷺ said, "If she had left him (his matter) would become clear."""[23]

This is the wording of Ḥumayd. Al-Hisinjānī narrated it with the wording, "So, he got down hiding himself with the stump of a date palm, attempting to hear something from Ibn Ṣayyād before the latter saw him. Ibn Ṣayyād was on a bed mumbling something. The mother of Ibn Ṣayyād saw the Prophet ﷺ and said, 'O Ṣāf, here is Muhammad' – meaning he was disturbed or something else. The Messenger ﷺ said, 'If she had left him, it would become clear.'"

This hadith is authentic. Al-Bukhārī narrated it from Abū al-Yamān. Likewise, many scholars informed us of it – a group of them with their chain of narration to al-Bukhārī, and by that, the level of its chain of narration was raised.

23 This hadith was sourced in hadith no. 1.

# 13 HADITH THIRTEEN

أَخْبَرَنَا أَحْمَدُ بْنُ هِبَةِ اللهِ بْنِ أَحْمَدَ سَنَةَ ثَلَاثٍ وَتِسْعِينَ عَنِ الْمُؤَيَّدِ الطُّوسِيِّ أَنَا مُحَمَّدُ بْنُ الْفَضْلِ الْعَتَبَةُ أَنَا عَبْدُ الْغَافِرِ بْنُ مُحَمَّدٍ الْفَارِسِيُّ أَنَا أَبُو أَحْمَدَ مُحَمَّدُ بْنُ عِيسَى بْنِ عَمْرَوَيْهِ نَا إِبْرَاهِيمُ بْنُ مُحَمَّدِ بْنِ سُفْيَانَ ثَنَا مُسْلِمُ بْنُ الْحَجَّاجِ ثَنَا مُحَمَّدُ بْنُ الْمُثَنَّى ثَنَا سَالِمُ بْنُ نُوحٍ أَنَا الْجُرَيْرِيُّ عَنْ أَبِي نَضْرَةَ عَنْ أَبِي سَعِيدٍ قَالَ خَرَجْنَا حُجَّاجًا أَوْ عُمَّارًا وَمَعَنَا ابْنُ صَائِدٍ فَنَزَلْنَا مَنْزِلًا فَتَفَرَّقَ النَّاسُ وَبَقِيتُ أَنَا وَهُوَ فَاسْتَوْحَشْتُ مِنْهُ وَحْشَةً شَدِيدَةً مِمَّا يُقَالُ عَلَيْهِ قَالَ وَجَاءَ بِمَتَاعِهِ فَوَضَعَهُ مَعَ مَتَاعِي فَقُلْتُ إِنَّ الْحَرَّ شَدِيدٌ فَلَوْ وَضَعْتَهُ تَحْتَ تِلْكَ الشَّجَرَةِ فَفَعَلَ قَالَ فَرُفِعَتْ لَنَا غَنَمٌ فَانْطَلَقَ فَجَاءَ بِعُسٍّ فَقَالَ اشْرَبْ أَبَا سَعِيدٍ فَقُلْتُ إِنَّ الْحَرَّ شَدِيدٌ وَاللَّبَنُ حَارٌّ مَا بِي إِلَّا أَنِّي أَكْرَهُ أَنْ أَشْرَبَ مِنْ يَدِهِ أَوْ قَالَ آخُذَ عَنْ يَدِهِ فَقَالَ أَبَا سَعِيدٍ لَقَدْ هَمَمْتُ أَنْ آخُذَ حَبْلًا فَأُعَلِّقَهُ بِشَجَرَةٍ ثُمَّ أَخْتَنِقَ مِمَّا يَقُولُ لِي النَّاسُ يَا أَبَا سَعِيدٍ مَنْ خَفِيَ عَلَيْهِ رَسُولُ اللهِ صَلَّى اللهُ عَلَيْهِ وَسَلَّمَ مَا خَفِيَ عَلَيْكُمْ مَعْشَرَ الْأَنْصَارِ أَلَسْتَ مِنْ أَعْلَمِ النَّاسِ بِحَدِيثِ رَسُولِ اللهِ صَلَّى اللهُ عَلَيْهِ وَسَلَّمَ أَلَيْسَ قَدْ قَالَ وَهُوَ كَافِرٌ وَأَنَا مُسْلِمٌ أَوَلَيْسَ قَدْ قَالَ هُوَ عَقِيمٌ لَا يُولَدُ لَهُ وَقَدْ تَرَكْتُ وَلَدِي بِالْمَدِينَةِ أَوَلَيْسَ قَدْ قَالَ لَا يَدْخُلُ الْمَدِينَةَ وَلَا مَكَّةَ وَقَدْ أَقْبَلْتُ مِنَ الْمَدِينَةِ وَأَنَا أُرِيدُ مَكَّةَ قَالَ أَبُو سَعِيدٍ حَتَّى كِدْتُ أَنْ أَعْذِرَهُ ثُمَّ قَالَ أَمَا وَاللهِ إِنِّي لَأَعْرِفُهُ وَأَعْرِفُ مَوْلِدَهُ وَأَيْنَ هُوَ الْآنَ فَقُلْتُ لَهُ تَبًّا لَكَ سَائِرَ الْيَوْمِ.

# 13 HADITH THIRTEEN

Aḥmad ibn Hibat Allāh ibn Aḥmad informed us in the year 93 (AH) from al-Mu'ayyad al-Ṭūsī: Muhammad ibn al-Faḍl al-ʿUtbah related: ʿAbd al-Ghāfir ibn Muhammad al-Fārisī related: Abū Aḥmad Muhammad ibn ʿĪsā ibn ʿAmrawayh related: Ibrāhīm ibn Muhammad ibn Sufyān related: Muslim ibn al-Ḥajjāj narrated to us: Muhammad ibn al-Muthannā narrated to us: Sālim ibn Nūḥ narrated to us: al-Jurayrī related from Abū Naḍrah that Abū Saʿīd said, "We set out to perform hajj – or ʿ*umrah*. With us was Ibn Ṣā'id. We came to a dwelling and people split up. Only he and I remained. I felt intense dread due to what had been said of him. He went for his possessions and placed them with mine. So, I said to him, 'The heat is intense. Why will you not place them under the tree?' He did so. Then, a sheep was served to us. He then went off and returned with a large container. He said, 'Drink, O Abū Saʿīd.' I said, 'The heat is intense and the milk is hot.' I only disliked to drink something from his hand (or he said "taking from his hand"). He said to me: 'Abū Saʿīd, I intended to take a rope, hang it from a tree, and strangle myself because of what people have said to me. O Abū Saʿīd, for whom did the Messenger of Allah ﷺ fear what he feared for you, O Anṣār? Are you not from the most knowledgeable of people of the hadith of the Messenger of Allah ﷺ? Did he not say, "He (the Dajjāl) is a disbeliever"? I am a believer. Did he not say, "He is sterile and no child will be born to him"? I left my son behind in Madinah. Did he not say, "He will neither enter Madinah nor Makkah"? I have left Madinah and am headed for Makkah.'" Abū Sa'īd said, "I almost apologized to him. But then he said, 'By Allah, I know him. I know his birthplace and where he is now.' So, I said to him, 'May you be cursed for the rest of the day.'"[24]

24 *Ṣaḥīḥ Muslim*, hadith no. 2927; *Sunan al-Tirmidhī*, hadith no. 2396.

# 14 HADITH FOURTEEN

جَرِيرٌ وَأَبُو مُعَاوِيَةَ عَنِ الْأَعْمَشِ عَنْ أَبِي وَائِلٍ عَنْ عَبْدِ اللَّهِ قَالَ كُنَّا مَعَ رَسُولِ اللَّهِ صَلَّى اللَّهُ عَلَيْهِ وَسَلَّمَ فَمَرَرْنَا بِصِبْيَانٍ فِيهِمُ ابْنُ صَائِدٍ فَفَرَّ الصِّبْيَانُ وَجَلَسَ ابْنُ صَائِدٍ فَكَأَنَّ رَسُولَ اللَّهِ صَلَّى اللَّهُ عَلَيْهِ وَسَلَّمَ كَرِهَ ذَلِكَ فَقَالَ لَهُ تَرِبَتْ يَدَاكَ أَتَشْهَدُ أَنِّي رَسُولُ اللَّهِ قَالَ لَا أَتَشْهَدُ أَنِّي رَسُولُ اللَّهِ فَقَالَ عُمَرُ يَا رَسُولَ اللَّهِ ذَرْنِي أَقْتُلَهُ قَالَ دَعْهُ فَإِنْ يَكُنِ الَّذِي تَخَافُ فَلَنْ تَسْتَطِيعَ قَتْلَهُ. وَقَعَ لَنَا فِي م.

Jarīr and Abū Muʿāwiyah narrate on the authority of al-Aʿmash from Abū Wā'il that ʿAbdullāh said, "We were with the Messenger of Allah ﷺ and we passed by some children, among whom were Ibn Ṣā'id. The children all ran off and Ibn Ṣā'id sat down. That seemed to upset the Messenger of Allah ﷺ. He said, 'May your hands be sifted in dust. Do you testify that I am the Messenger of Allah?' He said, 'No. Do you testify that I am the Messenger of Allah?' 'Umar said, 'O Messenger of Allah, allow me to kill him.' He replied, 'Leave him. For if he is the one that you fear, you will not be able to kill him.'"[25] It is also found in Muslim.

25 *Ṣaḥīḥ Muslim*, hadith no. 2924.

# HADITH FIFTEEN 15

أَخۡبَرَتۡنَا سِتُّ الۡأَهۡلِ أَنَا الۡبَهَاءُ الۡمَقۡدِسِيُّ أَنَا عَبۡدُ الۡحَقِّ أَنَا أَبُو سَعۡدِ بۡنُ خَشِيۡشٍ أَنَا ابۡنُ شَاذَانَ أَنَا ابۡنُ السِّمَاكِ ثَنَا حَنۡبَلٌ ثَنَا شُرَيۡحُ بۡنُ النُّعۡمَانِ ثَنَا حَمَّادٌ عَنِ الۡجُرَيۡرِيِّ عَنۡ أَبِي نَضۡرَةَ عَنۡ أَبِي سَعِيۡدٍ قَالَ حَجَجۡنَا فَنَزَلۡنَا تَحۡتَ شَجَرَةٍ فَجَاءَ ابۡنُ صَائِدٍ فَنَزَلَ فِيۡ مَا جَنۡبِهَا فَقُلۡتُ إِنَّا لِلَّهِ مِنۡ أَيۡنَ سَلَّطَ عَلَيَّ فَقَالَ يَا أَبَا سَعِيۡدٍ مَا أَلۡقَى مِنَ النَّاسِ يَقُوۡلُوۡنَ إِنِّي الدَّجَّالُ أَمَا سَمِعۡتَ رَسُوۡلَ اللهِ صَلَّى اللّٰهُ عَلَيۡهِ وَسَلَّمَ يَقُوۡلُ إِنَّ الدَّجَّالَ لَا يُوۡلَدُ لَهُ وَلَا يَدۡخُلُ الۡمَدِيۡنَةَ وَلَا مَكَّةَ قُلۡتُ بَلَى قَالَ قَدۡ وُلِدَ لِيۡ وَقَدۡ خَرَجۡتُ مِنَ الۡمَدِيۡنَةِ وَأَنَا أُرِيۡدُ مَكَّةَ فَقَالَ أَبُوۡ سَعِيۡدٍ كَأَنِّيۡ رَقَقۡتُ بِهِ فَقَالَ وَاللّٰهِ إِنَّ أَعۡلَمَ النَّاسِ بِمَكَانِهِ أَنَا فَقُلۡتُ تَبًّا لَكَ سَائِرَ الۡيَوۡمِ.

Sitt[26] al-Ahl informed us: al-Bahā' al-Maqdisī informed us: ʿAbd al-Ḥaqq informed us: Abū Saʿd ibn Khushaysh informed us: Ibn Shādhān informed us: Ibn al-Sammāk informed us: Ḥanbal narrated to us: Shurayḥ ibn al-Nuʿmān narrated to us: Ḥammād narrated to us from al-Jurayrī from Abū Naḍrah that Abū Saʿīd said, "We set out for hajj. On the way, we sat under a tree. Ibn Ṣā'id came and sat somewhere to our side. I said, 'We belong to Allah. From where have you

26 An abbreviated form of *sayyidah*. She was one of the female narrators of hadith that heard hadith directly from al-Bahā' al-Maqdisī, being the sole narrator from him of *Kitāb al-Zuhd*.

descended upon me?' He said, 'O Abū Sa'īd, regarding what has been transmitted from the people saying that I am the Dajjāl, have they not heard the Messenger of Allah ﷺ say, "The Dajjāl will not have children. Nor will he enter Makkah or Madinah"?' I responded, 'Yes.' He said, 'I have had a child and I exited Madinah and am heading for Makkah.'" Abū Sa'īd said, "I almost pitied him, but then he said, 'By Allah, I am the most knowledgeable of people of his place.' So, for the rest of the day, I said, 'May you be cursed.'"[27]





27 This hadith was sourced in Hadith no. 13.

# 16 HADITH SIXTEEN

عَبْدُ الرَّزَّاقِ أَنَا مَعْمَرٌ عَنْ أَبِي نَصْرٍ عَنْ سَالِمٍ عَنِ ابْنِ عُمَرَ قَالَ لَقِيتُ ابْنَ صَيَّادٍ يَوْمًا وَمَعَهُ رَجُلٌ مِنَ الْيَهُودِ فَإِذَا عَيْنُهُ قَدْ كُفِيَتْ وَكَانَتْ عَيْنُهُ خَارِجَةً مِثْلَ عَيْنِ الْجَمَلِ فَلَمَّا رَأَيْتُهَا قُلْتُ أَنْشُدُكَ اللَّهَ مَتَى كُفِيَتْ عَيْنُكَ فَمَسَحَهَا وَقَالَ لَا أَدْرِي وَالرَّحْمَٰنِ فَقُلْتُ كَذَبْتَ لَا تَدْرِي وَهِيَ فِي رَأْسِكَ فَنَخَرَ ثَلَاثًا فَقُلْتُ اخْسَأْ فَلَنْ تَعْدُوَ قَدْرَكَ قَالَ أَجَلْ لَعَمْرِي لَا أَعْدُو قَدْرِي فَذَكَرْتُ ذَٰلِكَ لِحَفْصَةَ فَقَالَتِ اجْتَنِبْ هَذَا الرَّجُلَ فَإِنَّا نَتَحَدَّثُ أَنَّ الدَّجَّالَ يَخْرُجُ مِنْ غَضْبَةٍ يَغْضَبُهَا.

إِسْنَادُهُ صَحِيحٌ أَخْرَجَاهُ.

ʿAbd al-Razzāq narrated: Maʿmar informed us from Abū Naṣr from Sālim that Ibn ʿUmar said, "I met Ibn Ṣayyād one day. With him was a Jewish man. His eye was swollen, and it protruded like a camel's eye. When I saw it, I said, 'I ask you by Allah to answer me. When did your eye become swollen?' He wiped it and said, 'I do not know, by the All Merciful.' So, I said, 'You have lied. How could you not know when it is on your face?' He snorted three times and I then said, 'Away with you, for you will not exceed your rank.' He replied, 'Yes. I will not exceed my rank.' I mentioned that to Ḥafṣah and she said, 'Avoid that man, for it was related to us that the Dajjāl would appear as a result of a severe fit of anger that would befall him.'"[28]

Its chain of transmission is sound. They (al-Bukhārī and Muslim) both narrated it[29].

28 *Ṣaḥīḥ Muslim*, hadith no. 2932a with slightly different wording. The wording of the hadith in Muslim is: "Ibn 'Umar said, 'I met Ibn Ṣayyād twice and said to some of them (his friends): You state that it was he (the Dajjāl). He said: By Allah, it is not so. I said: You have not told me the truth; by Allah, some of you informed me that he would not die until he would have the largest number of offspring and huge wealth and it is he about whom it is thought so. Then Ibn Ṣayyād talked to us. I then departed and met him again for the second time and his eye had become swollen. I said: What has happened to your eye? He said: I do not know. I said: Is this in your head and you do not know about it? He said: If Allah so wills He can create it (an eye) in your staff. He then produced a sound like the braying of a donkey. Some of my companions thought that I had struck him with the staff that was with me until it broke, yet, by Allah, I was not conscious of it. He then came to the Mother of the Faithful (Ḥafṣah) and narrated it to her and she said: What concern do you have with him? Do you not know that Allah's Apostle ﷺ said that the first thing (by the incitement of which) he would come out before the public would be his anger?'"

29 We did not find this hadith in al-Bukhārī.

# 17 HADITH SEVENTEEN

أَخْبَرَنَا عَبْدُ اللهِ بْنُ مُحَمَّدٍ أَنَا عَبْدُ الْقَادِرِ بْنُ مُحَمَّدٍ أَنَا الْحَسَنُ بْنُ عَلِيٍّ أَنَا أَحْمَدُ بْنُ جَعْفَرٍ ثَنَا عَبْدُ اللهِ حَدَّثَنِي أَبِي ثَنَا شُرَيْحٌ وَغَفَّارٌ وَيُونُسُ قَالُوا ثَنَا حَمَّادُ بْنُ سَلَمَةَ عَنْ أَيُّوبَ وَعُبَيْدِ اللهِ عَنْ نَافِعٍ عَنِ ابْنِ عُمَرَ أَنَّهُ رَأَى ابْنَ صَائِدٍ فِي سِكَّةِ الْمَدِينَةِ فَسَبَّهُ ابْنُ عُمَرَ وَوَقَعَ فِيهِ فَانْتَفَخَ حَتَّى سَدَّ الطَّرِيقَ فَضَرَبَهُ ابْنُ عُمَرَ بِعَصًى كَانَتْ مَعَهُ حَتَّى كَسَّرَهَا عَلَيْهِ فَقَالَتْ لَهُ حَفْصَةُ مَا شَأْنُكَ وَشَأْنُهُ مَا يُولِعُكَ بِهِ أَمَا سَمِعْتَ رَسُولَ اللهِ صَلَّى اللهُ عَلَيْهِ وَسَلَّمَ يَقُولُ إِنَّمَا يَخْرُجُ الدَّجَّالُ مِنْ غَضْبَةٍ يَغْضَبُهَا.

وَقَالَ يُونُسُ فِي حَدِيثٍ مَا يُولِعُكَ. أَنَا جَمَاعَةٌ إِجَازَةً قَالُوا نَا حَنْبَلٌ أَنَا ابْنُ الْحُصَيْنِ أَخْرَجَاهُ.

ʿAbdullāh ibn Muhammad informed us: ʿAbd al-Qādir ibn Muhammad informed us: al-Ḥasan ibn ʿAlī informed us: Aḥmad ibn Jaʿfar informed us: ʿAbdullāh narrated to us: My father ﵀ narrated to me: Shurayḥ, Ghaffār and Yūnus all narrated to us, saying: Ḥammād ibn Salamah narrated to us from Ayyūb and ʿUbayd Allāh from Nāfiʿ that Ibn ʿUmar saw Ibn Ṣāʾid on one of the streets of Madinah. Ibn ʿUmar cursed him and that impacted him. He then made himself bigger until he blocked the way. So, Ibn ʿUmar hit him with a staff he had with him until he broke it over him. Ḥafṣah said to him, "What is with you and him? Why do you concern yourself so much with him? Have you not heard the Messenger of Allah ﷺ say, 'The Dajjāl will emerge due to a fit of anger that befalls him'?"[30]

Yūnus said in his hadith, "Why do you concern yourself so much with him?"

Another group also informed us by way of *ijāzah*, saying, "Ḥanbal informed: Ibn al-Ḥusayn informed us." This was narrated by al-Bukhārī[31] and Muslim.

30 *Ṣaḥīḥ Muslim*, hadith no. 2932, with some omissions.

31 We did not find it in al-Bukhārī.

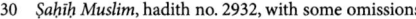

# HADITH EIGHTEEN 18

أَخْبَرَنَا مُحَمَّدُ بْنُ عَبْدِ الْبَاقِي أَنَا أَبُو الْفَضْلِ أَحْمَدُ بْنُ الْحَسَنِ بْنِ خَيْرُونَ أَنَا أَبُو عَمْرٍو عُثْمَانُ بْنُ مُحَمَّدِ بْنِ يُوسُفَ الْعَلَّافُ أَنَا مُحَمَّدُ بْنُ عَبْدِ اللهِ بْنِ إِبْرَاهِيمَ الشَّافِعِيُّ ثَنَا إِسْحَاقُ هُوَ ابْنُ الْحَسَنِ نَا عَفَّانُ ثَنَا حَمَّادٌ عَنْ أَيُّوبَ وَعُبَيْدِ اللهِ عَنْ نَافِعٍ عَنْ عُمَرَ أَنَّهُ رَأَى ابْنَ صَائِدٍ فِي سِكَّةٍ مِنْ سِكَكِ الْمَدِينَةِ فَسَبَّهُ وَوَقَعَ فِيهِ فَانْتَفَخَ حَتَّى سَدَّ الطَّرِيقَ فَضَرَبَهُ بِعَصًى كَانَتْ مَعَهُ حَتَّى كَسَّرَهَا عَلَيْهِ فَقَالَتْ لَهُ حَفْصَةُ مَا شَأْنُكَ وَشَأْنُهُ مَا يُولِعُكَ بِهِ أَمَا سَمِعْتَ رَسُولَ اللهِ صَلَّى اللهُ عَلَيْهِ وَسَلَّمَ يَقُولُ إِنَّمَا يَخْرُجُ الدَّجَّالُ عِنْدَ غَضْبَةٍ يَغْضَبُهَا.

أَنْبَأَنَاهُ أَحْمَدُ بْنُ سَلَامَةَ عَنْ عَبْدِ الْغَنِيِّ.

Muhammad ibn ʿAbd al-Bāqī informed us: Abū al-Faḍl Aḥmad ibn al-Ḥasan ibn Khayrūn informed us: Abū ʿAmr ʿUthmān ibn Muhammad ibn Yūsuf al-ʿAllāf informed us: Muhammad ibn ʿAbdullāh ibn Ibrāhīm al-Shāfiʿī informed us: Isḥāq – who is ibn al-Ḥasan – narrated to us: ʿAffān informed us: Ḥammād narrated to us from Ayyūb and ʿAbdullāh from Nāfiʿ that ʿUmar saw Ibn Ṣā'id on one of the streets of Madinah. He cursed him and that impacted him. So, he became very large until he blocked the way. So, he hit him with a staff that he had with him until he broke it.

# 18 HADITH EIGHTEEN

Ḥafṣah said to him, "What is with you and that man? What concerns you so much with him? Have you not heard the Messenger of Allah ﷺ say, 'The Dajjāl will only emerge due to a fit of anger that befalls him'?"[32]

Aḥmad ibn Salamah informed us of it on the authority of 'Abd al-Ghanī.

32 This hadith was sourced in the previous hadith (no. 17).

# HADITH NINETEEN 19

قَالَ أَحْمَدُ بْنُ عَلِيٍّ الْآبَارُ فِيْ تَارِيْخِهِ ثَنَا أَحْمَدُ بْنُ مُصْعَبٍ الْمَرْوَزِيُّ ثَنَا حَفْصٌ عَنْ مُجَالِدٍ عَنِ الشَّعْبِيِّ قَالَ كُنْيَةُ الدَّجَّالِ أَبُوْ يُوْسُفَ. قَالَ وَكِيْعٌ حَفْصٌ لَمْ يَسْمَعْ هٰذَا مِنْ مُجَالِدٍ وَسَمِعَهُ جُنَادَةُ مِنْ مُجَالِدٍ ثَنَا جُنَادَةُ عَنِ الشَّعْبِيِّ.

Aḥmad ibn ʿAlī al-Abbār said in his *Tārīkh*, "Aḥmad ibn Muṣʿab al-Marūzī narrated to us: Ḥafṣ narrated to us from Mujālid from al-Shaʿbī, 'The epithet of the Dajjāl is "Abū Yūsuf".'"

Wakīʿ said, "Ḥafṣ did not hear hadiths from Mujālid. Rather, it was Junādah who heard it (and said): Mujālid narrated to us from al-Shaʿbī."[33]

33 We did not find this hadith.

## 20 HADITH TWENTY

قَالَ قَتَادَةُ عَنْ أَبِي الطُّفَيْلِ عَامِرِ بْنِ وَاثِلَةَ سَمِعْتُ حُذَيْفَةَ بْنَ أُسَيْدٍ يَقُوْلُ فِيْ الدَّجَّالِ لَا يَسْخَرُ لَهُ مِنَ الْمَطَايَا إِلَّا الْحِمَارُ فَهُوَ رِجْسٌ عَلَى رِجْسٍ.

إِسْنَادُهُ صَحِيْحٌ.

Qatādah said: Abū al-Ṭufayl ʿĀmir ibn Wāthilah said: I heard Ḥudhayfah ibn Usayd say about the Dajjāl, "No animal other than a donkey will obey him. For he is impurity upon impurity."[34]





34 This hadith was sourced in hadith no. 4.

# HADITH TWENTY-ONE 21

مُسْلِمٌ مِنْ حَدِيثِ أَبِي سَعِيدٍ أَنَّ ابْنَ صَيَّادٍ سَأَلَ النَّبِيَّ صَلَّى اللَّهُ عَلَيْهِ وَسَلَّمَ عَنْ تُرْبَةِ الْجَنَّةِ فَقَالَ دَرْمَكَةٌ بَيْضَاءُ مِسْكٌ خَالِصٌ.

Muslim reported from the hadith of Abū Saʿīd that Ibn Ṣayyād asked the Prophet ﷺ about the soil of Paradise. He responded, "It is *darmakah*[35] – pure, white musk."[36]

35 "*Darmak*, when used for describing Paradise, such as in 'Its soil is *darmak*', means deep white. When *darmakah* is used in the hadith of Ibn Ṣayyād, it is as if the meaning is that it is unique in its deep whiteness" (Ibn Athīr, *al-Nihāyah fī Gharīb al-Ḥadīth wa al-Athar*, Dār Ibn al-Jawzī, p. 304).

36 *Ṣaḥīḥ Muslim*, hadith no. 2928a. However, the wording in Muslim is, "The Messenger of Allah ﷺ said to Ibn Ṣayyād, 'What is the soil of Paradise?' The latter responded, 'It is *darmakah* – deep white.' He (i.e., the Prophet ﷺ) responded, 'You have spoken the truth.'" So, the one who asked was the Prophet ﷺ.

# 22 HADITH TWENTY-TWO

أَخْبَرَنَا عَبْدُ اللهِ بْنُ مُحَمَّدٍ أَنَا عَبْدُ الْقَادِرِ بْنُ مُحَمَّدٍ أَنَا الْحُسَيْنُ بْنُ عَلِيٍّ أَنَا أَحْمَدُ بْنُ جَعْفَرٍ ثَنَا عَبْدُ اللهِ حَدَّثَنِي أَبِي ثَنَا رَوْحُ بْنُ عُبَادَةَ ثَنَا ابْنُ عَوْنٍ عَنْ نَافِعٍ عَنِ ابْنِ عُمَرَ قَالَ لَقِيتُ ابْنَ صَائِدٍ مَرَّتَيْنِ فَأَمَّا مَرَّةً فَلَقِيتُهُ وَمَعَهُ بَعْضُ أَصْحَابِهِ فَقُلْتُ لِبَعْضِهِمْ نَشَدْتُكُمْ بِاللهِ إِنْ نَشَدْتُكُمْ عَنْ شَيْءٍ لَتَصْدُقُنِّي قَالُوا نَعَمْ قُلْتُ أَتُحَدِّثُونَ أَنَّهُ هُوَ قَالُوا لَا قُلْتُ كَذَبْتُمْ وَاللهِ لَقَدْ حَدَّثَنِي بَعْضُكُمْ وَهُوَ يَوْمَئِذٍ أَقَلُّكُمْ مَالًا وَوَلَدًا أَنَّهُ لَا يَمُوتُ حَتَّى يَكُونَ أَكْثَرَكُمْ مَالًا وَوَلَدًا وَهُوَ كَذٰلِكَ فَتَحَدَّثْنَا ثُمَّ قَاذَفْتُهُ ثُمَّ لَقِيتُهُ مَرَّةً أُخْرَى وَقَدْ تَغَيَّرَتْ عَنْهُ فَقُلْتُ مَتَى فَعَلَتْ عَيْنُكَ مَا أَرَى قَالَ لَا أَدْرِي قُلْتُ لَا تَدْرِي وَهِيَ فِي رَأْسِكَ قَالَ مَا تُرِيدُ مِنِّي يَا ابْنَ عُمَرَ إِنْ شَاءَ اللَّهُ أَنْ يَخْلُقَهُ مِنْ عَصَاكَ هَذِهِ خَلَقَهُ وَنَخَرَ كَأَشَدِّ نَخِيرِ حِمَارٍ سَمِعْتُهُ قَطُّ فَزَعَمَ بَعْضُ أَصْحَابِي أَنِّي ضَرَبْتُهُ بِعَصًى كَانَتْ مَعِي حَتَّى تَكَسَّرَتْ وَأَمَّا أَنَا فَوَاللهِ مَا شَعَرْتُ قَالَ فَدَخَلَ عَلَى أُخْتِهِ حَفْصَةَ فَأَخْبَرَهَا فَقَالَتْ مَا تُرِيدُ مِنْهُ أَمَا عَلِمْتَ أَنَّهُ قَالَ تَعْنِي النَّبِيَّ صَلَّى اللَّهُ عَلَيْهِ وَسَلَّمَ أَوَّلُ مَا يَبْعَثُهُ عَلَى النَّاسِ غَضْبَةٌ يَغْضَبُهَا. هُوَ عِنْدِي مِنَ الْمُسْنَدِ. وَأَخْرَجَهُ مُسْلِمٌ عَنْ عَبْدٍ عَنْ رَوْحٍ عَنْ هِشَامِ بْنِ حَسَّانٍ عَنْ أَيُّوبَ عَنْ نَافِعٍ وَعَنْ أَبِي مُوسَى الزَّمِنِ عَنْ حُسَيْنِ بْنِ حَسَنٍ عَنِ ابْنِ عَوْنٍ بِهِ.

ʿAbdullāh ibn Muhammad informed us: ʿAbd al-Qādir ibn Muhammad informed us: al-Ḥusayn ibn ʿAlī informed us:

# HADITH TWENTY-TWO 22

Aḥmad ibn Jaʿfar informed us: ʿAbdullāh narrated to us: My father ﷺ narrated to me: Rawḥ ibn ʿUbādah narrated to us: Ibn ʿAwn narrated to us from Nāfiʿ that Ibn ʿUmar said, "I met Ibn Ṣā'id twice. The first time I met him was when he was with some of his companions. I said to some of them, 'I adjure you by Allah. If I adjure you about something, would you tell me the truth?' They said, 'Yes.' I said, 'Do you state that he (Ibn Ṣayyād) is he (the Dajjāl)?' They said, 'No.' I said, 'You have lied. By Allah, one of you informed me – while he (Ibn Ṣayyād) was the one among you with the least wealth and children – that he (the Dajjāl) would not die until he would have the most wealth and children among you. And he (Ibn Ṣayyād) today is like how you said he would be.' He then spoke to us and I left him. Then, I met him a second time and his eye had changed. I said to him, 'When did you do with your eye that which I see?' He said, 'I do not know.' I said, 'Do you not know while it is on your face?' He said, 'What do you want from me, O Ibn ʿUmar? If Allah ﷻ willed to create it in that staff of yours, He would do so.' He then snorted like the loudest snort that I have ever heard from a donkey. Some of my companions believe that I hit him with the staff that I had with me until it broke. However, as far as I am concerned, by Allah, I do not remember that." He then said that he entered upon his sister Ḥafṣah and told her about the incident. She said, "What do you want with him?

# 22 HADITH TWENTY-TWO

Do you not know that he – meaning the Prophet ﷺ – said, 'The first thing that will make him emerge to people is a fit of rage that will befall him'?"[37]

This hadith, as I have copied it, is from *al-Musnad* (of Imam Aḥmad). Muslim also narrated it on the authority of ʿAbdullāh from Rawḥ, from Hishām ibn Hassān, from Ayyūb from Nāfiʿ. In addition, Abū Mūsā al-Zaman narrated it from Ḥusayn ibn Ḥasan from Ibn ʿAwn.

37 *Musnad al-Imām Aḥmad*, Mu'assasah al-Risālah, hadith no. 26426; *Ṣaḥīḥ Muslim*, hadith no. 2932.

# 23 HADITH TWENTY-THREE

أَبُو دَاوُدَ فِي سُنَنِهِ نَا هُدْبَةُ نَا هُمَّامٌ عَنْ قَتَادَةَ عَنْ عَبْدِ الرَّحْمٰنِ بْنِ آدَمَ عَنْ أَبِي هُرَيْرَةَ عَنِ النَّبِيِّ ﷺ قَالَ لَيْسَ بَيْنِي وَبَيْنَ عِيسَى نَبِيٌّ وَإِنَّهُ نَازِلٌ فَإِذَا رَأَيْتُمُوهُ فَاعْرِفُوهُ رَجُلٌ مَرْبُوعٌ إِلَى الْحُمْرَةِ وَالْبَيَاضِ بَيْنَ مُمَصَّرَتَيْنِ كَأَنَّ رَأْسَهُ يَقْطُرُ وَإِنْ لَمْ يُصِبْهُ بَلَلٌ فَيُقَاتِلُ النَّاسَ عَلَى الإِسْلَامِ فَيَدُقُّ الصَّلِيبَ وَيَقْتُلُ الْخِنْزِيرَ وَيَضَعُ الْجِزْيَةَ وَيُهْلِكُ اللهُ فِي زَمَانِهِ الْمِلَلَ كُلَّهَا إِلَّا الإِسْلَامَ وَيُهْلِكُ الْمَسِيحَ الدَّجَّالَ فَيَمْكُثُ فِي الأَرْضِ أَرْبَعِينَ سَنَةً ثُمَّ يُتَوَفَّى فَيُصَلِّي عَلَيْهِ الْمُسْلِمُونَ.

سَنَدُهُ قَوِيٌّ فِي مُسْنَدِ الطَّيَالِسِيِّ نَا هِشَامٌ عَنْ قَتَادَةَ أَتَمَّ مِنْهُ وَسَيَأْتِي.

Abū Dāwūd reported in his *Sunan*: Hudbah narrated to us: Humām narrated to us on the authority of Qatādah from ʿAbd al-Raḥmān ibn Adam from Abū Hurayrah ﷺ that the Prophet ﷺ said, "Between ʿĪsā and I, there is no Prophet. He will descend. When you see him, you shall recognize him. He is a man of a complexion between red and white, wearing two robes of a slightly yellowish colour. It is as if his head drips, even if no water has touched it. He will fight people till they enter Islam. He will break the cross, kill the swine, and abolish the *jizyah*. In his time, Allah will cause all religions besides Islam to perish. He will kill the Dajjāl and remain on the Earth for forty years. Then, he will die and the

# 23 HADITH TWENTY-THREE

Muslims will pray over him."[38] Its chain of transmission is strong. It has been reported by al-Ṭayālisī in his *Musnad* in a more complete manner from Hishām from Qatādah. That report will be mentioned later.

38 *Sunan Abī Dāwūd*, Dār al-Risālah al-'Ālamiyyah, hadith no. 4324; *Musnad al-Imām Aḥmad*, Mu'assasah al-Risālah, hadith nos. 9270, 9632-9634; *Ṣaḥīḥ Ibn Ḥibbān*, hadith nos. 6814 and 6821; *Musnad al-Ṭayālisī*, hadith no. 2575.

# 24 HADITH TWENTY-FOUR

أَخْبَرَنَا عَبْدُ اللهِ بْنُ مُحَمَّدٍ أَنَا عَبْدُ الْقَادِرِ بْنُ مُحَمَّدٍ أَنَا الْحُسَيْنُ بْنُ عَلِيٍّ أَنَا أَحْمَدُ بْنُ جَعْفَرٍ ثَنَا عَبْدُ اللهِ بْنُ أَحْمَدَ بْنِ حَنْبَلٍ حَدَّثَنِي أَبِي نَا يَزِيدُ ثَنَا حَمَّادُ بْنُ سَلَمَةَ عَنْ عَلِيِّ بْنِ زَيْدٍ عَنْ عَبْدِ الرَّحْمٰنِ بْنِ أَبِي بَكْرَةَ عَنْ أَبِيهِ قَالَ قَالَ رَسُولُ اللّٰهِ صَلَّى اللهُ عَلَيْهِ وَسَلَّمَ يَمْكُثُ أَبَوَا الدَّجَّالِ ثَلَاثِينَ عَامًا لَا يُولَدُ لَهُمَا ثُمَّ يُولَدُ لَهُمَا غُلَامٌ أَعْوَرُ أَضَرُّ شَيْئًا وَأَقَلُّهُ نَفْعًا تَنَامُ عَيْنَاهُ وَلَا يَنَامُ قَلْبُهُ ثُمَّ نَعَتَ أَبَوَيْهِ فَقَالَ أَبُوهُ رَجُلٌ طُوَالٌ مُضْطَرِبُ اللَّحْمِ طَوِيلُ الْأَنْفِ كَأَنَّ أَنْفَهُ مِنْقَارٌ وَأُمُّهُ امْرَأَةٌ فِرْضَاخِيَّةٌ عَظِيمَةُ الثَّدْيَيْنِ قَالَ فَبَلَغَنَا أَنَّ مَوْلُودًا مِنَ الْيَهُودِ وُلِدَ بِالْمَدِينَةِ فَانْطَلَقْتُ أَنَا وَالزُّبَيْرُ بْنُ الْعَوَّامِ حَتَّى دَخَلْنَا عَلَى أَبَوَيْهِ فَرَأَيْنَا فِيهِمَا نَعْتَ رَسُولِ اللّٰهِ صَلَّى اللهُ عَلَيْهِ وَسَلَّمَ فَإِذَا هُوَ مُنْجَدِلٌ فِي الشَّمْسِ فِي قَطِيفَةٍ لَهُ هَمْهَمَةٌ فَسَأَلْنَا أَبَوَيْهِ فَقَالَا مَكَثْنَا ثَلَاثِينَ عَامًا لَا يُولَدُ لَنَا ثُمَّ وُلِدَ لَنَا غُلَامٌ أَعْوَرُ أَضَرُّ شَيْئًا وَأَقَلُّهُ نَفْعًا فَلَمَّا خَرَجْنَا مَرَرْنَا بِهِ فَقَالَ مَا كُنْتُمَا فِيهِ قُلْنَا وَسَمِعْتَ قَالَ نَعَمْ إِنَّهُ تَنَامُ عَيْنَايَ وَلَا يَنَامُ قَلْبِي وَإِذَا هُوَ ابْنُ صَيَّادٍ. أَخْرَجَهُ ت عَنْ عَبْدِ اللهِ بْنِ مُعَاوِيَةَ الْجُمَحِيِّ ثَنَا حَمَّادُ بْنُ سَلَمَةَ وَقَالَ حَسَنٌ غَرِيبٌ لَا نَعْرِفُهُ إِلَّا مِنْ حَدِيثِ حَمَّادٍ وَرَوَاهُ أَحْمَدُ بْنُ مَنِيعٍ عَنْ يَزِيدَ وَهُوَ ابْنُ هَارُونَ قُلْتُ وَقَعَ لَنَا فِي الْمُسْنَدِ بِالْإِجَازَةِ.

ʿAbdullāh ibn Muhammad informed us: ʿAbd al-Qādir ibn Muhammad narrated to us: al-Ḥusayn ibn ʿAlī narrated to

# 24 HADITH TWENTY-FOUR

us: Aḥmad ibn Ja'far narrated to us: 'Abdullāh ibn Aḥmad ibn Ḥanbal narrated to us: My father ﷺ narrated to me: Yazīd narrated to us: Ḥammād ibn Salamah narrated to us from 'Alī ibn Zayd from 'Abd al-Raḥmān ibn Abī Bakrah that his father said, "The Messenger of Allah ﷺ said, 'The parents of the Dajjāl will remain on Earth for thirty years without any child being born to them. Then, they will have a male child with a defective eye – the most harmful of things and the least beneficial. His eye will sleep but his heart will not.' Then he (the Prophet ﷺ) described his parents, saying, 'His father is a tall, thin man with a long nose, like a bird's beak. His mother is stocky with large breasts.' "It reached us that a child was born to some of the Jews of Madinah. So, I went with al-Zubayr ibn al-'Awwām until we entered upon his parents. We saw in them the description that the Messenger of Allah ﷺ had given. The child had been laid down on some twine in the Sun in a group of date palms. And he was mumbling. So, we asked his father and they said, 'We remained thirty years without a son. Then, a one-eyed son was born to us – the most harmful of things and the least beneficial.' When we left, we passed by him and he said, 'What are you two doing?' We said, 'Did you hear?' He said, 'Yes. My eyes sleep but my heart does not sleep.' That was Ibn Ṣayyād."[39] It was narrated by al-Tirmidhī on the authority of ʿAbdullāh ibn Muʿāwiyah al-Jumaḥī: Ḥammād ibn Salamah narrated to us. He (al-Tirmidhī) said, "This hadith is *ḥasan gharīb*. We only know this hadith by way of Ḥammād." However, it was narrated by Aḥmad ibn Manīʿ from Yazīd – who is Ibn Hārūn. I (al-Maqdisī) say: We also narrate it from *al-Musnad* by way of *ijāzah*.

39 *Sunan al-Tirmidhī*, Dār al-Risālah al-ʿĀlamiyyah, hadith no. 2399; *Musnad al-Imām Aḥmad*, hadith no. 20418.

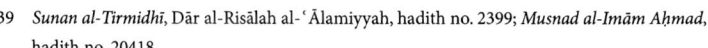

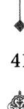

# 25 HADITH TWENTY-FIVE

وَأَخْبَرَنَاهُ عَالِيًا سِتُّ الْأَهْلِ الْبَعْلَبَكِّيَّةُ أَنَا الْبَهَاءُ عَبْدُ الرَّحْمٰنِ أَنَا أَبُو الْحُسَيْنِ الْيُوسُفِيُّ أَنَا ابْنُ خَشِيْشٍ أَنَا ابْنُ شَاذَانَ أَنَا ابْنُ السَّمَاكِ ثَنَا حَنْبَلٌ ثَنَا مُسْلِمُ بْنُ إِبْرَاهِيمَ ثَنَا حَمَّادُ بْنُ سَلَمَةَ نَا عَلِيُّ بْنُ زَيْدٍ عَنْ عَبْدِ الرَّحْمٰنِ بْنِ أَبِي بَكْرَةَ عَنْ أَبِيهِ أَنَّ رَسُولَ اللَّهِ صَلَّى اللهُ عَلَيْهِ وَسَلَّمَ قَالَ يَمْكُثُ أَبَوَا الدَّجَّالِ لَا يُولَدُ لَهُمَا ثَلَاثِيْنَ عَامًا ثُمَّ يُولَدُ لَهُمَا غُلَامٌ أَعْوَرُ أَضَرُّ شَيْءٍ وَأَقَلُّهُ نَفْعًا تَنَامُ عَيْنُهُ وَلَا يَنَامُ قَلْبُهُ ثُمَّ نَعَتَ أَبَوَيْهِ فَقَالَ أَبُوهُ رَجُلٌ طُوَالٌ مُضْطَرِبُ اللَّحْمِ طَوِيلُ الْأَنْفِ كَأَنَّ أَنْفَهُ مِنْقَارٌ وَأُمُّهُ فِرْضَاخِيَّةٌ عَظِيمَةُ الثَّدْيَيْنِ.

Sitt al-Ahl al-Baʿlabakiyyah informed us of the same hadith with a shorter chain: al-Bahāʾ ʿAbd al-Raḥmān narrated to us: Abū al-Ḥusayn al-Yūsufī narrated to us: Ibn Khushaysh narrated to us: Ibn Shādhān narrated to us: Ibn al-Sammāk narrated to us: Ḥanbal narrated to us: Muslim ibn Ibrāhīm narrated to us: Ḥammād ibn Salamah narrated to us: ʿAlī ibn Zayd narrated from ʿAbd al-Raḥmān ibn Abī Bakrah from his father that the Messenger of Allah ﷺ said, "The father and mother of the Dajjāl would remain for thirty years without having a son. Then, a one-eyed son will be born to them – the most harmful of things and least beneficial. His eyes will sleep, but his heart will not sleep." Then he described his parents by saying, "His father is a tall, thin man with a long nose like a bird's beak. His mother is stocky with large breasts."[40]

40 This hadith was sourced in the previous footnote.

# 26 HADITH TWENTY-SIX

أَخْبَرَنَا أَبُو مُوسَى ثَنَا أَبُو عَلِيٍّ الْحَدَّادُ سَنَةَ خَمْسٍ وَخَمْسِمِئَةٍ ثَنَا أَبُو نُعَيْمٍ
الْحَافِظُ سَنَةَ ثَلَاثٍ وَعِشْرِينَ وَأَرْبَعِمِئَةٍ وَثَنَا هِبَةُ اللهِ بْنُ مُحَمَّدِ بْنِ عَبْدِ
الْوَاحِدِ بْنِ الْحَسَنِ الشَّيْبَانِيُّ بِبَغْدَادَ ثَنَا أَبُو عَلِيٍّ بْنُ الْمُذْهِبِ قَالَا أَنَا أَبُو
بَكْرِ بْنُ مَالِكٍ الْقَطِيعِيُّ ثَنَا عَبْدُ اللهِ بْنُ أَحْمَدَ حَدَّثَنِي أَبِي نَا مُحَمَّدُ بْنُ سَابِقٍ
ثَنَا إِبْرَاهِيمُ بْنُ طَهْمَانَ عَنْ أَبِي الزُّبَيْرِ عَنْ جَابِرِ بْنِ عَبْدِ اللهِ أَنَّهُ قَالَ إِنَّ
امْرَأَةً مِنَ الْيَهُودِ بِالْمَدِينَةِ وَلَدَتْ غُلَامًا مَمْسُوحَةٌ عَيْنُهُ طَالِعَةٌ نَابُهُ
فَأَشْفَقَ رَسُولُ اللهِ صَلَّى اللَّهُ عَلَيْهِ وَسَلَّمَ أَنْ يَكُونَ الدَّجَّالَ فَوَجَدَهُ تَحْتَ
قَطِيفَةٍ يُهَمْهِمُ وَآذَنَتْهُ أُمُّهُ وَقَالَتْ يَا عَبْدَ اللهِ هَذَا أَبُو الْقَاسِمِ قَدْ جَاءَ
فَاخْرُجْ إِلَيْهِ فَقَالَ رَسُولُ اللهِ صَلَّى اللَّهُ عَلَيْهِ وَسَلَّمَ قَاتَلَهَا اللَّهُ لَوْ تَرَكَتْهُ
لَبَيَّنَ ثُمَّ قَالَ يَا بْنَ صَائِدٍ مَا تَرَى قَالَ أَرَى حَقًّا وَأَرَى بَاطِلًا وَأَرَى عَرْشًا
عَلَى الْمَاءِ قَالَ فَلُبِّسَ عَلَيْهِ فَقَالَ أَتَشْهَدُ أَنِّي رَسُولُ اللهِ فَقَالَ هُوَ أَتَشْهَدُ
أَنِّي رَسُولُ اللهِ قَالَ رَسُولُ اللهِ صَلَّى اللَّهُ عَلَيْهِ وَسَلَّمَ آمَنْتُ بِاللهِ وَرُسُلِهِ
ثُمَّ خَرَجَ وَتَرَكَهُ. ثُمَّ أَتَاهُ مَرَّةً أُخْرَى فَوَجَدَهُ فِي مَحَلٍّ لَهُمْ يُهَمْهِمُ فَآذَنَتْهُ أُمُّهُ
فَقَالَتْ يَا عَبْدَ اللهِ هَذَا أَبُو الْقَاسِمِ قَدْ جَاءَ فَقَالَ رَسُولُ اللهِ صَلَّى اللَّهُ
عَلَيْهِ وَسَلَّمَ مَا لَهَا قَاتَلَهَا اللَّهُ لَوْ تَرَكَتْهُ لَبَيَّنَ وَكَانَ رَسُولُ اللهِ صَلَّى اللَّهُ
عَلَيْهِ وَسَلَّمَ يَطْمَعُ أَنْ يَسْمَعَ مِنْ كَلَامِهِ شَيْئًا فَيَعْلَمَ هُوَ هُوَ أَمْ لَا قَالَ يَا ابْنَ
صَائِدٍ مَا تَرَى قَالَ أَرَى حَقًّا وَأَرَى بَاطِلًا وَأَرَى عَرْشًا قَالَ تَشْهَدُ أَنِّي
رَسُولُ اللهِ قَالَ هُوَ تَشْهَدُ أَنِّي رَسُولُ اللهِ فَقَالَ رَسُولُ اللهِ صَلَّى اللَّهُ عَلَيْهِ

وَسَلَّمَ آمَنْتُ بِاللَّهِ وَرُسُلِهِ فَلُبِّسَ عَلَيْهِ ثُمَّ خَرَجَ فَتَرَكَهُ ثُمَّ جَاءَ فِي الثَّالِثَةِ أَوِ الرَّابِعَةِ وَمَعَهُ أَبُو بَكْرٍ وَعُمَرُ بْنُ الْخَطَّابِ فِي نَفَرٍ مِنَ الْمُهَاجِرِينَ وَالأَنْصَارِ وَأَنَا مَعَهُ فَنَأَى رَسُولُ اللهِ صَلَّى اللَّهُ عَلَيْهِ وَسَلَّمَ بَيْنَ أَيْدِينَا رَجَاءَ أَنْ يَسْمَعَ مِنْ كَلَامِهِ شَيْئًا فَسَبَقَتْهُ أُمُّهُ إِلَيْهِ فَقَالَتْ يَا عَبْدَ اللهِ هَذَا أَبُو الْقَاسِمِ قَدْ جَاءَ فَقَالَ رَسُولُ اللهِ صَلَّى اللَّهُ عَلَيْهِ وَسَلَّمَ قَاتَلَهَا اللَّهُ لَوْ تَرَكَتْهُ لَبَيَّنَ فَقَالَ يَا بْنَ صَائِدٍ مَا تَرَى فَقَالَ أَرَى حَقًّا وَأَرَى بَاطِلًا وَأَرَى عَرْشًا عَلَى الْمَاءِ قَالَ أَتَشْهَدُ أَنِّي رَسُولُ اللهِ قَالَ أَتَشْهَدُ أَنْتَ أَنِّي رَسُولُ اللهِ فَقَالَ رَسُولُ اللهِ صَلَّى اللَّهُ عَلَيْهِ وَسَلَّمَ آمَنْتُ بِاللَّهِ وَرُسُلِهِ فَلُبِّسَ عَلَيْهِ فَقَالَ رَسُولُ اللهِ صَلَّى اللَّهُ عَلَيْهِ وَسَلَّمَ يَا ابْنَ صَائِدٍ إِنَّا قَدْ خَبَّأْنَا لَكَ خَبْأً فَمَا هُوَ قَالَ الدُّخُّ الدُّخُّ فَقَالَ رَسُولُ اللهِ صَلَّى اللَّهُ عَلَيْهِ وَسَلَّمَ اِخْسَأْ اِخْسَأْ فَقَالَ عُمَرُ اِئْذَنْ لِي فَأَقْتُلَهُ يَا رَسُولَ اللهِ فَقَالَ رَسُولُ اللهِ صَلَّى اللَّهُ عَلَيْهِ وَسَلَّمَ إِنْ يَكُنْ هُوَ فَلَسْتَ بِصَاحِبِهِ إِنَّمَا صَاحِبُهُ عِيسَى بْنُ مَرْيَمَ وَإِنْ لَّا يَكُنْ فَلَيْسَ لَكَ أَنْ تَقْتُلَ رَجُلًا مِنْ أَهْلِ الْعَهْدِ قَالَ فَلَمْ يَزَلْ رَسُولُ اللهِ صَلَّى اللَّهُ عَلَيْهِ وَسَلَّمَ مُشْفِقًا أَنَّهُ الدَّجَّالُ. هٰذَا حَدِيثٌ صَحِيحٌ وَقَعَ لَنَا فِي مُسْنَدِ الْإِمَامِ أَحْمَدَ.

Abū Mūsā informed us: Abū ʿAlī al-Ḥaddād narrated to us in the year 505 AH: Abū Nuʿaym, the Ḥāfiẓ, narrated to us in the year 423 AH. Hibat Allāh ibn Muhammad ibn ʿAbd al-Wāḥid ibn al-Ḥasan al-Shaybānī also narrated to us in Baghdad: Abū ʿAlī ibn al-Mudhib narrated to us. Both said: Abū Bakr ibn Mālik al-Qaṭīʿī narrated to us: ʿAbdullāh ibn Aḥmad narrated to us: My father narrated to me: Muhammad ibn Sābiq narrated to us: Ibrāhīm ibn Ṭahmān narrated to us from Abū al-Zubayr that Jābir ibn ʿAbdullāh said, "A woman from the Jews of Madinah gave birth to a son with a swollen eye, who was believed to be a bad omen. The Messenger of Allah ﷺ was concerned that he may have been the Dajjāl. So, he went to him and found him in a thicket of date palms mumbling. His mother alerted him and said, 'O ʿAbdullāh, here is Abū al-Qāsim. He has come.' So, he came out to him. The Messenger of Allah ﷺ said, 'May Allah punish her. If she had left him, his matter would have become clear.' Then, he said, 'O Ibn Ṣāʾid, what do you see?' He (Ibn Ṣāʾid) replied, 'I see true and false premonitions, and I see a throne over water.' That was inconclusive for him. So, he ﷺ said, 'Do you testify that I am the Messenger of Allah?' He (Ibn Ṣāʾid) replied, 'Do you testify that I am the Messenger of Allah?' So, the Messenger of Allah ﷺ replied, 'I believe in Allah and His Messengers.' Then he left him and went out.

"He came to him a second time and found him in a space that belonged to them, murmuring. His mother alerted him saying, 'O ʿAbdullāh. Abū al-Qāsim has come.' The Messenger of Allah ﷺ said, 'What is wrong with her? May

Allah punish her. If she had left him, his matter would have been clear.' The Messenger of Allah ﷺ had been intending to hear something of his speech so that he would know if he was indeed he (the Dajjāl) or not. He then said, 'O Ibn Ṣā'id, what do you see?' He (Ibn Ṣā'id) responded, 'I see true and false visions. And I see a throne.' He ﷺ said, 'Do you bear witness that I am the Messenger of Allah?' He (Ibn Ṣā'id) responded, 'Do you bear witness that I am the Messenger of Allah?' The Messenger of Allah ﷺ responded, 'I believe in Allah and His Messengers.' That was still inconclusive for him. Then, he left and went out.

"He came to him a third or fourth time. With him were Abū Bakr and 'Umar ibn al-Khaṭṭāb among a group of the Muhājirīn and Anṣār j. I was with them. The Messenger of Allah ﷺ distanced himself from us hoping to hear something of his speech. However, his mother caught him and said, 'O 'Abdullāh, here is Abū al-Qāsim. He has come.' The Messenger of Allah ﷺ said, 'May Allah punish her. If she had left him, his matter would have become clear.' He then said, 'O Ibn Ṣā'id, what do you see?' He said, 'I see true and false visions, and I see a throne upon water.' He ﷺ then said, 'Do you testify that I am the Messenger of Allah?' He (Ibn Ṣā'id) replied, 'Do you testify that I am the Messenger of Allah?' The Messenger of Allah ﷺ replied, 'I believe in Allah and His Messengers.' The matter remained indecisive for him. The Messenger of Allah ﷺ then said, 'O Ibn Ṣā'id, I have hidden something from you. What is it?' He (Ibn Ṣā'id) replied, '*Al-Dukh. Al-Dukh*[41].' The Messenger of Allah ﷺ then said, 'Away with you. Away with you.' 'Umar said, 'Permit me to kill him, O Messenger of Allah.' The Messenger of Allah ﷺ replied, 'If he is he (the Dajjāl), then you are not his companion.[42] His companion is only 'Īsā ibn Maryam. If it is not he, then you have no right to kill anyone from among the people of the treaty.' And the Messenger of Allah ﷺ never stopped being concerned that he may have been the Dajjāl."[43]

This hadith is authentic. It is found in *Musnad al-Imām Aḥmad.*

41 This was explained in hadith number 1.

42 I.e. you are not the one to kill him.

43 This hadith is a different version of the narrations in hadith number 1. Its source has been mentioned in the footnote for that hadith.

# HADITH TWENTY-SEVEN 27

أَبُوْ مُعَاوِيَةَ عَنِ الْأَعْمَشِ عَنْ خَيْثَمَةَ عَنْ عَبْدِ اللهِ بْنِ عَمْرٍو قَالَ تَجَيَّشَ الرُّوْمُ فَيِسْتَمِدُّ أَهْلُ الْإِسْلَامِ مُسْتَغِيْثِيْنَ فَلَا يَتَخَلَّفُ عَنْهُمْ مُؤْمِنٌ قَالَ فَيَهْزِمُوْنَ الرُّوْمَ حَتّٰى يَنْتَهُوْا بِهِمْ إِلٰى أُسْطُوَانَةَ قَدْ عَرَفُوْا مَكَانَهَا فَبَيْنَمَا هُمْ عِنْدَهَا إِذَا جَاءَهُمُ الصَّرِيْخُ أَلَا إِنَّ الدَّجَّالَ قَدْ خَلَفَ فِيْ عِيَالِكُمْ فَيَرْفُضُوْا مَا فِيْ أَيْدِيْهِمْ وَيَقْبَلُوْا نَحْوَهُ. مَوْقُوْفٌ.

Abū Muʿāwiyah narrated on the authority of al-Aʿmash from Khaythamah that ʿAbdullāh ibn ʿAmr said, "The Byzantines will prepare for war. The people of Islam will seek reinforcements for help. No believer will refuse them. They will defeat Byzantium and will rout them until they reach a column whose place is known. While they are near it, a loud call will come, 'The Dajjāl is taking your place with your children. So, they will leave everything that is in their hands and will head towards him.'"[44]

This hadith is *mawqūf*[45].



44 Narrated by al-Bazzār.
45 The chain of narration ends at the companion.

# 28 HADITH TWENTY-EIGHT

عَبْدُ الرَّحْمٰنِ بْنُ شَرِيْكٍ نَا أَبِي عَنِ ابْنِ إِسْحَاقَ عَنِ الزُّهْرِيِّ عَنْ عَبْدِ الرَّحْمٰنِ بْنِ يَزِيْدَ بْنِ جَارِيَةَ عَنْ مُجَمِّعِ بْنِ جَارِيَةَ سَمِعَ النَّبِيَّ ﷺ يَقُوْلُ يُقْتَلُ الدَّجَّالُ دُوْنَ بَابِ اللُّدِّ بِسَبْعِ عَشَرَةِ ذِرَاعًا. وَاللُّدُّ بِالرَّمْلَةِ. ابن شريك متروك الحديث واه.

ʿAbd al-Raḥmān ibn Sharīk narrated: My father narrated from Ibn Isḥāq from al-Zuhrī from ʿAbd al-Raḥmān ibn Sharīk ibn Jāriyah that Mujammiʿ ibn Jāriyah heard the Prophet ﷺ say, "The Dajjāl will be killed around seventeen cubits away from the gate of Ludd."[46] Ludd is in Ramallah.

Ibn Sharīk is a rejected narrator of hadith who is suspected of inventing reports.

46 The author narrated this hadith without the chain of narration. However, it has supporting narrations: *Ṣaḥīḥ Muslim*, hadith no. 2937; *Sunan al-Tirmidhī*, Dār al-Risālah al-ʿĀlamiyyah, hadith no. 2394; *Musnad al-Imām Aḥmad*, Mu'assasah al-Risālah, hadith no. 17629.

# HADITH TWENTY-NINE 29

عِيسَى الْخَيَّاطُ عَنْ مُحَمَّدِ بْنِ يَحْيَى بْنِ حِبَّانَ قَالَ سَمِعْتُ أَبَا سَعِيدٍ الْخُدْرِيَّ
يَقُولُ مَعَ الدَّجَّالِ امْرَأَةٌ يُقَالُ لَهَا طَيِّبَةٌ لَا يَقْدَمُ قَرْيَةً إِلَّا سَبَقَتْ إِلَيْهَا
تَقُولُ هَذَا الدَّجَّالُ دَخَلَ عَلَيْكُمْ فَاحْذَرُوهُ.

ʿĪsā ibn Khayyāṭ from Muhammad ibn Yaḥyā ibn Ḥibbān: I heard Abū Saʿīd al-Khudrī say, "With the Dajjāl will be a woman who is called Ṭaybah[47]. He will not enter any town, except that she will enter it before him and say, 'This is the Dajjāl who is entering upon you. So beware of him.'"[48]

47 The woman's name in the original text of the hadith is Laʿībah.

48 Narrated by Nuʿaym ibn Ḥammād in *al-Fitan*. It was also copied from that text, with reference, in *Kanz al-ʿUmmāl*, hadith no. 39691.

# 30 HADITH THIRTY

أَخْبَرَنَا عَبْدُ اللهِ بْنُ مُحَمَّدٍ وَالْمُبَارَكُ بْنُ عَلِيٍّ ثَنَا عَبْدُ الْقَادِرِ بْنُ مُحَمَّدٍ (ح) وَثَنَا عَبْدُ الْحَقِّ أَنَا عَمِّي ثَنَا الْحُسَيْنُ بْنُ عَلِيٍّ ثَنَا أَحْمَدُ بْنُ جَعْفَرٍ نَا عَبْدُ اللهِ حَدَّثَنِي أَبِي ثَنَا يَحْيَى ثَنَا التَّيْمِيُّ عَنْ أَبِي نَضْرَةَ عَنْ أَبِي سَعِيدٍ قَالَ لَقِيَنِي ابْنُ صَائِدٍ فَقَالَ عُدَّ النَّاسَ يَقُولُونَ أَوْ أَحْسِبُ النَّاسَ يَقُولُونَ وَأَنْتُمْ يَا أَصْحَابَ مُحَمَّدٍ سَمِعْتُ رَسُولَ اللهِ صَلَّى اللَّهُ عَلَيْهِ وَسَلَّمَ يَقُولُ أَوْ قَالَ رَسُولُ اللهِ صَلَّى اللَّهُ عَلَيْهِ وَسَلَّمَ هُوَ يَهُودِيٌّ وَأَنَا مُسْلِمٌ وَأَنَّهُ أَعْوَرُ وَأَنَا صَحِيحٌ وَلاَ يَأْتِي مَكَّةَ وَلاَ الْمَدِينَةَ وَقَدْ حَجَجْتُ وَأَنَا مَعَكَ الآنَ بِالْمَدِينَةِ وَلاَ يُولَدُ لَهُ وَقَدْ وُلِدَ لِي ثُمَّ قَالَ مَعَ ذٰلِكَ إِنِّي لَأَعْلَمُ أَيْنَ وُلِدَ وَمَتَىٰ يَخْرُجُ وَأَيْنَ هُوَ قَالَ فَلَبَّسَ عَلَيَّ.

مِنَ الْمُسْنَدِ. صَحِيحٌ رَوَاهُ مُسْلِمٌ عَنْ يَحْيَى بْنِ حُسَيْنٍ عَنْ أَبِي عَنْ مُعْتَمِرِ بْنِ سُلَيْمَانَ عَنْ أَبِيهِ وَعَنْ عُبَيْدِ اللهِ الْقَوَارِيرِيِّ وَأَبِي مُوسَىٰ عَنْ عَبْدِ الْأَعْلَىٰ الشَّامِيِّ عَنْ دَاوُدَ وَأَبِي هِنْدَ وَعَنْ أَبِي مُوسَىٰ عَنْ سَالِمِ بْنِ نُوحٍ عَنْ سَعِيدٍ الْجُرَيْرِيِّ ثَلاَثَتُهُمْ عَنْ أَبِي نَضْرَةَ عَنْ أَبِي سَعِيدٍ.

ʿAbdullāh ibn Muhammad and al-Mubārak ibn ʿAlī both informed us: ʿAbd al-Qādir ibn Muhammad narrated to us. ʿAbd al-Ḥaqq also narrated to us: My uncle narrated to us: al-Ḥusayn ibn ʿAlī narrated to us: Aḥmad ibn Jaʿfar narrated to us: ʿAbdullāh narrated to us: My father narrated to me: Yaḥyā narrated to us: al-Taymī narrated to us from Abū Naḍrah that Abū Sa'īd said, "Ibn Ṣā'id met me and said, 'Many people – or most people – say things. However, O Companions of Muhammad, have you heard the Messenger of Allah ﷺ say – or the Messenger of Allah ﷺ said, "He is a Jew", while I am a Muslim? That he is one-eyed, while I am healthy? That he will not enter Makkah nor Madinah, while I have performed hajj and I am, now, with you in Madinah? That he will not have children, while I have fathered a child?' Then he said, 'Despite that, I know where he will be born, when he will come out, and where he is.' So, it became confusing for me."[49]

This is reproduced from *al-Musnad*. It is an authentic hadith. It was also narrated by Muslim on the authority of Yaḥyā ibn Ḥusayn from his father from Mu'tamir ibn Sulaymān from his father, on the authority of 'Ubayd Allāh al-Qawārīrī, on the authority of Abū Mūsā from 'Abd al-A'lā al-Shāmī from Dāwūd from Abū Hind, and on the authority of Abū Mūsā from Sālim from Nūḥ from Sa'īd al-Jurayrī. All three of these routes are narrated from Naḍrah from Abū Sa'īd.



49 The source of this Hadith was mentioned with hadith no. 13.

# 31 HADITH THIRTY-ONE

أَخْبَرَنَا يَحْيَى بْنُ ثَابِتٍ ثَنَا أَبِي أَنَا الْبَرْقَانِيُّ أَنَا الْإِسْمَاعِيلِيُّ ثَنَا أَبُو عَمْرٍو عَبْدُ اللهِ بْنُ أَحْمَدَ بْنِ ذَكْوَانَ الدِّمَشْقِيُّ ثَنَا الْوَلِيدُ بْنُ مُسْلِمٍ ثَنَا شَيْبَانُ (ح) وَأَخْبَرَنِي أَبُو يَعْلَى ثَنَا أَبُو خَيْثَمَةَ (ح) وَثَنَا الْقَاسِمُ ثَنَا الْمَخْرَمِيُّ وَزُهَيْرٌ وَالرَّمَادِيُّ قَالُوا ثَنَا حُسَيْنُ بْنُ مُحَمَّدٍ ثَنَا شَيْبَانُ قَالَ وَحَدَّثَنِي قَاسِمُ بْنُ دِينَارٍ ثَنَا عُبَيْدُ اللهِ بْنُ مُوسَى عَنْ شَيْبَانَ (ح) وَأَخْبَرَنِي الْحَسَنُ ثَنَا أَبُو بَكْرِ بْنُ أَبِي شَيْبَةَ ثَنَا الْحُسَيْنُ بْنُ مُوسَى ثَنَا شَيْبَانُ وَقَالَ نَا عُبَيْدُ اللهِ بْنُ عُمَرَ الْجُعْفِيُّ ثَنَا الْفَضْلُ بْنُ دُكَيْنٍ نَا شَيْبَانُ عَنْ يَحْيَى عَنْ أَبِي سَلَمَةَ عَنْ أَبِي هُرَيْرَةَ سَمِعْتُهُ يَقُولُ قَالَ رَسُولُ اللَّهِ صَلَّى اللهُ عَلَيْهِ وَسَلَّمَ أَلَا أُحَدِّثُكُمْ عَنِ الدَّجَّالِ مَا حَدَّثَهُ نَبِيٌّ قَوْمَهُ إِنَّهُ أَعْوَرُ وَإِنَّهُ يَجِيءُ بِمِثَالِ الْجَنَّةِ وَالنَّارِ فَالَّتِي يَقُولُ إِنَّهَا الْجَنَّةُ هِيَ النَّارُ وَإِنِّي أُنْذِرُكُمْ بِهِ كَمَا أَنْذَرَ نُوحٌ قَوْمَهُ.

حَدِيثُهُمْ مُتَقَارِبُ اللَّفْظِ وَالْمَعْنَى إِلَّا الْوَلِيدُ فَإِنَّهُ لَمْ يَرِدْ عَلَى قَوْلِهِ قَالَ رَسُولُ اللهِ ﷺ أُنْذِرُكُمْ مِنَ الدَّجَّالِ مَا أَنْذَرَ نُوحٌ قَوْمَهُ. وَقَعَ لَنَا فِي الْبُخَارِيِّ وَغَيْرِهِ.

Yaḥyā ibn Thābit informed us: My father narrated to us: al-Burqānī narrated to us: al-Ismāʿīlī narrated to us: Abū ʿAmr ʿAbdullāh ibn Aḥmad ibn Dhakwān al-Dimashqī narrated to us: al-Walīd ibn Muslim narrated to us: Shaybān narrated to us. Abū Yaʿlā also informed me: Abū Khaythamah narrated to us. Al-Qāsim narrated to us: al-Mukharramī narrated to us: Zuhayr and al-Ramādī narrated to us; they all said: Ḥusayn ibn Muhammad narrated to us: Shaybān narrated to us, saying: And Qāsim ibn Dīnār narrated to me: 'Ubayd Allāh ibn Mūsā narrated to us from Shaybān.

And al-Ḥasan informed me: Abū Bakr ibn Abī Shaybah narrated to us: al-Ḥusayn ibn Mūsā narrated to us: Shaybān narrated to us, saying: 'Ubayd Allāh ibn 'Umar al-Ju'fī informed us: al-Faḍl ibn Dukayn narrated to us: Shaybān informed us from Yaḥyā from Abū Salamah that Abū Hurayrah said, "I heard the Messenger of Allah ﷺ say, 'Shall I not relate to you concerning the Dajjāl that which no Prophet related to his people? He is one-eyed. He will come with semblances of Paradise and the Fire. That about which he says, "It is Paradise" is really the Fire. I warn you about him just as Nūḥ warned his people.'"[50]

The hadiths from all the chains mentioned above are similar in wording and meaning, except for al-Walīd's version. He did not mention that the Messenger of Allah ﷺ said, "I warn you about the Dajjāl just as Nūḥ warned his people."

50 *Ṣaḥīḥ al-Bukhārī*, hadith no. 3338; *Ṣaḥīḥ Muslim*, hadith no. 2936.

# 32 HADITH THIRTY-TWO

أَخْبَرَنَا مُحَمَّدُ بْنُ عَبْدِ الْبَاقِيِّ بْنُ أَحْمَدَ بْنِ سَلْمَانَ نَا أَبُو الْفَضْلِ أَحْمَدُ بْنُ الْحُسَيْنِ بْنِ خَيْرُونَ ثَنَا أَبُو عَلِيٍّ الْحُسَيْنُ بْنُ أَحْمَدَ بْنِ إِبْرَاهِيمَ أَنَا أَبُو سَهْلٍ أَحْمَدُ بْنُ مُحَمَّدِ بْنِ عَبْدِ اللهِ بْنِ أَبِي الْقَطَّانِ ثَنَا أَبُو الْعَبَّاسِ أَحْمَدُ بْنُ مُحَمَّدِ بْنِ عِيسَى نَا أَبُو نُعَيْمٍ ثَنَا شَيْبَانُ عَنْ يَحيَى بْنِ أَبِي كَثِيرٍ عَنْ أَبِي سَلَمَةَ عَنْ أَبِي هُرَيْرَةَ قَالَ قَالَ رَسُولُ اللهِ ﷺ لَأُحَدِّثَنَّكُمْ بِحَدِيثٍ عَنِ الدَّجَّالِ مَا حَدَّثَ بِهِ نَبِيٌّ قَوْمَهُ إِنَّهُ أَعْوَرُ وَإِنَّهُ لَحَيٌّ يُمَثِّلُ الْجَنَّةَ وَالنَّارَ فَالَّتِي يَقُولُ إِنَّهَا الْجَنَّةُ فَهِيَ النَّارُ وَإِنِّي أُنْذِرُكُمُوهُ كَمَا أَنْذَرَ نُوحٌ قَوْمَهُ.

قُلْتُ أَخْبَرَنَاهُ أَبُو الْمَعَالِي الْأَبَرْقُوهِيُّ أَنَا ابْنُ سَابُورَ أَنَا عَبْدُ الْعَزِيزِ بْنُ آدَمَ أَنَا رِزْقُ اللهِ التَّمِيمِيُّ.

صَحِيحٌ مُتَّفَقٌ عَلَيْهِ رَوَاهُ الْبُخَارِيُّ عَنْ أَبِي نُعَيْمٍ وَمُسْلِمٌ عَنْ مُحَمَّدِ بْنِ رَافِعٍ عَنْ حُسَيْنٍ إِمْلَاءً أَنَا أَبُو الْحَسَنِ عَلِيُّ بْنُ أَحْمَدَ بْنِ عُمَرَ بْنِ حَفْصٍ الْحَمَامِيُّ الْمُقْرِيُّ أَنَا أَبُو سَهْلٍ الْقَطَّانُ فَذَكَرَهُ بِنَصِّهِ الْمَرْوَزِيُّ كِلَاهُمَا عَنْ شَيْبَانَ وَهُوَ أَبُو مُعَاوِيَةَ شَيْبَانُ النَّحْوِيُّ الْكُوفِيُّ.

Muhammad ibn ʿAbd al-Bāqī ibn Aḥmad ibn Salmān informed us: Abū al-Faḍl Aḥmad ibn al-Ḥusayn ibn Khayrūn informed us: Abū ʿAlī al-Ḥusayn ibn Aḥmad ibn

# HADITH THIRTY-TWO 32

Ibrāhīm narrated to us: Abū Sahl Aḥmad ibn Muhammad ibn ʿAbdullāh ibn Abī al-Qaṭṭān informed us: Abū al-ʿAbbās Aḥmad ibn Muhammad ibn ʿĪsā narrated to us: Abū Nuʿaym narrated to us: Shaybān narrated to us from Yaḥyā ibn Abī Kathīr from Abī Salamah that Abū Hurayrah said, "The Messenger of Allah ﷺ said, 'I will relate to you about the Dajjāl something which no Prophet has related to his people. He is one-eyed. He will have a valley that resembles Paradise and (one that resembles) the Fire. That which he says is Paradise is the Fire. I warn you of him just as Nūḥ warned his people.'"[51]

I say: Abū al-Maʿālī al-Abarqūhī informed us of it (this hadith, saying): Ibn Sābūr informed us: ʿAbd al-ʿAzīz ibn Adam informed us: Rizq Allāh al-Tamīmī informed us.

It is an authentic hadith, being reported both in al-Bukhārī from Abū Nuʿaym and in Muslim from Muhammad ibn Rāfiʿ from Ḥusayn by way of dictation: Abū al-Ḥasan ʿAlī ibn Aḥmad ibn ʿUmar ibn Ḥafṣ al-Ḥamāmī al-Muqrī informed us: Abū Sahl al-Qaṭṭān informed us. He then mentioned it with the text of al-Marūzī. Each of them narrated from Shaybān – who is Muʿāwiyah Shaybān al-Naḥwī al-Kūfī.

51 See sourcing in the footnote above.

قَرَأْتُ عَلَى أَبِي جَعْفَرٍ الْمَوَازِينِيُّ أَخْبَرَنِي الْبَهَاءُ عَبْدُ الرَّحْمٰنِ أَنَا أَبُو نَصْرٍ
بْنُ يُوسُفَ أَنَا أَبُو عَلِيِّ بْنُ نَبْهَانَ أَنَا أَبُو عَلِيِّ بْنُ شَاذَانَ أَنَّ عُثْمَانَ بْنَ أَحْمَدَ
أَنَا الْحَسَنُ بْنُ سَلَامٍ ثَنَا عُبَيْدُ اللهِ بْنُ مُوسَى نَا الْحَسَنُ بْنُ دِينَارٍ عَنْ أَبِي
التَّيَّاحِ حَدَّثَنِي الْمُغِيرَةُ عَنْ عَمْرِو بْنِ حُرَيْثٍ قَالَ شَهِدْتُ أَبَا بَكْرٍ
الصِّدِّيقِ فِي مَرَضِهِ الَّذِي قُبِضَ فِيهِ فَأُغْمِيَ عَلَيْهِ إِغْمَاءَةً ثُمَّ أَفَاقَ فَقَالَ
وَاللهِ لَا آلُوكُمْ خَيْرًا يَعْنِي عُمَرَ ثُمَّ قَالَ إِنِّي مُحَدِّثُكُمْ حَدِيثًا سَمِعْتُهُ مِنْ
رَسُولِ اللهِ ﷺ يَقُولُ إِنَّ الدَّجَّالَ يَخْرُجُ مِنْ خُرَاسَانَ.

I recited to Abū Jaʿfar al-Mawāzīnī: al-Bahāʾ ʿAbd al-Raḥmān informed me: Abū Naṣr ibn Yūsuf informed us: Abū ʿAlī ibn Nabhān informed us: Abū ʿAlī ibn Shādhān informed us: ʿUthmān ibn Aḥmad informed us: al-Ḥasan ibn Salām informed us: ʿUbayd Allāh ibn Mūsā narrated to us: al-Ḥasan ibn Dīnār narrated to us from Abū al-Ṭayyāḥ: al-Mughīrah narrated to me that ʿAmr ibn Ḥārith said, "I was present with Abū Bakr al-Ṣiddīq during the illness from which he passed away. He fainted for a time and then awoke. He then said, 'By Allah, I will give you a little good' – referring to ʿUmar. He said, 'I am narrating to you a hadith that I heard from the Messenger of Allah ﷺ, where he said: "The Dajjāl will emerge from Khurasan."'"[52]

---

52 *Sunan al-Tirmidhī*, Dār al-Risālah al-ʿĀlamiyyah, hadith no. 2387; *Sunan Ibn Mājah*, Dār al-

# HADITH THIRTY-FOUR

# 34

أَخْبَرَنَا أَحْمَدُ بْنُ إِسْحَاقَ أَنَا مُحَمَّدُ بْنُ أَبِي الْفَتْحِ وَعَبْدُ الرَّحْمٰنِ بْنُ صَيْلَاءَ قَالَا أَنَا أَبُو الْوَقْتِ أَنَا أَبُو الْحَسَنِ أَنَا ابْنُ حَمَوَيْهِ أَنَا إِبْرَاهِيمُ بْنُ خُزَيْمٍ أَنَا عَبْدُ بْنُ حُمَيْدٍ ثَنَا رَوْحُ بْنُ عُبَادَةَ ثَنَا سَعِيدُ بْنُ عَرَفَةَ عَنْ أَبِي التَّيَّاحِ عَنِ الْمُغِيرَةِ وَهُوَ ابْنُ سُبَيْعٍ عَنْ عَمْرِو بْنِ حُرَيْثٍ عَنْ أَبِي بَكْرٍ الصِّدِّيقِ قَالَ قَالَ رَسُولُ اللهِ صَلَّى اللهُ عَلَيْهِ وَسَلَّمَ إِنَّ الدَّجَّالَ يَخْرُجُ مِنْ أَرْضٍ بِالْمَشْرِقِ يُقَالُ لَهَا خُرَاسَانُ يَتْبَعُهُ أَقْوَامٌ كَأَنَّ وُجُوهَهُمُ الْمَجَانُّ الْمُطْرَقَةُ.

هٰذَا حَدِيثٌ صَحِيحٌ غَرِيبٌ وَهُوَ مُخَالِفٌ لِحَدِيثِ تَمِيمٍ الدَّارِيِّ.

Aḥmad ibn Isḥāq informed us: Muhammad ibn Abī al-Fatḥ and ʿAbd al-Raḥmān ibn Ṣaylāʾ both informed us, saying: Abū al-Waqt informed us: Abū al-Ḥasan informed us: Ibn Ḥamawayh informed us: Ibrāhīm ibn Khuzaym informed us: ʿAbd ibn Ḥumayd informed us: Rawḥ ibn ʿUbādah narrated to us: Saʿīd ibn ʿArafah narrated to us from Abū al-Tayyāḥ from al-Mughīrah – from ʿUmar ibn Ḥārith that Abū Bakr al-Ṣiddīq said, "The Messenger of Allah ﷺ said, 'The Dajjāl will emerge from a land in the East called Khurasan. He will be followed by some peoples whose faces are like

Risālah al-ʿĀlamiyyah, hadith no. 4082.

# 34 HADITH THIRTY-FOUR

flattened shields.'"[53] This hadith is a singular narration but *ṣaḥīḥ*. However, it contradicts the hadith of Tamīm al-Dārī.



53 See the footnote above for the source of this hadith.

# 35 HADITH THIRTY-FIVE

أَخْبَرَنَا مُحَمَّدُ بْنُ عَبْدِ الْبَاقِيِّ ثَنَا أَبُو الْفَضْلِ أَحْمَدُ بْنُ الْحُسَيْنِ بْنِ خَيْرُونَ ثَنَا أَبُو عَلِيٍّ الْحُسَيْنُ بْنُ أَحْمَدَ بْنِ إِبْرَاهِيمَ بْنِ شَاذَانَ أَنَا عَبْدُ اللهِ بْنُ جَعْفَرٍ النَّحْوِيُّ ثَنَا يَعْقُوبُ بْنُ سُفْيَانَ ثَنَا مُحَمَّدُ بْنُ عَبْدِ اللهِ الْخُزَاعِيُّ ثَنَا حَمَّادُ بْنُ سَلَمَةَ عَنْ خَالِدٍ الْحَذَّاءِ عَنْ عَبْدِ اللَّهِ بْنِ شَقِيقٍ عَنْ عَبْدِ اللَّهِ بْنِ سُرَاقَةَ عَنْ أَبِي عُبَيْدَةَ بْنِ الْجَرَّاحِ قَالَ سَمِعْتُ رَسُولَ اللَّهِ صَلَّى اللهُ عَلَيْهِ وَسَلَّمَ يَقُولُ إِنَّهُ لَمْ يَكُنْ نَبِيٌّ بَعْدَ نُوحٍ إِلَّا وَقَدْ أَنْذَرَ الدَّجَّالَ أُمَّتَهُ وَإِنِّي أُنْذِرُكُمُوهُ فَوَصَفَهُ لَنَا رَسُولُ اللَّهِ صَلَّى اللهُ عَلَيْهِ وَسَلَّمَ وَقَالَ سَيُدْرِكُهُ بَعْضُ مَنْ رَآنِي وَ سَمِعَ كَلَامِي قَالُوا يَا رَسُولَ اللهِ كَيْفَ قُلُوبُنَا يَوْمَئِذٍ أَمِثْلُهَا الْيَوْمَ قَالَ أَوْ خَيْرًا.

رَوَاهُ عَفَّانُ عَنْ حَمَّادٍ وَفِيهِ زِيَادَةٌ وَسَأَكْشِفُهُ نَعَمْ . أَنْبَأَنَاهُ أَبُو الْحَسَنِ الْمَقْدِسِيُّ عَنِ اللَّبَّانِ عَنْ غَانِمٍ الْبُرْجِيِّ عَنْ أَبِي عَلِيِّ بْنِ شَاذَانَ أَخْبَرَتْنَا بِهِ بِنْتُ الْعَدْكَمِ أَنَا الْكَاشْفِرِيُّ حُضُورًا أَنَا الْكَاغِدِيُّ.

Muhammad ibn ʿAbd al-Bāqī informed us: Abū al-Faḍl Aḥmad ibn al-Ḥusayn ibn Khayrūn narrated to us: Abū ʿAlī al-Ḥusayn ibn Aḥmad ibn Ibrāhīm ibn Shādhān narrated to us: ʿAbdullāh ibn Jaʿfar al-Naḥwī narrated to us: Yaʿqūb ibn Sufyān narrated to us: Muhammad ibn ʿAbdullāh al-Khuzāʿī narrated to us: Ḥammād ibn Salamah narrated to us from Khālid al-Ḥadhdhā' from 'Abdullāh ibn Shaqīq from 'Abdullāh ibn Surāqah that Abū 'Ubaydah ibn al-Jarrāḥ said, "I heard the Messenger of Allah ﷺ say, 'No Prophet came after Nūḥ except that he warned his people of the Dajjāl. And I too will warn you of him.' The Messenger of Allah ﷺ then described him and said, 'Some of those who see me or hear my words will live to witness him.' The people said, 'O Messenger of Allah, will our hearts be in the same condition as today?' He said, 'Or better.'"[54]

'Affān narrated it from Ḥammād with the addition, "I will remove all ambiguity from him."

54 *Sunan Abū Dāwūd*, Dār al-Risālah al-'Ālamiyyah, hadith no. 4756; *Sunan al-Tirmidhī*, Dār al-Risālah al-'Ālamiyyah, hadith no. 2384; *Musnad al-Imām Aḥmad*, Mu'assasah al-Risālah, hadith no. 1693.

# HADITH THIRTY-SIX 36

أَخْبَرَنَا مُحَمَّدُ بْنُ عَبْدِ السَّلَامِ بْنِ أَبِي عَصْرُونَ عَنْ أَبِي رَوْحٍ أَنَا تَمِيمُ الْجُرْجَانِيُّ أَنَا أَبُو سَعْدٍ اللَّنْجَرُوذِيُّ أَنَا أَبُو عَمْرِو بْنُ حَمْدَانَ أَنَا أَبُو يَعْلَى الْمَوْصِلِيُّ ثَنَا عَبْدُ اللهِ بْنُ مُعَاوِيَةَ ثَنَا حَمَّادُ بْنُ سَلَمَةَ فَذَكَرَ مِثْلَ مَا تَقَدَّمَ إِلَّا أَنَّهُ قَالَ فِيهِ لَعَلَّهُ سَيُدْرِكُهُ.

وَقَدْ رَوَاهُ شُعْبَةُ عَنْ خَالِدٍ الْحَذَّاءِ كَذَلِكَ أَخْرَجَهُ ت د وَحَسَّنَهُ التِّرْمِذِيُّ.

Muhammad ibn ʿAbd al-Salām ibn Abī ʿAṣrūn from Abī Rawḥ informed us: Tamīm al-Jurjānī informed us: Abū Saʿd al-Lanjarūdhī informed us: Abū ʿAmr ibn Ḥamdān informed us: Abū Yaʿlā al-Mawṣilī informed us: ʿAbdullāh ibn Muʿāwiyah narrated to us: Ḥammād ibn Salamah narrated to us: a similar hadith as the previous one. However, in it he said, "Perhaps someone (who sees me or hears my words) will live to see him."[55]

Shuʿbah also narrated it from Khālid al-Ḥadhdhāʾ. It was included in *Sunan al-Tirmidhī* and *Sunan Abū Dāwūd*. Al-Tirmidhī declared it *ḥasan*.

55 See the footnote above for the source.

# 37 HADITH THIRTY-SEVEN

أَخْبَرَنَا مُحَمَّدُ بْنُ عَبْدِ الْبَاقِي بْنِ أَحْمَدَ بْنِ سَلْمَانَ أَنَا أَبُو الْفَضْلِ أَحْمَدُ بْنُ الْحَسَنِ بْنِ خَيْرُونَ وَيَحْيَى بْنُ ثَابِتٍ ثَنَا أَبِي قَالَا أَنَا أَبُو بَكْرٍ أَحْمَدُ بْنُ مُحَمَّدِ بْنِ غَالِبٍ قَالَ قَرَأْتُ عَلَى أَبِي الْعَبَّاسِ بْنِ حَمْدَانَ حَدَّثَكُمْ مُحَمَّدُ بْنُ أَيُّوبَ أَنَا أَبُو عُمَرَ الْحَوْضِيُّ ثَنَا شُعْبَةُ سَمِعْتُ قَتَادَةَ يُحَدِّثُ عَنْ أَنَسٍ أَنَّ النَّبِيَّ صَلَّى اللهُ عَلَيْهِ وَسَلَّمَ قَالَ مَا بُعِثَ نَبِيٌّ إِلَّا أَنْذَرَ أُمَّتَهُ الدَّجَّالَ الْأَعْوَرَ الْكَذَّابَ أَلَا إِنَّهُ أَعْوَرُ وَإِنَّ بَيْنَ عَيْنَيْهِ مَكْتُوبٌ كَافِرٌ.

أَخْبَرَنَا بِهِ ابْنُ الْفَرَّاءِ أَنَا الشَّيْخُ الْمُوَفَّقُ بِسَمَاعِهِ مِنَ الشَّيْخَيْنِ.

صَحِيحٌ رَوَاهُ مُسْلِمٌ عَنْ أَبِي مُوسَى وَبُنْدَارٌ عَنْ غُنْدَرَ عَنْ شُعْبَةَ وَرَوَاهُ الْبُخَارِيُّ عَنْ أَبِي عُمَرَ الْحَوْضِيِّ وَسُلَيْمُ بْنُ حَرْبٍ عَنْ شُعْبَةَ.

Muhammad ibn ʿAbd al-Bāqī ibn Aḥmad ibn Salmān informed us: Abū al-Faḍl Aḥmad ibn al-Ḥasan ibn Khayrūn and Yaḥyā ibn Thābit both informed us, the latter from his father: Abū Bakr Aḥmad ibn Muhammad ibn Ghālib informed us, saying: I recited to Abū al-ʿAbbās ibn Hamdan: Muhammad ibn Ayyūb narrated to us: Abū ʿUmar al-Ḥawḍī informed us: Shuʿbah narrated to us: I heard Qatādah narrating on the authority of Anas that the Prophet ﷺ said, "No Prophet was sent except that he warned his nation of the lying, one-eyed Dajjāl. Indeed, he is one-eyed. And between his two eyes is written *kāfir*."[56]

Ibn al-Farrā' informed us of this hadith saying: Sheikh al-Muwaffaq informed us of it after hearing it from the two Sheikhs. It is an authentic hadith narrated by Muslim from Abū Mūsā and Bundār from Ghundar from Shu'bah. And al-Bukhārī narrated it from Abū 'Umar al-Ḥawḍī and Sālim ibn Ḥarb from Shu'bah.

56 *Ṣaḥīḥ al-Bukhārī*, hadith nos. 3450 and 7130; *Ṣaḥīḥ Muslim*, hadith no. 2934; *Sunan Abū Dāwūd*, hadith no. 4316.

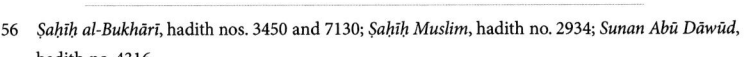

# 38 HADITH THIRTY-EIGHT

أَخْبَرَنَا أَبُو طَاهِرٍ الْبِيلِيُّ ثَنَا أَبُو الْفَضْلِ مُحَمَّدُ بْنُ عَبْدِ السَّلَامِ بْنِ أَحْمَدَ بْنِ مُحَمَّدٍ الْأَنْصَارِيُّ أَنَا أَبُو عَلِيٍّ الْحُسَيْنُ بْنُ أَحْمَدَ بْنِ إِبْرَاهِيمَ بْنِ شَاذَانَ أَنَا أَبُو عَلِيٍّ حَامِدُ بْنُ مُحَمَّدِ بْنِ عَبْدِ اللهِ الْهَرَوِيُّ ثَنَا مُحَمَّدُ بْنُ صَالِحٍ ثَنَا ذَكْوَانُ بْنُ إِبْرَاهِيمَ ثَنَا شُعْبَةُ قَالَ سَمِعْتُ قَتَادَةَ يُحَدِّثُ عَنْ أَنَسِ بْنِ مَالِكٍ قَالَ سَمِعْتُ رَسُولَ اللهِ صَلَّى اللَّهُ عَلَيْهِ وَسَلَّمَ يَقُولُ إِنَّ اللهَ لَمْ يَبْعَثْ نَبِيًّا إِلَّا أَنْذَرَ أُمَّتَهُ الدَّجَّالَ مَكْتُوبٌ بَيْنَ عَيْنَيْهِ كَافِرٌ يَقْرَأُهُ كُلُّ مُؤْمِنٍ وَكَافِرٍ فَإِنَّهُ أَعْوَرُ وَإِنَّ رَبَّكُمْ لَيْسَ بِأَعْوَرَ.

وَقَعَ لَنَا فِي جُزْءِ ابْنِ الرَّفَاءِ وَفِي كِتَابِ حَنْبَلٍ رَوَاهُ عَنْ أَبِي الْوَلِيدِ الطَّيَالِسِيِّ ثَنَا شُعْبَةُ.

Abū Ṭāhir al-Bīlī informed us: Abū al-Faḍl Muhammad ibn ʿAbd al-Salām ibn Aḥmad ibn Muhammad al-Anṣārī informed us: Abū al-Ḥusayn ibn Aḥmad ibn Ibrāhīm ibn Shādhān informed us: Abū ʿAlī Ḥāmid ibn Muhammad ibn ʿAbdullāh al-Harawī informed us: Muhammad ibn Ṣāliḥ narrated to us: Dhakwān ibn Ibrāhīm narrated to us: Shuʿbah narrated to us, saying, "I heard Qatādah narrate on the authority of Anas ibn Mālik, who said, 'I heard the Messenger of Allah ﷺ say, "Indeed, Allah (Mighty and Majestic is He) did not send any Prophet except that he warned his nation of the Dajjāl. Between his two eyes is written *kāfir*. Every believer and disbeliever will be able to read it. Indeed, he is one-eyed and your Lord is not one-eyed."""'[57]

We found this hadith in a short book by Ibn al-Rifā and in the book of Ḥanbal. It was also narrated by Abū al-Walīd al-Ṭayālisī, who narrated it from Shu'bah.

57 This hadith was narrated with the author's own chain of narration. We did not find it in any of the famous books of Hadith.

# 39 HADITH THIRTY-NINE

أَخْبَرَنَا يَحْيَى بْنُ ثَابِتٍ ثَنَا أَبِي ثَنَا الْبَرْقَانِيُّ أَنَا الْإِسْمَاعِيلِيُّ أَخْبَرَنِي الْحَسَنُ ثَنَا عَبَّاسٌ الْقَوْسِيُّ ثَنَا يَحْيَى بْنُ سَعِيدٍ ثَنَا إِسْمَاعِيلُ ثَنَا قَيْسٌ قَالَ قَالَ الْمُغِيرَةُ بْنُ شُعْبَةَ مَا سَأَلَ رَسُولَ اللهِ صَلَّى اللَّهُ عَلَيْهِ وَسَلَّمَ عَنِ الدَّجَّالِ أَحَدٌ أَكْثَرَ مِمَّا سَأَلْتُهُ فَإِنَّهُ قَالَ لِي مَا يَضُرُّكَ مِنْهُ قَالَ قُلْتُ إِنَّ مَعَهُ جَبَلَ خُبْزٍ وَنَهَرَ مَاءٍ قَالَ هُوَ أَهْوَنُ عَلَى اللهِ مِنْ ذَلِكَ. رَوَاهُ الْبُخَارِيُّ عَنْ مُسَدَّدٍ عَنْ يَحْيَى بْنِ سَعِيدٍ وَقَعَ لَنَا مِنَ الْبُخَارِيِّ عَالِيًا.

Yaḥyā ibn Thābit informed us: My father narrated to us: al-Burqānī narrated to us: al-Ismāʿīlī related to us: al-Ḥasan informed me: ʿAbbās al-Qūsī narrated to us: Yaḥyā ibn Saʿīd narrated to us: Ismāʿīl narrated to us: Qays narrated to us, saying: al-Mughīrah ibn Shuʿbah said, "No one would ask the Messenger of Allah ﷺ about the Dajjāl more than what I asked him. He then said to me, 'What is it that concerns you so much about him?' I said, 'With him is a mountain of rice and a river of water.' He said, 'He is more despised by Allah b than that.'"[58] It was narrated by al-Bukhārī from Musaddad from Yaḥyā ibn Saʿīd. And we took it from al-Bukhārī with a shorter chain of transmission.

58 *Ṣaḥīḥ Muslim*, hadith no. 2939.

# HADITH FORTY 40

أَخْبَرَنَا سَعْدُ اللهِ بْنُ نَصْرِ بْنِ سَعِيدٍ وَأَحْمَدُ بْنُ عَبْدِ الْغَنِيِّ بْنِ حَنِيفَةَ ثَنَا مُحَمَّدُ بْنُ أَحْمَدَ ثَنَا عَبْدُ الْغَفَّارِ بْنُ مُحَمَّدِ بْنِ جَعْفَرٍ نَا مُحَمَّدُ بْنُ أَحْمَدَ بْنِ الْحَسَنِ بْنِ الصَّوَّافِ ثَنَا حُسَيْنُ بْنُ مُوسَى ثَنَا الْحُمَيْدِيُّ نَا سُفْيَانُ ثَنَا مُخَلَّدٌ قَالَ سَمِعْتُ قَيْسَ بْنَ مُجَاشِعٍ يَقُولُ سَمِعْتُ الْمُغِيرَةَ بْنَ شُعْبَةَ يَقُولُ مَا سَأَلَ أَحَدٌ رَسُولَ اللَّهِ صَلَّى اللَّهُ عَلَيْهِ وَسَلَّمَ عَنِ الدَّجَّالِ مَا سَأَلْتُهُ قَالَ وَمَا مَسْأَلَتُكَ عَنْهُ إِنَّكَ لَنْ تُدْرِكَهُ.

رَوَاهُ ابْنُ مَاجه عَنْ مُحَمَّدِ بْنِ عَبْدِ اللهِ بْنِ يَحْيَى وَعَلِيِّ بْنُ مُحَمَّدٍ عَنْ وَكِيعٍ عَنْ إِسْمَاعِيلَ بْنِ أَبِي خَالِدٍ وَهُوَ صَحِيحٌ رَوَاهُ مُسْلِمٌ عَنِ ابْنِ أَبِي عُمَرَ عَنِ ابْنِ عُيَيْنَةَ وَقَعَ لَنَا مِنْ سُنَنِ ابْنِ مَاجه وَرَوَاهُ هِشَامٌ وَإِبْرَاهِيمُ بْنُ حُمَيْدٍ وَجَرِيرٌ وَوَكِيعٌ وَأَبُو أُسَامَةَ وَغَيْرُهُمْ عَنْ إِسْمَاعِيلَ.

Sa'd Allāh ibn Naṣr ibn Sa'īd and Aḥmad ibn 'Abd al-Ghanī ibn Ḥanafiyyah both informed us: Muhammad ibn Aḥmad narrated to us: 'Abd al-Ghaffār ibn Muhammad ibn Ja'far narrated to us: Muhammad ibn Aḥmad ibn al-Ḥasan ibn al-Ṣawwāf related to us: Ḥusayn ibn Mūsā narrated to us: al-Ḥumaydī narrated to us: Sufyān related to us: Mukhallad narrated to us, saying, "I heard Qays ibn Mujāshi' say, 'I heard al-Mughīrah ibn Shu'bah say, "No one would ask the Messenger of Allah ﷺ more about the Dajjāl than I. So, he said, 'What is your concern with him? You will not see him.'"""[59] It was narrated by Ibn Mājah from Muhammad ibn 'Abdullāh ibn Yaḥyā and from 'Alī ibn Muhammad from Wakī' from Ismā'īl ibn Abī Khālid. It is an authentic hadith. Muslim narrated it from Ibn Abī 'Umar on the authority of Ibn 'Uyaynah. We found it in *Sunan Ibn Mājah*. And it was narrated by Hishām, Ibrāhīm ibn Ḥamīd, Jarīr, Wakī', Abū Usāmah, and others on the authority of Ismā'īl.



59 See footnote above for source.

# HADITH FORTY-ONE 41

أَخْبَرَنَا عَلِيُّ بْنُ عُثْمَانَ وَأَبُو الْحُسَيْنِ الْبُوَيْنِيُّ قَالَا أَنَا أَحْمَدُ بْنُ مُحَمَّدٍ الْمَحْمُودِيُّ أَنَا أَحْمَدُ بْنُ مُحَمَّدٍ الْحَافِظُ أَنَا الْقَاسِمُ بْنُ الْفَضْلِ إِجَازَةً إِنْ لَمْ يَكُنْ سِمَاعًا سَأَلْتُ مَرْدَوَيْهِ نَا عَبْدُ اللهِ بْنُ إِسْحَاقَ نَا الْحَسَنُ بْنُ مُكْرَمٍ ثَنَا يَزِيدُ بْنُ هَارُونَ أَنَا إِسْمَاعِيلُ بْنُ أَبِي خَالِدٍ عَنْ قَيْسٍ عَنِ الْمُغِيرَةِ قَالَ مَا سَأَلَ أَحَدٌ رَسُولَ اللهِ صَلَّى اللَّهُ عَلَيْهِ وَسَلَّمَ عَنِ الدَّجَّالِ أَكْثَرَ مِمَّا سَأَلْتُهُ قَالَ أَيْ بُنَيَّ وَمَا يُصِيبُكَ مِنْهُ إِنَّهُ لَنْ يَضُرَّكَ قُلْتُ إِنَّهُمْ يَزْعُمُونَ أَنَّ مَعَهُ جِبَالُ خُبْزٍ وَأَنْهَارُ مَاءٍ قَالَ نَعَمْ هُوَ أَهْوَنُ عَلَى اللهِ مِنْ ذَلِكَ.

ʿAlī ibn ʿUthmān and Abū al-Ḥusayn al-Buwaynī both informed us, saying: Aḥmad ibn Muhammad al-Maḥmūdī informed us: Aḥmad ibn Muhammad al-Ḥāfiẓ informed us: al-Qāsim ibn al-Faḍl informed us, by way of the license he gave us – if we indeed did not hear it from him: I asked Mardawayh: ʿAbdullāh ibn Isḥāq informed us: al-Ḥasan ibn Mukarram informed us: Yazīd ibn Hārūn narrated to us: Ismāʿīl ibn Abī Khālid informed us from Qays that al-Mughīrah said, "No one asked the Messenger of Allah ﷺ about the Dajjāl more than me. So, he said, 'O my son, why does he worry you so much? He will not harm you.' I said, 'It is believed that he will have with him a mountain of bread and rivers of water.' He replied, 'Yes, he is more trifling to Allah than that.'"[60]

60 *Ṣaḥīḥ al-Bukhārī*, hadith no. 7122; *Ṣaḥīḥ Muslim*, hadith no. 2152.

# 42 HADITH FORTY-TWO

أَخْبَرَنَا عَبْدُ اللهِ بْنُ مُحَمَّدٍ ثَنَا أَبُو الْحُسَيْنِ الْمُبَارَكُ بْنُ عَبْدِ الْجَبَّارِ بْنِ أَحْمَدَ الصَّيْرَفِيُّ ثَنَا أَبُو مَنْصُورٍ مُحَمَّدُ بْنُ مُحَمَّدِ بْنِ عُثْمَانَ السَّوَّاقُ نَا أَبُو عَلِيٍّ مَخْلَدُ بْنُ جَعْفَرٍ الْبَاقَرْجِيُّ ثَنَا أَحْمَدُ بْنُ يَحْيَى الْحُلْوَانِيُّ ثَنَا مُحَمَّدُ بْنُ الصَّبَّاحِ ثَنَا مُحَمَّدُ ابْنُ عُبَيْدٍ ثَنَا إِسْمَاعِيلُ بْنُ أَبِي خَالِدٍ عَنْ قَيْسٍ عَنِ الْمُغِيرَةِ بْنِ شُعْبَةَ قَالَ مَا سَأَلَ رَسُولَ اللَّهِ صَلَّى اللَّهُ عَلَيْهِ وَسَلَّمَ أَحَدٌ عَنِ الدَّجَّالِ أَكْثَرَ مِمَّا سَأَلْتُهُ أَنَا فَقَالَ مَا يُهِمُّكَ مِنْهُ يَا بُنَيَّ قَالَ يَزْعُمُونَ أَنَّ مَعَهُ أَنْهَارُ مَاءٍ وَطَعَامٌ قَالَ هُوَ أَهْوَنُ عَلَى اللَّهِ مِنْ ذَٰلِكَ.

وَقَالَ مُحَمَّدُ بْنُ الصَّبَّاحِ مَرَّةً حَدَّثَنِي مُحَمَّدُ بْنُ عُبَيْدٍ وَيَزِيدُ بْنُ هَارُونَ قَالَ مُحَمَّدٌ ثَنَا يَزِيدُ وَقَالَ يَزِيدُ ثَنَا إِسْمَاعِيلُ وَقَعَ لَنَا فِي سُنَنِ ابْنِ الصَّبَّاحِ أَنَا سِنْفَرُ الْفُضَالِيُّ أَنَا عَبْدُ اللَّطِيفِ بْنُ يُوسُفَ.

صَحِيحٌ مُتَّفَقٌ عَلَيْهِ رَوَاهُ الْبُخَارِيُّ عَنْ مُسَدَّدٍ عَنْ يَحْيَى الْقَطَّانِ وَرَوَاهُ مُسْلِمٌ عَنْ أَبِي بَكْرِ بْنِ أَبِي شَيْبَةَ وَابْنُ أَبِي عُمَرَ عَنْ يَزِيدَ بْنِ هَارُونَ كِلَاهُمَا عَنْ إِسْمَاعِيلَ بْنِ أَبِي خَالِدٍ وَرَوَاهُ مُسْلِمٌ مِنْ طُرُقٍ.

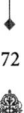

ʿAbdullāh ibn Muhammad informed us: Abū al-Ḥusayn al-Mubārak ibn ʿAbd al-Jabbār ibn Aḥmad al-Ṣayrafī narrated to us: Abū Manṣūr Muhammad ibn Muhammad ibn ʿUthmān al-Sawwāq narrated to us: Abū ʿAlī Mukhallad ibn Jaʿfar al-Bāqirjī informed us: Aḥmad ibn Yaḥyā al-Ḥulwānī narrated to us: Muhammad ibn al-Ṣabbāḥ narrated to us: Muhammad ibn ʿUbayd narrated to us: Ismāʿīl ibn Abī Khālid narrated to us from Qays that al-Mughīrah ibn Shuʿbah said, "No one asked the Messenger of Allah ﷺ about the Dajjāl more than I did. So, he (once) said to me, 'What is your worry about him, O my son?' I replied, 'It is believed that he will have with him rivers of water and food.' He said, 'He is more trifling to Allah b than that.'"[61]

Muhammad ibn al-Ṣabbāḥ once narrated it with the following chain, "Muhammad ibn ʿUbayd and Yazīd ibn Hārūn narrated to me, saying: Muhammad said: Yazīd narrated to us: Yazīd said: Ismāʿīl narrated to us."

We also found it in *Sunan Ibn al-Ṣabbāḥ* with the chain of transmission: Sinfar al-Fuḍālī informed us: ʿAbd al-Laṭīf ibn Yūsuf informed us.

It is an authentic hadith that is narrated by al-Bukhārī from Musaddad from Yaḥyā al-Qaṭṭān, and by Muslim from Abū Bakr ibn Abī Shaybah and Ibn Abī ʿUmar from Yazīd ibn Hārūn – both from Ismāʿīl ibn Abī Khālid. Muslim narrated it with a number of different chains of transmission.

61 *Ṣaḥīḥ al-Bukhārī*, hadith no. 7122; *Ṣaḥīḥ Muslim*, hadith no. 2939.

# 43 HADITH FORTY-THREE

أَخْبَرَنَا يَحْيَى بْنُ ثَابِتٍ ثَنَا أَبِي ثَنَا الْبَرْقَانِيُّ أَنَا الْإِسْمَاعِيلِيُّ أَخْبَرَنِي الْحَسَنُ ثَنَا فِيَاضٌ ثَنَا عَبْدُ الرَّزَّاقِ ح وَثَنَا الْقَاسِمُ ثَنَا ابْنُ زَنْجَوَيْهِ (ح) وَأَخْبَرَنَا ابْنُ صَالِحٍ ثَنَا مُحَمَّدُ بْنُ سَهْلٍ وَأَحْمَدُ بْنُ مَنْصُورٍ وَأَخْبَرَنِي ابْنُ نَاجِيَةَ ثَنَا زُهَيْرُ بْنُ مُحَمَّدِ بْنِ قُمَيْنٍ وَحَدَّثَنِي إِبْرَاهِيمُ بْنُ هَانِئٍ ثَنَا الرَّمَادِيُّ قَالُوا ثَنَا عَبْدُ الرَّزَّاقِ عَنْ مَعْمَرٍ عَنِ الزُّهْرِيِّ عَنْ سَالِمٍ عَنْ أَبِيهِ قَامَ رَسُولُ اللهِ ﷺ فِي النَّاسِ وَأَثْنَى عَلَى اللهِ بِمَا هُوَ أَهْلُهُ ثُمَّ ذَكَرَ الدَّجَّالَ فَقَالَ إِنِّي لَأُنْذِرُكُمُوهُ وَمَا مِنْ نَبِيٍّ إِلَّا قَدْ أَنْذَرَ قَوْمَهُ لَقَدْ أَنْذَرَهُ نُوحٌ قَوْمَهُ وَلَكِنْ سَأَقُولُ لَكُمْ فِيهِ قَوْلًا لَمْ يَقُلْهُ نَبِيٌّ لِقَوْمِهِ تَعْلَمُونَ أَنَّهُ أَعْوَرُ وَأَنَّ اللهَ لَيْسَ بِأَعْوَرَ.

وَزَادَ ابْنُ نَاجِيَةَ قَالَ الزُّهْرِيُّ فَأَخْبَرَنِي عُمَرُ بْنُ ثَابِتٍ فِي حَدِيثٍ ذَكَرَهُ فِي الدَّجَّالِ وَقَعَ لَنَا إِسْنَادٌ صَحِيحٌ لِلْإِسْمَاعِيلِيِّ.

Yaḥyā ibn Thābit informed us: My father narrated to us: al-Burqānī narrated to us: al-Ismāʿīlī informed us: al-Ḥasan informed us: Fayāḍ narrated to us: ʿAbd al-Razzāq narrated to us.

Al-Qāsim narrated to us: Ibn Zanjawayh narrated to us.

Ibn Ṣāliḥ informed me: Muhammad ibn Sahl and Aḥmad ibn Manṣūr both narrated to me and Ibn Nājiyah informed me: Zuhayr ibn Muhammad ibn Qummayn narrated to us:

# HADITH FORTY-THREE 43

Ibrāhīm ibn Hāni' narrated to me: al-Ramādī narrated to us, all saying: 'Abd al-Razzāq narrated to us from Ma'mar from al-Zuhrī from Sālim that his father said, "The Messenger of Allah ﷺ stood up in front of the people, praised Allah as He deserved, and then mentioned the Dajjāl. He said, 'I warn you of him. There came no Prophet except that he warned his people about him. Even Nūḥ warned his people of him. However, I will tell you something about him that no other Prophet told his people. You should know that he is one-eyed and that Allah is not one-eyed.'"[62]

Nājiyah added: al-Zuhrī said: 'Umar ibn Thābit informed of it in the narrations that he mentioned about the Dajjāl.

We also received it with an authentic chain to al-Ismā'īlī.

62 *Ṣaḥīḥ al-Bukhārī*, hadith no. 7184; *Ṣaḥīḥ Muslim*, hadith no. 2931.

# 44 HADITH FORTY-FOUR

أَخْبَرَنَا الْأَبَرْقُوهِيُّ أَنَا مُحَمَّدُ بْنُ هِبَةِ اللهِ الدِّينَوَرِيُّ أَنَا عَمِّي مُحَمَّدُ بْنُ أَبِي حَامِدٍ أَنَا عَاصِمُ بْنُ الْحَسَنِ أَنَا ابْنُ مَهْدِيٍّ نَا الْمَحَامِلِيُّ نَا يُوسُفُ بْنُ مُوسَى ثَنَا جَرِيرٌ عَنْ إِسْمَاعِيلَ عَنْ قَيْسٍ عَنِ الْمُغِيرَةِ قُلْتُ يَا رَسُولَ اللهِ بَلَغَنِي أَنَّ مَعَ الدَّجَّالِ أَنْهَارُ مَاءٍ وَجِبَالُ خُبْزٍ فَقَالَ هُوَ أَهْوَنُ عَلَى اللهِ مِنْ ذَلِكَ وَقَالَ لَيْسَ بِالَّذِي يَضُرُّكَ. م عَنِ ابْنِ رَاهَوَيْهِ عَنْ جَرِيرٍ.

Al-Abarqūhī informed us: Muhammad ibn Hibat Allāh al-Dīnūrī informed us: My uncle Muhammad ibn Abī Ḥāmid informed us: ʿĀṣim ibn al-Ḥasan informed us: Ibn Mahdī informed us: al-Muḥāmilī informed us: Yūsuf ibn Mūsā informed us: Jarīr narrated to us from Ismāʿīl from Qays that al-Mughīrah said, "O Messenger of Allah, it has reached me that with the Dajjāl there will be rivers of water and mountains of bread. He responded, 'He is more trifling to Allah than that.' He then said, 'He is not the one that will harm you.'"[63]





63 *Ṣaḥīḥ al-Bukhārī*, hadith no. 7122; *Ṣaḥīḥ Muslim*, hadith no. 2152.

# 45 HADITH FORTY-FIVE

أَخْبَرَنَا عُمَرُ بْنُ عَبْدِ الْمُنْعِمِ أَنْبَأَنَا عَبْدُ الْجَلِيلِ بْنُ مَنْدَوَيْةِ أَنَا نَصْرُ بْنُ الْمَظَفَّرِ أَنَا ابْنُ النَّقُّورِ أَنَا أَبُو الْحَسَنِ الْحَرْبِيُّ ثَنَا مُحَمَّدُ بْنُ هَارُونَ بْنِ الْمُحْدِرِ إِمْلَاءً ثَنَا هَمَّامٌ ثَنَا الْوَلِيدُ بْنُ مُسْلِمٍ عَنِ الْأَوْزَاعِيِّ عَنْ إِسْحَاقَ بْنِ عَبْدِ اللَّهِ بْنِ أَبِي طَلْحَةَ عَنْ أَنَسٍ قَالَ قَالَ رَسُولُ اللَّهِ صَلَّى اللَّهُ عَلَيْهِ وَسَلَّمَ يَتْبَعُ الدَّجَّالَ مِنْ يَهُودِ أَصْبَهَانَ سَبْعُونَ أَلْفًا.

ʿUmar ibn ʿAbd al-Munʿim informed us: ʿAbd al-Jalīl ibn Mandawiyyah informed us: Naṣr ibn al-Muẓaffar informed us: Ibn al-Naqqūr informed us: Abū al-Ḥasan al-Ḥarbi informed us: Muhammad ibn Hārūn ibn al-Muḥaddar narrated to us by dictation: Humām narrated to us: al-Walīd ibn Muslim narrated to us from al-Awzāʿī from Isḥāq ibn ʿAbdullāh ibn Abī Ṭalḥah that Anas said, "The Messenger of Allah ﷺ said, 'The Dajjāl will be followed by seventy thousand of the Jews of Isfahan.'"[64]

64 *Ṣaḥīḥ Muslim*, hadith no. 2944.

# 46 HADITH FORTY-SIX

أَخْبَرَنَا يَحْيَى بْنُ ثَابِتٍ ثَنَا أَبِي أَنَا الْبَرْقَانِيُّ أَنَا الْإِسْمَاعِيلِيُّ أَخْبَرَنِي أَبُو يَعْلَى ثَنَا أَحْمَدُ بْنُ عِيسَى ثَنَا ابْنُ وَهْبٍ أَخْبَرَنِي عُمَرُ بْنُ مُحَمَّدٍ أَنَّ أَبَاهُ حَدَّثَهُ عَنْ عَبْدِ اللَّهِ بْنِ عُمَرَ قَالَ كُنَّا نَتَحَدَّثُ فِي حَجَّةِ الْوَدَاعِ وَرَسُولُ اللَّهِ صَلَّى اللَّهُ عَلَيْهِ وَسَلَّمَ بَيْنَ أَظْهُرِنَا لَا نَدْرِي مَا حَجَّةُ الْوَدَاعِ فَحَمِدَ اللَّهَ وَحْدَهُ وَأَثْنَى عَلَيْهِ ثُمَّ ذَكَرَ الْمَسِيحَ الدَّجَّالَ فَأَطْنَبَ فِي ذِكْرِهِ ثُمَّ قَالَ مَا بَعَثَ اللَّهُ مِنْ نَبِيٍّ إِلَّا قَدْ أَنْذَرَهُ أُمَّتَهُ لَقَدْ أَنْذَرَهُ نُوحٌ وَالنَّبِيُّونَ مِنْ بَعْدِهِ وَإِنَّهُ يَخْرُجُ فِيكُمْ فَمَا خَفِيَ عَلَيْكُمْ مِنْ شَأْنِهِ فَلَا يَخْفَى عَلَيْكُمْ أَنَّهُ أَعْوَرُ الْعَيْنِ الْيُمْنَى كَأَنَّهَا عِنَبَةٌ طَافِيَةٌ ثُمَّ قَالَ أَلَا إِنَّ اللَّهَ حَرَّمَ عَلَيْكُمْ دِمَاءَكُمْ وَأَمْوَالَكُمْ كَحُرْمَةِ يَوْمِكُمْ هَذَا فِي بَلَدِكُمْ هَذَا فِي شَهْرِكُمْ هَذَا أَلَا هَلْ بَلَّغْتُ قَالُوا نَعَمْ قَالَ اللَّهُمَّ اشْهَدْ ثُمَّ قَالَ وَيْحَكُمْ أَوْ وَيْلَكُمْ انْظُرُوا لَا تَرْجِعُوا بَعْدِي كُفَّارًا يَضْرِبُ بَعْضُكُمْ رِقَابَ بَعْضٍ.

وَقَعَ لَنَا فِي الصَّحِيحَيْنِ صَحِيحٌ مُتَّفَقٌ عَلَيْهِ رَوَاهُ الْبُخَارِيُّ عَنْ يَحْيَى بْنِ سُلَيْمَانَ وَمُسْلِمٌ عَنْ حَرْمَلَةَ كِلَاهُمَا عَنِ ابْنِ وَهْبٍ.

Yaḥyā ibn Thābit informed us: My father narrated to us: al-Burqānī informed us: al-Ismāʿīlī informed us: Abū Yaʿlā informed me: Aḥmad ibn ʿĪsā narrated to us: Ibn Wahb narrated to us: ʿUmar ibn Muhammad informed him that our father narrated to him that ʿAbdullāh ibn ʿUmar said,

"We were speaking among ourselves about the farewell pilgrimage, and the Messenger of Allah ﷺ was behind us. We did not know what the farewell pilgrimage was. Then, he praised Allah in His oneness and extolled him. Then, he mentioned al-Masīḥ al-Dajjāl and did so in detail. Then he said, 'No Prophet was sent except that he warned his people of him. Nūḥ and all the Prophets after him warned their people of him. However, he will emerge among you. So, nothing of his affair should be hidden from you. He is one-eyed. His right eye will be like a floating grape.' Then he said, 'Indeed, Allah has made inviolable between you your blood and your wealth, just like the inviolability of this day of yours in this land of yours in this month of yours. Have I not delivered the message?' The people said, 'Yes.' He said, 'O Allah, bear witness.' Then he said, 'Woe to you. Be diligent and do not turn back after me as disbelievers, striking each other's necks.'"[65]

We found it in Ṣaḥīḥ al-Bukhārī and *Ṣaḥīḥ Muslim*. It is an authentic hadith that is agreed upon. Al-Bukhārī narrated it from Yaḥyā ibn Sulaymān and Muslim from Ḥarmalah – both from Wahb.

65 *Ṣaḥīḥ al-Bukhārī*, nos. 4402 and 4403.

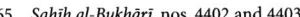

# 47 HADITH FORTY-SEVEN

قَرَأْتُ عَلَى إِسْمَاعِيلَ بْنِ عَبْدِ الرَّحْمٰنِ أَخْبَرَكُمْ أَبُوْ مُحَمَّدِ بْنُ قُدَامَةَ أَنَا اِبْنُ الدَّلْحِيِّ أَنَا رِزْقُ اللهِ التَّمِيْمِيُّ أَنَا عَلِيُّ بْنُ مُحَمَّدٍ نَا أَبُوْ جَعْفَرِ بْنُ الْبُحْتَرِيِّ ثَنَا مُحَمَّدُ بْنُ عُبَيْدِ اللهِ ثَنَا إِسْحَاقُ الْأَزْرَقُ ثَنَا عَوْفٌ عَنْ أَنَسِ بْنِ سِيْرِيْنَ عَنْ أَبِيْ عُبَيْدَةَ عَنْ عَبْدِ اللهِ بْنِ مَسْعُوْدٍ قَالَ مَا ذَكَرْنَا مِنَ الْآيَاتِ فَقَدْ مَضَيْنَ غَيْرَ أَرْبَعٍ طُلُوْعُ الشَّمْسِ مِنْ مَغْرِبِهَا وَالدَّجَّالُ وَدَابَّةُ الْأَرْضِ وَخُرُوْجُ يَأْجُوْجَ وَمَأْجُوْجَ قَالَ وَالْآيَةُ الَّتِيْ تُخْتَمُ الْأَعْمَالُ طُلُوْعُ الشَّمْسِ مِنْ مَغْرِبِهَا أَلَمْ تَرَ أَنَّ اللهَ يَقُوْلُ يَوْمَ يَأْتِيْ بَعْضُ آيَاتِ رَبِّكَ لَا يَنْفَعُ نَفْسًا إِيْمَانُهَا لَمْ تَكُنْ آمَنَتْ مِنْ قَبْلُ أَوْ كَسَبَتْ فِيْ إِيْمَانِهَا خَيْرًا. فَهُوَ طُلُوْعُ الشَّمْسِ مِنْ مَغْرِبِهَا.

إِسْنَادُهُ جَيِّدٌ.

I recited to Ismāʿīl ibn ʿAbd al-Raḥmān: Abū Muhammad ibn Qudāmah informs you: Ibn al-Dalḥī informed us: Rizq Allāh al-Tamīmī informed us: ʿAlī ibn Muhammad informed us: Abū Jaʿfar ibn al-Baḥtarī informed us: Muhammad ibn ʿUbayd Allāh narrated to us: Isḥāq al-Azraq narrated to us: ʿAwf narrated to us from Anas ibn Sīrīn from Abū ʿUbaydah that ʿAbdullāh ibn Masʿūd said, "Whatever signs we have mentioned have already passed, except four: the rising of the Sun from its place of setting, the Dajjāl, the Beast of the

Earth, and the emergence of Ya'jūj and Ma'jūj." He added, "The sign which cuts off deeds is the rising of the Sun from its place of setting. Have you not seen that Allah says, 'On the Day your Lord's signs arrive, belief will not benefit those who did not believe earlier or those who did no good through their faith.'[66] This refers to the rising of the Sun from its place of setting."

This hadith's chain of narration is good.[67]

66 *Al-An'ām*, 158.

67 Al-Ṭabarānī, *al-Mu'jam al-Kabīr*, hadith no. 9019.

# 48 HADITH FORTY-EIGHT

أَنبَأَنَا أَحْمَدُ بْنُ سَلَامَةَ عَنْ أَبِي الْمَكَارِمِ الْأَصْبَهَانِيِّ أَنَا أَبُو عَلِيٍّ الْحَدَّادُ أَنَا أَبُو نُعَيْمٍ ثَنَا عَبْدُ اللهِ بْنُ فَارِسَ ثَنَا يُوسُفُ بْنُ حُبَيْبٍ ثَنَا أَبُو دَاوُدَ ثَنَا هِشَامٌ عَنْ قَتَادَةَ عَنْ عَبْدِ الرَّحْمَنِ بْنِ آدَمَ عَنْ أَبِي هُرَيْرَةَ قَالَ قَالَ رَسُولُ اللهِ صَلَّى اللهُ عَلَيْهِ وَسَلَّمَ الْأَنْبِيَاءُ إِخْوَةٌ لِعَلَّاتٍ وَأُمَّهَاتُهُمْ شَتَّى وَدِينُهُمْ وَاحِدٌ وَأَنَا أَوْلَى النَّاسِ بِعِيسَى بْنِ مَرْيَمَ لِأَنَّهُ لَمْ يَكُنْ بَيْنِي وَبَيْنَهُ نَبِيٌّ فَإِذَا رَأَيْتُمُوهُ فَاعْرِفُوهُ فَإِنَّهُ رَجُلٌ مَرْبُوعٌ إِلَى الْحُمْرَةِ وَالْبَيَاضِ بَيْنَ مُمَصَّرَتَيْنِ كَأَنَّ رَأْسَهُ يَقْطُرُ وَإِنْ لَمْ يُصِبْهُ بَلَلٌ إِنَّهُ يُكَسِّرُ الصَّلِيبَ وَيَقْتُلُ الْخِنْزِيرَ وَيَقْبَضُ الْمِلَلَ حَتَّى يَهْلِكَ فِي زَمَانِهِ الْمِلَلُ كُلُّهَا غَيْرَ الْإِسْلَامِ وَحَتَّى يُهْلِكَ اللهُ فِي زَمَانِهِ مَسِيحَ الضَّلَالَةِ الْأَعْوَرَ الْكَذَّابَ وَتَقَعُ الْأَمَنَةُ فِي الْأَرْضِ حَتَّى يَرْعَى الْأَسَدُ مَعَ الْإِبِلِ وَالنَّمِرُ مَعَ الْبَقَرِ وَالذِّئَابُ مَعَ الْغَنَمِ وَيَلْعَبَ الصِّبْيَانُ بِالْحَيَّاتِ وَلَا يَضُرُّ بَعْضُهُمْ بَعْضًا ثُمَّ يَبْقَى فِي الْأَرْضِ أَرْبَعِينَ سَنَةً ثُمَّ يَمُوتُ وَيُصَلِّي عَلَيْهِ الْمُسْلِمُونَ وَيَدْفِنُونَهُ.

أَخْرَجَهُ أَبُو دَاوُدَ عَنْ قَتَادَةَ عَنْ هُدْبَةَ وَهَمَّامٍ.

Aḥmad ibn Salamah related to us from Abū al-Makārim al-Aṣbahānī: Abū ʿAlī al-Ḥaddād informed us: Abū Nuʿaym informed us: ʿAbdullāh ibn Fāris narrated to us: Yūsuf ibn Ḥabīb narrated to us: Abū Dāwūd narrated to us: Hishām narrated to us from Qatādah from ʿAbd al-Raḥmān ibn

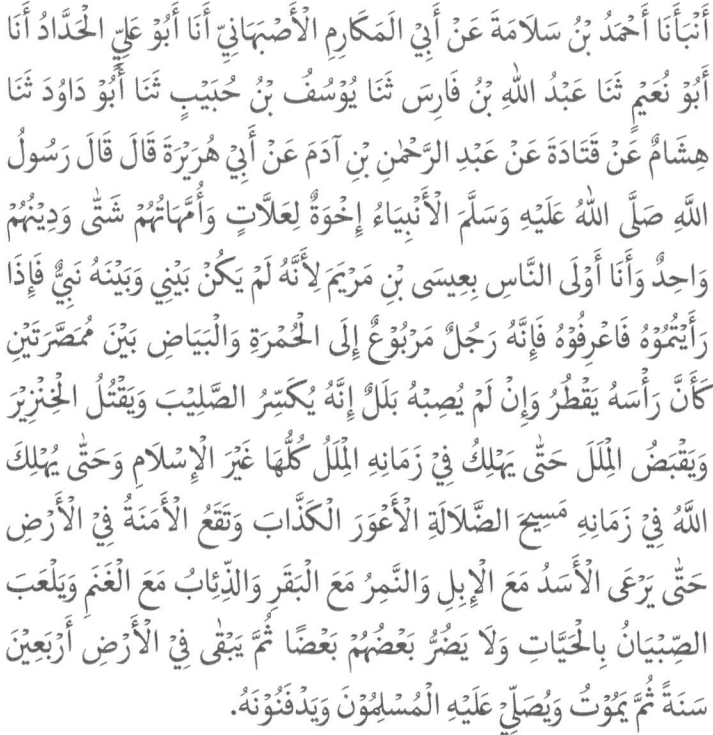

Adam that Abū Hurayrah said, "The Messenger ﷺ said, 'The Prophets are brothers from different mothers. Their mothers are different but their religion is one. I am the closest of people to 'Īsā ibn Maryam because there was no Prophet between us. So, when you see him, recognize him. He is a man of average height and complexion, tending towards reddish white. It is as if his head is dripping even though water had not touched it. He will break the cross and kill the swine. He will subdue all religions until Allah destroys, in his time, all the religions except Islam. And Allah will destroy, in his time, the misguidance of the one-eyed arch-liar. Security will follow on the Earth to the extent that the lion grazes with camels, the tiger with cattle, and wolves with sheep. Children will play with snakes and none of them will harm each other. He will then remain upon the Earth for forty years. Then he will die and the Muslims will pray over him and bury him.'"[68]

This hadith was narrated by Abū Dāwūd from Qatādah from Hudbah and Humām.

68 *Sunan Abī Dāwūd*, Dār al-Risālah al-'Ālamiyyah, hadith no. 4324; *Musnad al-Imām Aḥmad*, Mu'assasah al-Risālah, hadith nos. 9270, 9632-9634; *Ṣaḥīḥ Ibn Ḥibbān*, hadith nos. 6814 and 6821; *Musnad al-Ṭayālisī*, hadith no. 2575.

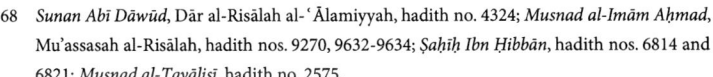

# 49 HADITH FORTY-NINE

أَخْبَرَنَا يَحْيَى بْنُ ثَابِتٍ أَنَا أَبِي ثَنَا الْبَرْقَانِيُّ ثَنَا الْإِسْمَاعِيلِيُّ ثَنَا الْقَاسِمُ بْنُ زَكَرِيَّا ثَنَا أَحْمَدُ بْنُ مَنْصُورٍ ذَاجَ أَنَا النَّضْرُ وَقَالَ نَا حُمَيْدُ بْنُ مِسْعَدَةَ ثَنَا يَزِيدُ بْنُ زُرَيْعٍ ثَنَا عَبْدُ اللهِ بْنُ عَوْنٍ عَنْ مُجَاهِدٍ قَالَ كُنَّا جُلُوسًا عِنْدَ ابْنِ عَبَّاسٍ فَقَالَ مَا يَقُولُونَ قَالَ يَقُولُونَ مَكْتُوبٌ بَيْنَ عَيْنَيْهِ ك ف ر قَالَ لَمْ أَسْمَعْهُ يَقُولُ ذَلِكَ وَلَكِنْ قَالَ أَمَّا إِبْرَاهِيمُ فَانْظُرُوا إِلَى صَاحِبِكُمْ وَأَمَّا مُوسَى فَرَجُلٌ جَعْدٌ آدَمُ جَعْدٌ عَلَى جَمَلٍ أَحْمَرَ مَخْطُومٌ يَخْلُبُهُ كَأَنِّي أَنْظُرُ إِلَيْهِ قَدِ انْحَدَرَ فِي الْوَادِي يُلَبِّي. قَالَ النَّضْرُ فِي حَدِيثِهِ كُنْتُ عِنْدَ ابْنِ عَبَّاسٍ فَذَكَرُوا الدَّجَّالَ قَالَ إِنَّهُ مَكْتُوبٌ بَيْنَ عَيْنَيْهِ كَافِرٌ أَوْ ك ف ر وَقَالَ ابْنُ عَبَّاسٍ فَمَا يَقُولُونَ قَالَ يَقُولُونَ إِنَّهُ مَكْتُوبٌ بَيْنَ عَيْنَيْهِ كَافِرٌ أَوْ ك ف ر.

قَالَ ابْنُ عَبَّاسٍ لَمْ أَسْمَعْهُ قَالَ ذَاكَ ثُمَّ ذَكَرَ مَتْنَهُ. صَحِيحٌ مُتَّفَقٌ عَلَيْهِ رَوَاهُ الْبُخَارِيُّ عَنْ أَبِي مُوسَى عَنْ مُحَمَّدِ بْنِ أَبِي عَدِيٍّ وَعَنْ بَيَانَ بْنِ عَمْرٍو عَنِ النَّضْرِ بْنِ شُمَيْلٍ كِلَاهُمَا عَنِ ابْنِ عَوْنٍ وَرَوَاهُ مُسْلِمٌ عَنْ أَبِي مُوسَى كَذَلِكَ وَرَوَاهُ الْبُخَارِيُّ عَنْ مُحَمَّدِ بْنِ كَثِيرٍ عَنْ إِسْمَاعِيلَ عَنْ عُثْمَانَ بْنِ الْمُغِيرَةِ عَنْ مُجَاهِدٍ عَنِ ابْنِ عُمَرَ هَكَذَا. قَالَ الْبُخَارِيُّ فِي جَمِيعِ الرِّوَايَاتِ عَنْهُ عَنِ ابْنِ عُمَرَ وَخَالَفَ أَصْحَابُ مُحَمَّدِ بْنِ كَثِيرٍ وَأَصْحَابُ إِسْرَائِيلَ قَالُوا كُلُّهُمْ عَنْ مُجَاهِدٍ عَنِ ابْنِ عَبَّاسٍ وَهُوَ الصَّوَابُ. مُخَرَّجٌ مِنَ الْبُخَارِيِّ عَنْ مُحَمَّدِ بْنِ كَثِيرٍ بِعُلُوٍّ.

# HADITH FORTY-NINE 49

Yaḥyā ibn Thābit informed us: My father informed us: al-Burqānī narrated to us: al-Ismāʿīlī narrated to us: al-Qāsim ibn Zakariyyā narrated to us: Aḥmad ibn Manṣūr Dhāj narrated to us: al-Naḍar informed us, saying: Ḥumayd ibn Masʿadah informed us: Yazīd ibn Zurayʿ narrated to us: ʿAbdullāh ibn ʿAwn narrated to us that Mujāhid said, "We were sitting with Ibn ʿAbbās and he said, 'What do you say?' It was said, 'People say that between his eyes will be written *kāf-fā'-rā*.' He responded, 'I did not hear him say that. However, he did say, "As for Ibrāhīm, look at your companions. As for Mūsā, he is a brown-skinned, stocky man, riding on a red Bactrian camel. It is as if I see him having dismounted in the valley reciting the *talbiyah*."'"[69]

In his narration, al-Naḍar said, "I was with Ibn ʿAbbās and some people mentioned the Dajjāl. Someone said, 'Written between his eyes is the word "*kāfir*" or the letters *kāf-fā'-rā*.' Ibn ʿAbbās said, 'What do you all say?' They said, 'Between his eyes is written the word "*kāfir*" or the letters *kāf-fā'-rā*.' Ibn ʿAbbās said, 'I did not hear him say that.'" Then he mentioned the rest of the text.

This hadith is authentic and agreed upon. Al-Bukhārī narrated it from Abū Mūsā from Muhammad ibn Abī ʿAdiyy and from Bayān from ʿAmr from al-Naḍar ibn Shumayl.

69 *Ṣaḥīḥ al-Bukhārī*, hadith no. 5913; *Ṣaḥīḥ Muslim*, hadith no. 166.

# 49 HADITH FORTY-NINE

Each of these two chains are on the authority of Ibn ʿAwn. Muslim narrated it from Abū Mūsā with the same chain. Al-Bukhārī also narrated it from Muhammad ibn Kathīr from Ismāʿīl from ʿUthmān ibn al-Mughīrah from Mujāhid on the authority of Ibn ʿUmar. And in all the different chains, al-Bukhārī said that it was on the authority of Ibn ʿUmar. However, the companions of Muhammad ibn Kathīr and the companions of Isrāʾīl all said, "It is from Mujāhid on the authority of Ibn ʿAbbās." And that is the correct opinion.

We copied it from al-Bukhārī for the higher chain of narration.

# HADITH FIFTY 50

عُثْمَانُ بْنُ عَبْدِ الرَّحْمٰنِ الْجُمَحِيُّ النَّصرِيُّ عَنْ عَبْدِ اللهِ بْنِ طَاوُوسٍ عَنْ أَبِيهِ عَنْ أَبِي هُرَيْرَةَ قَالَ ذُكِرَ الدَّجَّالُ عِنْدَ رَسُولِ اللهِ ﷺ فَقَالَ تَلِدُهُ أُمُّهُ وَهِيَ مَقْبُورَةٌ فِي قَبْرِهَا فَإِذَا وَلَدَتْهُ حَمَلَتِ النِّسَاءُ الْخَطَّاؤُونَ.

تَفَرَّدَ بِهِ عُثْمَانُ قَالَ أَبُو حَاتِمٍ الرَّازِيُّ لَا يُحْتَجُّ بِهِ.

'Uthmān ibn 'Abd al-Raḥmān al-Jumaḥī al-Naṣrī narrated from 'Abdullāh ibn Ṭāwūs from his father that Abū Hurayrah said, "The Dajjāl was mentioned in front of the Messenger of Allah ﷺ and he said, 'His mother will give birth to him (and he will be wrapped) in a thick covering of skin. When she gives birth to him, sinful women will carry him away.'"

'Uthmān is the only one to narrate this. Abū Ḥātim al-Rāzī said, "His hadiths are not taken as evidence."

# 51 HADITH FIFTY-ONE

الأَسْوَدُ بْنُ شَيْبَانَ ثَنَا عَبْدُ اللهِ بْنُ مُضَارِبٍ عَنِ الْعُرْيَانِ بْنِ الْهَيْثَمِ قَالَ وَفَدَ أَبِيْ إِلَى مُعَاوِيَةَ وَأَنَا غُلَامٌ فَلَمَّا دَخَلَ عَلَيْهِ قَالَ مَرْحَبًا مَرْحَبًا وَرَجُلٌ مَعَهُ عَلَى السَّرِيْرِ قَالَ مَنْ هٰذَا الَّذِيْ تُرَحِّبُ بِهِ قَالَ هَذَا الْهَيْثَمُ سَيِّدُ أَهْلِ الْمَشْرِقِ قُلْتُ مَنْ هَذَا قَالُوْا هٰذَا عَبْدُ اللهِ بْنُ عَمْرِو بْنِ الْعَاصِ قُلْتُ لَهُ يَا أَبَا فُلَانٍ مِنْ أَيْنَ يَخْرُجُ الدَّجَّالُ قَالَ مِنْ كُوْثَى.

Al-Aswad ibn Shaybān narrated: ʿAbdullāh ibn al-Muḍārib narrated that al-ʿIryān ibn al-Haytham said, "My father went in a caravan to Muʿāwiyah while I was a child. When he entered upon him, he (Muʿāwiyah) said, 'Welcome. Welcome.' A man on a couch asked, 'Who is the one that you are welcoming?' He said, 'This is Haytham, the master of the people of the East.' My father said, 'Who is this?' He said, 'This is ʿAbdullāh ibn ʿAmr ibn al-ʿĀṣ.' My father said to him, 'O so and so, from where will the Dajjāl emerge?' He said, 'From Kūthī[70].'"[71]

70 A place in Iraq.

71 *Muṣannaf Ibn Abī Shaybah*, vol. 15, p. 162.

# HADITH FIFTY-TWO 52

عَبْدُ الرَّزَّاقِ أَنَا مَعْمَرٌ عَنْ مُحَمَّدِ بْنِ شَبِيبٍ عَنِ الْعُرْيَانِ بْنِ الْهَيْثَمِ قَالَ وَفَدْتُ
عَلَى مُعَاوِيَةَ فَبَيْنَا أَنَا عِنْدَهُ إِذْ جَاءَهُ رَجُلٌ عَلَيْهِ طِمْرَانِ فَرَحَّبَ بِهِ مُعَاوِيَةُ
وَأَجْلَسَهُ عَلَى السَّرِيرِ فَقُلْتُ مَنْ هَذَا يَا أَمِيرَ الْمُؤْمِنِينَ قَالَ هَذَا عَبْدُ اللَّهِ بْنُ
عَمْرِو بْنِ الْعَاصِ قُلْتُ مَا هٰذَا الَّذِي تَقُولُ لَا يَعِيشُ النَّاسُ بَعْدَ مِائَةِ سَنَةٍ
فَأَقْبَلَ عَلَيَّ وَقَالَ أَوَقُلْتُ ذَلِكَ أَنَا غَيْرُهُمْ يَعِيشُونَ بَعْدَ مِائَةِ سَنَةٍ دَهْرًا طَوِيلًا
وَلَكِنَّ هَذِهِ الْأُمَّةَ أُجِّلَتْ مِائَةً وَّثَلَاثِينَ سَنَةً قَالَ ثُمَّ قَالَ مِمَّنْ أَنْتَ قُلْتُ مِنَ
الْعِرَاقِ فَقَالَ أَتَعْرِفُ كُوثَى قُلْتُ نَعَمْ قَالَ مِنْهَا يَخْرُجُ الدَّجَّالُ.

ʿAbd al-Razzāq narrated: Maʿmar informed us from Muhammad ibn Shabīb that ʿIryān ibn al-Haytham said, "I went in a caravan to Muʿāwiyah. While I was in his presence, a man came wearing two tattered robes. Muʿāwiyah welcomed him and sat him on a couch. I said, 'Who is that, O Commander of the Faithful?' He said, 'That is ʿAbdullāh ibn ʿAmr ibn al-ʿĀṣ.' I said, 'What is this matter of where you say that people will no longer live one hundred years?' He turned to him and said, 'Have I really said that? Others will live long lives after one hundred. However, this *ummah's* term is 130 years.' Then he said, 'From which people are you?' I said, 'From Iraq.' He said, 'Do you know Kūthī?' I said, 'Yes.' He said, 'From there, the Dajjāl will emerge.'"[72]





72 *Muṣannaf ʿAbd al-Razzāq*, vol. 11, p. 395; *Muṣannaf Ibn Abī Shaybah*, vol. 15, p. 150.

# 53 HADITH FIFTY-THREE

أَخْبَرَنَا أَبُو رُشَيْدٍ إِسْمَاعِيلُ بْنُ عَلِيٍّ حَدَّثَنَا خَالِدٌ الْبَيِّعُ بِأَصْبَهَانَ ثَنَا أَبُو الْعَلَاءِ مُحَمَّدُ بْنُ عَبْدِ الْجَبَّارِ بْنِ مُحَمَّدٍ الْعَرْشَانِيُّ قِرَاءَةً عَلَيْهِ وَأَنَا حَاضِرٌ أَنَا أَبُو بَكْرٍ مُحَمَّدُ بْنُ أَحْمَدَ بْنِ عَبْدِ الرَّحْمَٰنِ الْهَمْدَانِيُّ حَدَّثَنَا عَبْدُ اللهِ بْنُ جَعْفَرِ بْنِ أَحْمَدَ ابْنِ عَاصِمٍ ثَنَا وَهْبُ بْنُ جَرِيرٍ ثَنَا أَبِي قَالَ سَمِعْتُ عَبْدَ الْمَلِكِ بْنَ عُمَيْرٍ يُحَدِّثُ عَنْ رِبْعِيِّ بْنِ خِرَاشٍ قَالَ أَتَانِي حُذَيْفَةُ وَأَبُو مَسْعُودٍ الْبَدْرِيُّ وَنَحْنُ ثَلَاثَةٌ لَيْسَ مَعَنَا أَحَدٌ فَقَالَ أَبُو مَسْعُودٍ لِحُذَيْفَةَ يَا أَبَا عَبْدِ اللهِ هَلْ سَمِعْتَ رَسُولَ اللهِ ﷺ يَذْكُرُ الدَّجَّالَ قَالَ نَعَمْ سَمِعْتُهُ يَقُولُ إِنَّ مَعَهُ نَهْرَ مَاءٍ وَإِنَّ مَعَهُ نَارًا فَنَهْرُهُ الَّذِي يَرَاهُ النَّاسُ نَهْرُ نَارٍ تَأَجَّجُ وَنَارُهُ الَّتِي يَرَاهَا النَّاسُ نَارًا مَا نَارٌ دَعْدٌ مُطِيبٌ فَمَنْ أَدْرَكَ ذَٰلِكَ مِنْكُمْ فَلْيَقَعْ فِي النَّارِ الَّتِي يَرَاهَا نَارًا فَقَالَ أَبُو مَسْعُودٍ وَأَنَا قَدْ سَمِعْتُهُ مِنْهُ ثُمَّ قَالَ أَبُو مَسْعُودٍ هَلْ سَمِعْتَ رَسُولَ اللهِ ﷺ يَذْكُرُ الرَّجُلَ الَّذِي حَضَرَتْهُ الْوَفَاةُ؟ فَقَالَ نَعَمْ سَمِعْتُ رَسُولَ اللهِ ﷺ يَقُولُ يُؤْتَىٰ بِرَجُلٍ فَيُقَالُ هَلْ عَمِلْتَ مِنْ خَيْرٍ فَنُجْزِيَكَ فَقَالَ مَا أَعْتَدُّ مِنْ عَمَلِي بِشَيْءٍ غَيْرَ أَنِّي كُنْتُ أُبَايِعُ النَّاسَ فَأُيَسِّرُ عَنِ الْمُوسِرِ وَأَتَجَاوَزُ عَنِ الْمُعْسِرِ قَالَ فَغُفِرَ لَهُ بِهَا وَأُدْخِلَ الْجَنَّةَ. ثُمَّ قَالَ أَبُو مَسْعُودٍ هَلْ سَمِعْتَ رَسُولَ اللهِ ﷺ يَذْكُرُ حَدِيثَ الرَّجُلِ الَّذِي كَانَ يَنْبُشُ الْقُبُورَ فَلَمَّا حَضَرَتْهُ الْوَفَاةُ دَعَا بَنِيهِ فَقَالَ أَيَّ أَبٍ كُنْتُ لَكُمْ قَالُوا خَيْرَ أَبٍ قَالَ فَإِنِّي سَائِلُكُمْ سُؤَالًا قَالُوا مَا هُوَ -[٥١]- قَالَ إِذَا أَنَا مِتُّ فَأَحْرِقُونِي ثُمَّ اطْحَنُونِي أَشَدَّ طَحْنٍ طَحَنْتُمُوهُ شَيْئًا قَطُّ ثُمَّ انْظُرُوا يَوْمًا

## HADITH FIFTY-THREE 53

رَاحِيًا فَاذْرُوْنِي فِي الرِّيحِ فَإِنَّ اللهِ إِنْ يَقْدِرَ عَلَيَّ يُعَذِّبْنِي قَالَ فَبَعَثَهُ اللهُ فَقَالَ مَا حَمَلَكَ عَلَى مَا صَنَعْتَ قَالَ مَخَافَتُكَ قَالَ فَغَفَرَ لَهُ. أُثْبِتُهُ عَنْ عَبْدِ الْغَنِيِّ صَحِيحٌ مُتَّفَقٌ عَلَيْهِ.

Abū Rashīd Ismā'īl ibn 'Alī informed us: Khālid al-Bay' narrated to us in Isfahan: Abū al-'Alā' Muhammad ibn 'Abd al-Jabbār ibn Muhammad al-'Irshānī narrated to us by way of someone reciting it to him while I was present: Abū Bakr Muhammad ibn Aḥmad ibn 'Abd al-Raḥmān al-Hamdānī informed us: 'Abdullāh ibn Ja'far ibn Aḥmad ibn 'Iṣām narrated to us: Wahb ibn Jarīr narrated to us: My father narrated to us saying, "I heard 'Abd al-Malik ibn 'Umayr narrating on the authority of Rib'ī ibn Khirāsh saying, 'Ḥudhayfah and Abū Mas'ūd al-Badrī came to me. We were a group of three with no one else. Abū Mūsā said to Ḥudhayfah, 'O Abū 'Abdillāh, did you hear the Messenger of Allah ﷺ mentioning the Dajjāl?' He said, 'Yes. I heard the Messenger of Allah ﷺ say, "With him is a river of water and with him is a fire. His river which people see as water is really a blazing fire. His blaze, which people will see as a fire, is really pure water. So, if anyone of you sees that, let him enter that which he sees as fire."'" "'Abū Mas'ūd said, "I also heard it from him." "'Abū Mas'ūd then said, "Did you hear the Messenger ﷺ mentioning the man whom death approached?" He said, "Yes. I heard the Messenger of Allah ﷺ say, 'A man will be brought and it will be said to him, "Did you do any good work so that we may reward you?" He will respond, "I have not prepared any good deed except that I used to do business with people. And I would be lenient with those in good circumstances and forgive those in difficult circumstances." So, he was forgiven because of that and admitted into Paradise.'" "'Abū Mas'ūd then said, "Did you hear the Messenger of Allah ﷺ mention a hadith about the man that used to rob graves? When death approached him, he called his children and said, 'What kind of father have I been to you all?' They responded, 'The best father.' He said, 'So, I will request something of you.' They said, 'What is it?' He said, 'When I die, incinerate me. Then grind me into the finest powder you have ever ground. Then, wait for a windy day and cast me into the wind. For if Allah seizes me, He will punish me.' When Allah ﷻ resurrected him, He asked, 'What made you do what you did?' He said, 'Fear of You.' So, He forgave him.'"""[73]

This hadith is confirmed from 'Abd al-Ghanī. And it is *ṣaḥīḥ* due to it being reported by both al-Bukhārī and Muslim.

73 *Ṣaḥīḥ al-Bukhārī*, hadith nos. 3450, 3451, 3452; *Ṣaḥīḥ Muslim*, nos. 1560 and 2934.

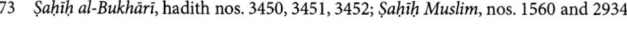

# HADITH FIFTY-FOUR 54

أَخْبَرَنَا الْحَسَنُ بْنُ عَلِيٍّ أَنَا مُكْرَمٌ أَنَا حَمْزَةُ بْنُ أَسَدٍ أَنَا سَهْلُ بْنُ بِشْرٍ أَنَا مُحَمَّدُ بْنُ الْحُسَيْنِ الطَّفَّالُ أَنَا الْحَسَنُ بْنُ رُشَيْقٍ ثَنَا عَلِيُّ بْنُ سَعِيدِ بْنِ بَشِيرٍ ثَنَا عَبْدُ الْعَزِيزِ بْنُ يَحْيَى ثَنَا سُلَيْمَانُ بْنُ بِلَالٍ عَنْ مُحَمَّدِ بْنِ عُقْبَةَ عَنْ أَبِيهِ عَنْ أَبِي هُرَيْرَةَ قَالَ قَالَ رَسُولُ اللَّهِ صَلَّى اللَّهُ عَلَيْهِ وَسَلَّمَ يَخْرُجُ الدَّجَّالُ عَلَى حِمَارٍ أَقْمَرَ مَا بَيْنَ أُذُنَيْهِ سَبْعُونَ بَاعًا مَعَهُ سَبْعُونَ أَلْفَ يَهُودِيٍّ عَلَيْهِمُ الطَّيَالِسَةُ الْخُضْرُ حَتَّى يَنْزِلُوا كَوْمَ أَبِي الْحَمْرَاءِ. عَبْدُ الْعَزِيزِ ضَعَّفُوهُ وَالْحَدِيثُ مُنْكَرٌ.

Al-Ḥasan ibn ʿAlī informed us: Mukarram informed us: Ḥamzah ibn Asad informed us: Sahl ibn Bishr informed us: Muhammad ibn al-Ḥusayn al-Ṭaffāl informed us: al-Ḥasan ibn Rashīq informed us: ʿAlī ibn Saʿīd ibn Bashīr narrated to us: ʿAbd al-ʿAzīz ibn Yaḥyā narrated to us: Sulaymān ibn Bilāl informed us from Muhammad ibn ʿUqbah from his father that Abū Hurayrah said, "The Messenger of Allah ﷺ said, 'The Dajjāl will emerge upon a green donkey between whose ears is (the length of) seventy arms. With him will be seventy thousand Jews wearing green tallises until they reach the trash heap of Abū al-Ḥamrā.'"[74]

The narrator ʿAbd al-ʿAzīz is considered weak. And this is a *munkar* hadith.

74 Al-Bukhārī, *al-Tārīkh*, vol. 1, p. 199.

# 55 HADITH FIFTY-FIVE

أَخْبَرَتْنَا سِتُّ الْأَهْلِ بِنْتُ عَلْوَانَ أَنَا الْبَهَاءُ عَبْدُ الرَّحْمَنِ أَنَا أَبُو الْحُسَيْنِ عَبْدُ الْحَقِّ أَنَا أَبُو سَعْدِ بْنُ خَشِيْشٍ أَنَا أَبُو عَلِيِّ بْنِ شَاذَانَ أَنَا عُثْمَانُ بْنُ أَحْمَدَ ثَنَا حَنْبَلُ بْنُ إِسْحَاقَ ثَنَا حَجَّاجُ بْنُ مِنْهَالٍ ثَنَا عَبْدُ الْحَمِيْدِ بْنُ بَهْرَامَ ثَنَا شَهْرُ بْنُ حَوْشَبٍ حَدَّثَتْنِي أَسْمَاءُ بِنْتُ يَزِيْدَ إِنَّ رَسُوْلَ اللَّهِ صَلَّى اللَّهُ عَلَيْهِ وَسَلَّمَ جَلَسَ فَحَدَّثَهُمْ عَنْ أَعْوَرَ الدَّجَّالِ حَتَّى خَلَعَ قُلُوبَنَا فَرَقًا مِنَ الدَّجَّالِ ثُمَّ خَرَجَ إِلَى الْكَلَا وَالْقَوْمُ فِي الْبَيْتِ فَرَجَعَ وَلَهُمْ خَنِيْنٌ فِيْ الْبَيْتِ يَبْكُوْنَ فَرَقًا مِنَ الدَّجَّالِ فَلَمَّا هَمَّ أَنْ يَدْخُلَ أَرَابَهُ انْكِبَابَ الْقَوْمِ فَقَالَ مَهْيَمْ قَالَتْ أَسْمَاءُ فَقُلْتُ يَا رَسُوْلَ اللَّهِ خَلَعَتْ قُلُوبَنَا فَرَقًا مِنَ الدَّجَّالِ. إِسْنَادُهُ قَوِيٌّ.

Sitt al-Ahl bint ʿAlwān informed us: al-Bahāʾ ʿAbd al-Raḥmān informed us: Abū al-Ḥusayn ʿAbd al-Ḥaqq informed us: Abū Saʿd ibn Khushaysh informed us: Abū ʿAlī ibn Shādhān informed us: ʿUthmān ibn Aḥmad informed us: Ḥanbal ibn Isḥāq narrated to us: Ḥajjāj ibn Minhāl narrated to us: ʿAbd al-Ḥamīd ibn Bahrām narrated to us: Shahr ibn Ḥawshab informed us: Asmāʾ bint Yazīd narrated to me that the Messenger of Allah ﷺ sat and spoke to them about the one-eyed Dajjāl until their hearts were split with fear of the Dajjāl. Then, he departed to the orchards leaving the people in the house. When he returned, they were crying in the house because of their fear of the Dajjāl. When he intended to enter, he became suspicious regarding the situation of the people. So, he said, "What is the matter with you?" Asmā' said, "I said to him, 'O Messenger of Allah, our hearts were split with fear of the Dajjāl.'"[75]

This hadith's chain of transmission is strong.

75 Part of this hadith is reported in *Musnad al-Imām Aḥmad*, Mu'assasah al-Risālah, hadith no. 27568.

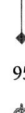

# 56 HADITH FIFTY-SIX

وَبِهِ إِلَى حَنْبَلٍ قَالَ ثَنَا أَحْمَدُ بْنُ الْوَلِيدِ الْأَزْرَقِيُّ ثَنَا دَاوُدُ بْنُ عَبْدِ الرَّحْمَٰنِ عَنْ أَبِي خَيْثَمَةَ عَنْ شَهْرِ بْنِ حَوْشَبٍ عَنْ أَسْمَاءَ بِنْتِ يَزِيدَ سَمِعْتُ رَسُولَ اللهِ يَقُولُ يَخْرُجُ الدَّجَّالُ وَهُوَ أَعْوَرُ وَلَيْسَ اللهُ أَعْوَرَ بَيْنَ عَيْنَيْهِ كَافِرٌ يَقْرَأُهُ أُمِّيٌّ وَكَاتِبٌ وَتَبْعَثُ مَعَهُ الشَّيَاطِينُ عَلَى صُوَرِ مَنْ قَدْ مَاتَ مِنَ الْآبَاءِ وَالْأُمَّهَاتِ فَيَأْتِي أَحَدُهُمْ إِلَى ابْنِهِ وَإِلَى أَخِيهِ وَذَوِي رَحِمِهِ فَيَقُولُ تَعْرِفُنِي أَلَسْتُ فَلَانًا اتَّبِعْهُ هُوَ رَبُّكَ يَعْمَرُ أَرْبَعِينَ سَنَةَ السَّنَةُ كَالشَّهْرِ وَالشَّهْرُ كَالْجُمُعَةِ وَالْجُمُعَةُ كَالْيَوْمِ وَالْيَوْمُ كَاحْتِرَاقِ السَّعْفَةِ. رَوَاهُ عَبْدُ الْحَمِيدِ بْنُ بَهْرَامَ عَنْ شَهْرٍ مُخْتَصَرًا.

With the same chain of transmission to Ḥanbal, who said: Aḥmad ibn al-Walīd al-Azraqī narrated to us: Dāwūd ibn ʿAbd al-Raḥmān narrated to us from Abū Khaythamah from Shahr ibn Ḥawshab that Asmāʾ bint Yazīd (said), "I heard the Messenger of Allah ﷺ say, 'The Dajjāl will emerge. He is one-eyed. Allah is not one-eyed. Between his eyes is (the word) *kāfir*. Every unlettered person and scribe will be able to read it. Some devils will be sent with him who will take on the form of people's mothers and fathers who had passed away. One of them will come to his son, his brother, or some relatives and say, "Do you recognize me? Am I not so-and-so? Follow him. He is your lord." He will remain for forty years. The year will be like a month, the month will be like a week, the week like a day, and the day like the burning of palm leaves.'"[76]

It was narrated by ʿAbd al-Ḥamīd ibn Bahrām from Shahr in an abridged form.

76 Part of this hadith is reported in *Musnad al-Imām Aḥmad*, Mu'assasah al-Risālah, hadith no. 27568.

# 57 HADITH FIFTY-SEVEN

وَبِهِ ثَنَا حَجَّاجٌ ثَنَا عَبْدُ الْحَمِيدِ بْنُ بَهْرَامَ ثَنَا شَهْرُ بْنُ حَوْشَبٍ حَدَّثَتْنِي أَسْمَاءُ أَنَّ عَامَّةَ أَتْبَاعِهِ بَعْدَ الْيَهُودِ أَعَارِيبُ النَّاسِ وَنَصَارَى الْعَرَبِ وَالنِّسَاءُ يَسْحَرُونَ أَعْيُنَ النَّاسِ فَيَقُولُ لِلْأَعْرَابِ مَا تَنْقِمُونَ مِنِّي إِلَّا أَنِّي أُحْيِي لَكُمْ أَنْعَامَكُمْ يَعْظُمُ دَرُّهَا وَتَنْتَفِخُ خَوَاصِيرُهَا وَتَدُرُّ أَلْبَانُهَا وَيَمُرُّ عَلَى الْخَرِبِ فَيَقُولُ أَنْبِتْ مَا فِيكَ فَلَا تَدَعُ فِي بَطْنِهَا شَيْئًا إِلَّا أَخْرَجَتْهُ.

With the same chain of transmission to Ḥajjāj: ʿAbd al-Ḥamīd ibn Bahrām narrated to us: Shahr ibn Ḥawshab narrated to us: Asmā' narrated to me that after the Jews, his (the Dajjāl's) followers will be nomadic peoples, the Christian Arabs, and women. They will bewitch the eyes of people and he will say to the people, "What is it of me that vexes you, except that I revive for you your cattle? Their milk is increased, their flanks fatten, and their milk flows." He will pass by ruins and say, "Let what is in you grow forth. And no seed will remain hidden within it without sprouting."[77]

77 *Muṣannaf ʿAbd al-Razzāq*, hadith no. 20821; *Muṣannaf Ibn Abī Shaybah*, vol. 15, p. 132.

# HADITH FIFTY-EIGHT 58

وَبِهِ ثَنَا حَجَّاجٌ نَا حَمَّادُ بْنُ سَلَمَةَ أَنَا الْحَجَّاجُ عَنْ عَطِيَّةَ عَنْ أَبِي سَعِيدٍ أَنَّ النَّبِيَّ صَلى اللّٰهُ عَلَيْهِ وَسَلَّمَ قَالَ إِنَّهُ لَمْ يَكُنْ نَبِيٌّ إِلاَّ وَقَدْ أَنْذَرَ أُمَّتَهُ الدَّجَّالَ إِنَّهُ أَعْوَرُ لاَ ذُوْ حَدَقَةٍ جَاحِظَةٍ وَلاَ تَخْفٰى كَأَنَّهَا نُخَاعَةٌ فِي جَنْبِ جِدَارٍ وَعَيْنُهُ الْيُسْرٰى كَأَنَّهَا كَوْكَبٌ دُرِّيٌّ مَعَهُ مِثْلُ الْجَنَّةِ وَمِثْلُ النَّارِ جَنَّتُهُ عَيْنُ ذَاتِ دُخَانٍ وَنَارُهُ رَوْضَةٌ خَضْرَاءُ وَبَيْنَ يَدَيْهِ رَجُلاَنِ يُنْذِرَانِ أَهْلَ الْقُرٰى كُلَّمَا خَرَجَا مِنْ قَرْيَةٍ دَخَلَ أَوَائِلُهُمْ فَيُسَلَّطُ عَلٰى رَجُلٍ لاَ يُسَلَّطُ عَلَى غَيْرِهِ فَيَذْبَحُهُ ثُمَّ يَضْرِبُهُ بِعَصًا فَيَقُوْلُ قُمْ فَيَقُوْمُ. وَذَكَرَ الْحَدِيْثَ. رَوَاهُ عَبْدٌ فِيْ مُسْنَدِهِ عَنْ حَجَّاجٍ بِطُوْلِهِ

With the same chain of transmission: Ḥajjāj narrated to us: Ḥammād ibn Salamah informed us: al-Ḥajjāj informed us from ʿAtiyyah from Abū Saʿīd that the Prophet ﷺ said, "Indeed, no Prophet came except that he warned his people of the Dajjāl. Indeed, he is one-eyed. His (right) pupil will bulge and will not be hidden (by his eyelids), as if it is phlegm on the side of a wall. His left eye will be like a glittering star. He will have with him something similar to Paradise and something similar to the Fire. His garden is the Fire itself and his fire is a green garden. He will be heralded by two men who will warn the people of the towns. Every time they exit from a town, the first of the Dajjāl's followers) will enter. He will attack a man – the only man he will attack – and he will slaughter him. He will then hit him with a staff and say, 'Stand up', and he will stand up."[78]

The narrator then mentioned the rest of the hadith.

It was narrated in full by ʿAbd in his *Musnad* from Ḥajjāj.

78 *Musnad Abū Yaʿlā*, vol. 2, p. 332.

# 59 HADITH FIFTY-NINE

أ - وَبِهِ ثَنَا أَحْمَدُ بْنُ عَبْدِ الْمَلِكِ ثنا مُحَمَّدُ بْنُ سَلَمَةَ عَنِ ابْنِ إِسْحَاقَ عَنْ مُحَمَّدِ بْنِ طَلْحَةَ عَنْ سَالِمٍ عَنِ ابْنِ عُمَرَ قَالَ قَالَ رَسُولُ اللَّهِ صَلَّى اللهُ عَلَيْهِ وَسَلَّمَ يَنْزِلُ الدَّجَّالُ فِيْ هَذِهِ النَّسَخَةِ مَجْرَى قَنَاةٍ فَيكُونُ أَكْثَرُ مَنْ يَخْرُجُ إِلَيْهِ النِّسَاءُ حَتَّى أَنَّ الرَّجُلَ لِيَرْجِعُ إِلَى حَمِيمَتِهِ وَإِلَى أُمِّهِ فَيُوْثِقُهَا رِبَاطًا مَخَافَةَ أَنْ تَخْرُجَ إِلَيْهِ

ب - وَبِهِ ثَنَا قَبِيْصَةُ ثَنَا سُفْيَانُ عَنْ سَلَمَةَ عَنْ خَيْثَمَةَ قَالَ تَذَاكَرُوْا الدَّجَّالَ عِنْدَ ابْنِ مَسْعُوْدٍ فَقَالُوْا لَوْ خَرَجَ لَرَجَمْنَاهُ فَقَالَ لَوْ أَصْبَحَ بِبَابِلَ لَأَوْشَكَ بَعْضُهُمْ أَنْ يَّشْكُوْا الْحَفَاءَ مِنَ السُّرْعَةِ إِلَيْهِ.

A) With the same chain of transmission: Aḥmad ibn ʿAbd al-Mālik narrated to us: Muhammad ibn Salamah narrated to us from Ibn Isḥāq from Muhammad ibn Ṭalḥah from Sālim that Ibn ʿUmar said, "The Messenger of Allah ﷺ said, 'The Dajjāl will descend into this marsh in Marr Qanāt[79]. Most of the people who will go out to him will be women to the point that a man will turn to his womenfolk and his mother and tie them up with rope out of fear that they will go out to him.'"[80]

79 A valley near Madinah.

80 *Musnad al-Imām Aḥmad*, Mu'assasah al-Risālah, hadith no. 5353.

# 59 HADITH FIFTY-NINE

B) With the same chain of narration: Qabīṣah narrated to us: Sufyān narrated to us from Salamah that Khaythamah said, "People discussed the Dajjāl in the presence of Ibn Mas'ūd. They said, 'If he were to emerge, we would surely stone him', to which he replied, 'If he were to appear in Babel, some of them would probably go to him so fast that they would complain to him of their exhaustion.'"[81]



81 *Muṣannaf Ibn Abī Shaybah*, vol. 13, p. 333.

# HADITH SIXTY 60

وَبِهِ ثَنَا حَجَّاجٌ نَا حَمَّادٌ عَنْ أَيُّوبَ عَنْ أَبِي قِلَابَةَ قَالَ دَخَلْتُ الْمَسْجِدَ فَإِذَا النَّاسُ قَدْ تَكَابُّوا عَلَى رَجُلٍ فَسَمِعْتُهُ يَقُولُ سَمِعْتُ رَسُولَ اللَّهِ صَلَّى اللَّهُ عَلَيْهِ وَسَلَّمَ يَقُولُ إِنَّ بَعْدِي الْكَذَّابَ الْمُضِلَّ وَإِنَّ رَأْسَهُ مِنْ وَرَائِهِ حُبُكٌ حُبُكٌ فَيَقُولُ أَنَا رَبُّكُمْ فَمَنْ قَالَ رَبِّيَ اللَّهُ لَا إِلَهَ إِلَّا هُوَ عَلَيْهِ تَوَكَّلْتُ وَإِلَيْهِ أُنِيبُ فَلَا سَبِيلَ لَهُ عَلَيْهِ.

With the same chain of transmission: Ḥajjāj narrated to us: Ḥammād informed us from Ayyūb that Abū Qilābah said, "I entered the *masjid* and people were crowding around a man. I heard him say, 'I heard the Messenger of Allah ﷺ say, "After me there will be a misguiding arch-liar. Behind his head are thick locks. He will say, 'I am your lord'. Whoever says, 'My Lord is Allah. There is no god but He. Upon Him I rely and to Him I will return', he (the Dajjāl) will not have any advantage over him."'"[82]



82 *Muṣannaf 'Abd al-Razzāq*, hadith no. 20828.

# 61 HADITH SIXTY-ONE

وَبِهِ ثَنَا قَبِيصَةُ ثَنَا سُفْيَانُ عَنْ سَلَمَةَ بْنِ كُهَيْلٍ عَنْ أَبِي الزَّعْرَاءِ قَالَ تَذَاكَرْنَا الدَّجَّالَ عِنْدَ عَبْدِ اللَّهِ فَقَالَ تَفْتَرِقُونَ أَيُّهَا النَّاسُ لِخُرُوجِهِ ثَلَاثَ فِرَقٍ فِرْقَةٌ تَتْبَعُهُ وَفِرْقَةٌ تَلْحَقُ بِأَرْضِ آبَائِهَا بِمَنَابِتِ الشِّيحِ وَفِرْقَةٌ تَأْخُذُ بِشَطِّ الْفُرَاتِ يُقَاتِلُهُمْ وَيُقَاتِلُونَهُ حَتَّى يَجْتَمِعَ الْمُؤْمِنُونَ بِقُرَى الشَّامِ وَيَبْعَثُونَ إِلَيْهِمْ طَلِيعَةً فِيهِمْ فَارِسٌ فَرَسُهُ أَشْقَرُ أَوْ أَبْلَقُ فَيَقْتَتِلُونَ فَلَا يَرْجِعُ مِنْهُمْ بَشَرٌ. وَهٰذِهِ أَسَانِيدُ جَيِّدَةٌ.

With the same chain of transmission: Qabīṣah narrated to us: Sufyān informed us from Salamah ibn Kuhayl that Abū al-Zaʿrāʾ said, "We were discussing the Dajjāl in the presence of ʿAbdullāh (Ibn Masʿūd). He said, 'O people, you will divide into three groups when he emerges. One group will follow him. One group will return to the land of their ancestors with dry crops. And a group will take to the shores of the Euphrates. He will fight them and they will fight him until the believers are gathered in the towns of Shām. He will send his advanced guard against them, among whom there will be a knight on a black and white horse. They will fight until no man among them returns.'"[83]

These chains of transmission are good.

83 *Muṣannaf Ibn Abī Shaybah*, vol. 15, p. 191.

# HADITH SIXTY-TWO 62

وَبِهِ ثَنَا حَجَّاجٌ نَا حَمَّادُ بْنُ سَلَمَةَ حَدَّثَنَا أَيُّوبُ عَنْ نَافِعٍ عَنِ ابْنِ عُمَرَ أَنَّ رَسُولَ اللَّهِ صَلَّى اللهُ عَلَيْهِ وَسَلَّمَ قَالَ إِنَّ الدَّجَّالَ أَعْوَرُ عَيْنِ الْيُمْنَى وَعَيْنُهُ الْأُخْرَى كَأَنَّهَا عِنَبَةٌ طَافِيَةٌ. وَأَخْبَرَنِي بِهَذَيْنِ الْحَدِيثَيْنِ أَيْضًا عَبْدُ الْكَرِيمِ بْنُ زَيْدٍ بِبَعْلَبَكَّ ثَنَا الْبَهَاءُ عَبْدُ الرَّحْمَنِ.

With the same chain of transmission: Ḥajjāj narrated to us: Ḥammād ibn Salamah informed us: Ayyūb narrated to us from Nāfiʿ from Ibn ʿUmar that the Messenger of Allah ﷺ said, "Indeed, the Dajjāl's right eye is defective. His other eye is like a floating grape."[84]

ʿAbd al-Karīm ibn Zayd also informed me of these two hadiths from the narration of al-Bahā' ʿAbd al-Raḥmān in Baalbek.

84 *Ṣaḥīḥ al-Bukhārī*, hadith no. 7123; *Ṣaḥīḥ Muslim*, hadith no. 2932.

# 63 HADITH SIXTY-THREE

أَخْبَرَنَا عَبْدُ اللهِ بْنُ مُحَمَّدٍ ثَنَا عَبْدُ الْقَادِرِ بْنُ مُحَمَّدٍ ثَنَا الْحَسَنُ بْنُ عَلِيٍّ أَنَا أَحْمَدُ بْنُ جَعْفَرٍ ثَنَا عَبْدُ اللهِ بْنُ أَحْمَدَ بْنِ حَنْبَلٍ حَدَّثَنِي أَبِي ثَنَا يَزِيدُ ثَنَا الْمَسْعُودِيُّ عَنْ عَاصِمِ بْنِ كُلَيْبٍ عَنْ أَبِيهِ عَنْ أَبِي هُرَيْرَةَ قَالَ قَالَ رَسُولُ اللهِ صَلَّى اللَّهُ عَلَيْهِ وَسَلَّمَ خَرَجْتُ إِلَيْكُمْ وَقَدْ بُيِّنَتْ لِي لَيْلَةُ الْقَدْرِ وَمَسِيحُ الضَّلَالَةِ وَكَانَ تَلَاحٍ بَيْنَ رَجُلَيْنِ بِسُدَّةِ الْمَسْجِدِ فَأَتَيْتُهُمَا لِأَحْجِزَ بَيْنَهُمَا فَأُنْسِيتُهُمَا وَسَأَشْدُو لَكُمْ مِنْهُمَا شَدْوًا أَمَّا لَيْلَةُ الْقَدْرِ فَالْتَمِسُوهَا فِي الْعَشْرِ الْأَوَاخِرِ وَأَمَّا مَسِيحُ الضَّلَالَةِ فَإِنَّهُ أَعْوَرُ الْعَيْنِ أَجْلَى الْجَبْهَةِ عَرِيضُ النَّحْرِ فِيهِ دَفًا كَأَنَّهُ قَطَنُ بْنُ عَبْدِ الْعُزَّى قَالَ يَا رَسُولَ اللهِ هَلْ يَضُرُّنِي شَبَهُهُ قَالَ لَا أَنْتَ امْرُؤٌ مُسْلِمٌ وَهُوَ امْرُؤٌ كَافِرٌ.

أَخْبَرَنَاهُ الشَّيْخُ شَمْسُ الدِّينِ بْنُ قُدَامَةَ كِتَابَةً أَنَا حَنْبَلٌ أَنَا ابْنُ الْحُصَيْنِ أَنَا الْحَسَنُ بْنُ عَلِيٍّ فَذَكَرَهُ.

ʿAbdullāh ibn Muhammad informed us: ʿAbd al-Qādir ibn Muhammad narrated to us: al-Ḥasan ibn ʿAlī narrated to us: Aḥmad ibn Jaʿfar informed us: ʿAbdullāh ibn Aḥmad ibn Ḥanbal narrated to us: My father ﷺ narrated to me: Yazīd narrated to us: al-Masʿūdī narrated to us from ʿĀṣim ibn Kulayb from his father that Abū Hurayrah said, "The Messenger of Allah ﷺ said, 'I came out to you after the (date) of the Night of Decree and the (identity) of the Messiah of

Misguidance had been made clear to me. However, two men were arguing under the canopy of the *masjid*. So, I went to them in order to restrain them and I was made to forget them. However, I will give you a small clue to each of them. As for the night of Decree, seek it in the last ten nights. As for the Messiah of Misguidance, he is one-eyed, has a broad forehead, and has a large bulging neck, as if he is Qaṭan ibn ʿAbd al-ʿUzzā'. He (Qaṭan) said, 'O Messenger of Allah, are you saying that I am his likeness?' He replied, 'No. You are a Muslim man. He is a disbeliever.'"[85]

Sheikh Samar al-Dīn ibn Qudāmah also informed me of this hadith in writing with the chain: Ḥanbal informed us: Ibn al-Ḥusayn informed us: al-Ḥasan ibn ʿAlī informed us. Then he mentioned the hadith.

85 *Musnad al-Imām Aḥmad*, Mu'assasah al-Risālah, hadith no. 7095; *Muṣannaf Ibn Abī Shaybah*, vol. 15, p. 291.

# 64 HADITH SIXTY-FOUR

أَخْبَرَتْنَا فَاطِمَةُ بِنْتُ سَعْدِ الدِّيْنِ بْنِ مُحَمَّدِ بْنِ سَهْلٍ الْأَنْصَارِيَّةُ ثَنَا أَبُوْ الْقَاسِمِ زَاهِرُ بْنُ طَاهِرِ بْنِ مُحَمَّدٍ السَّحَامِيُّ ثَنَا أَبُوْ سَعْدٍ مُحَمَّدُ بْنُ عَبْدِ الرَّحْمٰنِ النَّنْجِرُوْدِيُّ ثَنَا أَبُوْ عَمْرِو بْنُ حَمْدَانَ ثَنَا أَبُوْ يَعْلَى الْمُوْصِلِيُّ ثَنَا زُهَيْرٌ ثَنَا الْحَسَنُ بْنُ مُوْسٰى ثَنَا ثَابِتٌ أَبُوْ زَيْدٍ عَنْ هِلَالٍ عَنْ عِكْرِمَةَ عَنِ ابْنِ عَبَّاسٍ قَالَ أُسْرِيَ بِالنَّبِيِّ صَلَّى اللّٰهُ عَلَيْهِ وَسَلَّمَ إِلَى بَيْتِ الْمَقْدِسِ ثُمَّ جَاءَ مِنْ لَيْلَتِهِ فَحَدَّثَهُمْ بِسِيْرِهِ وَبِعَلَامَةِ بَيْتِ الْمَقْدِسِ وَبِعِيْرِهِمْ قَالَ قَالَ أُنَاسٌ نَحْنُ لَا نُصَدِّقُ مُحَمَّدًا فَارْتَدُّوْا كُفَّارًا فَضَرَبَ اللّٰهُ أَعْنَاقَهُمْ مَعَ أَبِيْ جَهْلٍ قَالَ وَقَالَ أَبُو جَهْلٍ يُخَوِّفُنَا مُحَمَّدٌ بِشَجَرَةِ الزَّقُّوْمِ فَهَاتُوْا تَمْرًا وَزُبْدًا وَعَمُّوْا قَالُوْا رَأَى الدَّجَّالَ فِيْ صُوْرَتِهِ رُؤْيَا عَيْنٍ لَيْسَ رُؤْيَا مَنَامٍ وَعِيسَى بْنَ مَرْيَمَ وَإِبْرَاهِيمَ قَالَ فَسُئِلَ النَّبِيُّ صَلَّى اللّٰهُ عَلَيْهِ وَسَلَّمَ عَنِ الدَّجَّالِ فَقَالَ رَأَيْتُهُ فَيْلَمَانِيًّا أَقْمَرَ هِجَانَ إِحْدٰى عَيْنَيْهِ قَائِمَةٌ كَأَنَّهَا كَوْكَبٌ دُرِّيٌّ كَأَنَّ شَعْرَهُ أَغْصَانُ شَجَرَةٍ وَرَأَيْتُ عِيسٰى شَابًّا جَعْدًا الرَّأْسِ حَدِيْدَ الْبَصَرِ مُنَطَّقَ الْخَلْقِ وَرَأَيْتُ مُوْسٰى أَسْحَمَ آدَمَ كَثِيْرَ الشَّعْرِ شَدِيْدَ الْخَلْقِ وَرَأَيْتُ إِبْرَاهِيمَ فَلَا أَنْظُرُ إِلٰى أَرَبٍ مِنْ آرَابِهِ إِلَّا نَظَرْتُ إِلَيْهِ كَأَنَّهُ صَاحِبُكُمْ قَالَ وَقَالَ لِيْ جِبْرِيْلُ سَلِّمْ عَلٰى أَبِيكَ فَسَلَّمْتُ عَلَيْهِ.

أَخْبَرَنَاهُ أَحْمَدُ بْنُ عَسَاكِرٍ عَنْ عَبْدِ الْمُعِزِّ بْنِ مُحَمَّدٍ أَنَا تَمِيمُ الْجُرْجَانِيُّ أَنَا أَبُوْ سَعِيْدٍ فَوَقَعَ عَالِيًا.

# HADITH SIXTY-FOUR 64

رَوَاهُ أَحْمَدُ فِي مُسْنَدِهِ عَنِ الْحَسَنِ بْنِ مُوسَى وَعَبْدِ الظَّاهِرِ قَالَا ثَنَا ثَابِتٌ وَأَنْبَأَنَاهُ عَالِيًا أَحْمَدُ بْنُ سَلَامَةَ عَنْ خَلِيلٍ الدَّارَانِيِّ نَا الْحَدَّادُ أَنَا أَبُو نُعَيمٍ ثَنَا ابْنُ حَدَّادٍ نَا الْحَارِثُ بْنُ أَبِي أُسَامَةَ ثَنَا الْحَسَنُ الْأَشْيَبُ نَا الْحَرَّارُ وَنَزَلَ مِنْ مَسْنَدِ الْحَارِثِ.

Fāṭimah bint Saʿd al-Din ibn Muhammad ibn Sahl al-Anṣāriyyah informed us: Abū al-Qāsim Zāhir ibn Ṭāhir ibn Muhammad al-Suḥāmī narrated to us: Abū Saʿd Muhammad ibn ʿAbd al-Raḥmān al-Najrūdī narrated to us: Abū ʿUmar ibn Ḥamdān narrated to us: Abū Yaʿlā al-Mawṣilī narrated to us: Zuhayr narrated to us: al-Ḥasan ibn Mūsā narrated to us: Thābit Abū Zayd narrated to us from Hilāl from ʿIkrimah that Ibn ʿAbbās said, "The Prophet ﷺ was made to journey to Jerusalem. Then, he came back in the same night. He told people about his journey and about the sign of Jerusalem and of other things. So, some people said, 'We do not believe Muhammad'. They became disbelievers and Allah struck their necks together with Abū Jahl. Abū Jahl said, 'Muhammad threatens us with the tree of Zaqqūm. So, bring us dates and ghee.' And they gorged themselves. He (the Prophet ﷺ) saw the Dajjāl in his true form with his physical eyes and not in a dream vision. He also saw ʿĪsā ibn Maryam, Mūsā, and Ibrāhīm. The Prophet ﷺ was asked about the Dajjāl and said, 'I saw him as a stocky person of extremely white complexion. One of his eyes stuck out as if it was a twinkling star. His hair was like the branches of a tree. I saw 'Īsā as a young man with curly hair, piercing vision, and average physique. I saw Mūsā as very dark-skinned, with a lot of hair and a large physique. When I saw Ibrāhīm, I did not see any aspect of his except that it resembled those of your companion. Jibrīl said to me, "Greet your father." So, I greeted him.'"[86]

Aḥmad ibn 'Asākir informed us of it on the authority of 'Abd al-Mu'izz ibn Muhammad (saying): Tamīm al-Jurjānī informed us: Abū Sa'īd informed us. Thus, we received it with a shorter transmission.

Aḥmad narrated it in his *Musnad* from al-Ḥasan ibn Mūsā and 'Abd al-Ẓāhir. They both mentioned narrating from Thābit.

Aḥmad ibn Salamah also informed us of it with a shorter chain from Khalīl al-Daranī: al-Ḥaddād informed us: Abū Nu'aym informed us: Ibn Ḥaddād narrated to us: al-Ḥārith ibn Abī Usāmah informed us: al-Ḥasan al-Ushayb narrated to us: al-Ḥarrār[87] informed us. He transmitted it from *Musnad al-Ḥārith.*

86 *Musnad al-Imām Aḥmad*, Mu'assasah al-Risālah, hadith no. 3546; *Musnad Abī Ya'lā*, vol. 5, p. 108.

87 After al-Ḥarrār, there is an unclear word.

# HADITH SIXTY-FIVE 65

أَخْبَرَنَا مُحَمَّدُ بْنُ عَبْدِ الْبَاقِي ثَنَا أَحْمَدُ بْنُ أَحْمَدَ بْنِ الْحَسَنِ الْأَصْبَهَانِيُّ ثَنَا أَحْمَدُ بْنُ عَبْدِ اللهِ ثَنَا عَبْدُ اللهِ بْنُ جَعْفَرٍ ثَنَا يُونُسُ بْنُ حَبِيبٍ ثَنَا أَبُو دَاوُدَ الطَّيَالِسِيُّ ثَنَا شُعْبَةُ عَنْ حَبِيبِ بْنِ الزُّبَيْرِ قَالَ سَمِعْتُ عَبْدَ اللهِ بْنَ أَبِي الْهُذَيْلِ يُحَدِّثُ عَنْ عَبْدِ الرَّحْمٰنِ بْنِ أَبْزٰى، قَالَ سَمِعْتُ عَبْدَ اللهِ بْنَ خَبَّابٍ يَقُولُ سَمِعْتُ أُبَيَّ بْنَ كَعْبٍ قَالَ ذُكِرَ الدَّجَّالُ عِنْدَ النَّبِيِّ صَلَّى اللهُ عَلَيْهِ وَسَلَّمَ أَوْ ذَكَرَ النَّبِيُّ صَلَّى اللهُ عَلَيْهِ وَسَلَّمَ الدَّجَّالَ فَقَالَ إِحْدٰى عَيْنَيْهِ كَأَنَّهَا زُجَاجَةٌ خَضْرَاءُ وَتَعَوَّذُوا بِاللهِ مِنْ عَذَابِ الْقَبْرِ.

أَنْبَأَنَا بِهِ عَلِيٌّ الْبُخَارِيُّ وَغَيْرُهُ أَنَا أَبُو الْمَكَارِمِ اللَّبَّانُ وَحَدَّثَنِي بِهِ مَنْ سَمِعَ يُوسُفَ بْنَ خَلِيلٍ عَنِ اللَّبَّانِ أَوْ غَيْرِهِ أَنَّ أَبَا عَلِيِّ بْنِ أَدَاخِرِهِمِ أَنَا أَحْمَدُ بْنُ عَبْدِ اللهِ الْحَافِظُ فَذَكَرَهُ.

Muhammad ibn ʿAbd al-Bāqī informed us: Aḥmad ibn Aḥmad ibn al-Ḥusayn al-Aṣbahānī narrated to us: Aḥmad ibn ʿAbdullāh narrated to us: ʿAbdullāh ibn Jaʿfar narrated to us: Yūnus ibn Ḥabīb narrated to us: Abū Dāwūd al-Ṭayālisī narrated to us: Shuʿbah narrated to us that Ḥabīb ibn al-Zubayr said, "I heard ʿAbdullāh ibn Abī al-Hudhayl narrate that ʿAbd al-Raḥmān ibn Abzā said, 'I heard ʿAbdullāh ibn Khabbāb say, "I heard Ubayy ibn Kaʿb say, 'The Dajjāl was mentioned in the presence of the Prophet ﷺ – or the

65 HADITH SIXTY-FIVE

Prophet ﷺ mentioned the Dajjāl – and he said, "One of his eyes is as if it were green glass. And seek refuge in Allah from the punishment of the grave."""""[88]

ʿAlī ibn al-Bukhārī and others also related it to us, saying: Abū al-Makārim al-Labbān informed us.

Additionally, someone who heard Yūsuf ibn Khalīl narrated from al-Labbān – or someone else – that Abū ʿAlī mentioned to them: Aḥmad ibn ʿAbdullāh al-Ḥāfiẓ informed us. And then he mentioned the hadith.

88 *Musnad al-Imām Aḥmad*, Mu'assasah al-Risālah, hadith no. 21145; *Musnad Abū Dāwūd al-Ṭayālisī*, hadith no. 546; Abū Nuʿaym, *Ḥilyah al-Awliyā'*, vol. 4, p. 363.

# HADITH SIXTY-SIX 66

أَخْبَرَنَا مُحَمَّدُ بْنُ مُحَمَّدٍ وَحَبِيبُ بْنُ إِبْرَاهِيمَ ثَنَا مُحَمَّدُ بْنُ إِسْمَاعِيلَ ثَنَا أَحْمَدُ بْنُ مُحَمَّدِ بْنِ الْحُسَيْنِ ثَنَا سُلَيْمُ بْنُ أَحْمَدَ بْنِ أَيُّوبَ ثَنَا عَلِيُّ بْنُ عَبْدِ الْعَزِيزِ ثَنَا مُسْلِمُ بْنُ إِبْرَاهِيمَ ثَنَا سَعِيدٌ عَنْ سِمَاكِ بْنِ حَرْبٍ عَنْ عِكْرِمَةَ عَنِ ابْنِ عَبَّاسٍ أَنَّ النَّبِيَّ صَلَّى اللَّهُ عَلَيْهِ وَسَلَّمَ ذَكَرَ الدَّجَّالَ فَقَالَ أَعْوَرُ جَعْدٌ هِجَانٌ أَزْهَرُ كَأَنَّ رَأْسَهُ أَصَلَةٌ أَشْبَهُ النَّاسِ بِعَبْدِ الْعُزَّى بْنِ قَطَنٍ وَلَكِنِ الْهُلْكُ كُلَّ الْهُلْكِ إِنَّهُ أَعْوَرُ وَإِنَّ رَبَّكُمْ لَيْسَ بِأَعْوَرَ. أُثْبِتُهُ عَنِ الْكَرَّانِيِّ أَنَا مَحْمُودٌ.

Muhammad ibn Muhammad and Ḥabīb ibn Ibrāhīm informed us: Muhammad ibn Ismāʿīl narrated to us: Aḥmad ibn Muhammad ibn al-Ḥusayn narrated to us: Sulaymān ibn Aḥmad ibn Ayyūb narrated to us: ʿAlī ibn ʿAbd al-ʿAzīz narrated to us: Muslim ibn Ibrāhīm narrated to us: Saʿīd narrated to us from Simāk ibn Ḥarb from ʿIkrimah from Ibn ʿAbbās that the Prophet ﷺ mentioned the Dajjāl. He said, "One-eyed, curly-headed, extremely white. It is as if he has snakes coming out of his head. The person that resembles him most is ʿAbd al-ʿUzzā ibn Qaṭan. However, beware of perishing. He is one-eyed. Your Lord is not one-eyed."[89] It was affirmed by way of al-Karrānī, who said: "Maḥmūd informed us."

89 Al-Ṭabarānī, *al-Muʿjam al-Kabīr*, vol. 11, p. 273; *Musnad al-Imām Aḥmad*, Mu'assasah al-Risālah, hadith no. 2148.

# 67 HADITH SIXTY-SEVEN

يَزِيدُ بْنُ هَارُونَ نَا أَبُو مَالِكٍ الْأَشْجَعِيُّ ثَنَا رِبْعِيٌّ عَنْ حُذَيْفَةَ قَالَ قَالَ رَسُولُ اللَّهِ صَلَّى اللَّهُ عَلَيْهِ وَسَلَّمَ أَنَا أَعْلَمُ النَّاسِ بِمَا مَعَ الدَّجَّالِ مَعَهُ نَهْرَانِ يَجْرِيَانِ أَحَدُهُمَا رَأْيَ الْعَيْنِ مَاءٌ أَبْيَضُ وَالْآخَرُ رَأْيَ الْعَيْنِ نَارٌ تَأَجَّجُ فَإِنْ أَدْرَكَهُ أَحَدٌ مِنْكُمْ ذٰلِكَ فَلْيَأْتِ النَّهَرَ الَّذِي يَرَاهُ نَارًا فَلْيُغْمِضْ عَيْنَهُ ثُمَّ لِيُطَأْطِئْ رَأْسَهُ فَلْيَشْرَبْ فَإِنَّهُ مَاءٌ بَارِدٌ فَإِنَّ الدَّجَّالَ يَعْرِفُهُ كُلُّ مُؤْمِنٍ مَمْسُوحُ الْعَيْنِ الْيُسْرَى عَلَيْهَا ظَفَرَةٌ غَلِيظَةٌ وَإِنَّهُ مَكْتُوبٌ بَيْنَ عَيْنَيْهِ كَافِرٌ يَقْرَأُهُ كُلُّ مُؤْمِنٍ كَاتِبٍ وَغَيْرِ كَاتِبٍ.

وَكَذَا رَوَاهُ مَرْوَانُ بْنُ مَعَاوِيَةَ وَغَيْرُهُ عَنْ أَبِي مَالِكٍ.

From Yazīd ibn Hārūn: Abū Mālik al-Ashjaʿī informed us: Ribʿī narrated to us that Ḥudhayfah said, "The Messenger of Allah ﷺ said, 'I am the most knowledgeable of people of what the Dajjāl will have[90]. He will have with him two flowing rivers. One of them will appear to the eyes to be white water. The other will appear to the eye to be raging flames. If one of you sees that, let him come to the one that he sees as fire and close his eyes. Then let him dip his head

90 In the narration of Muslim, the wording is, "I know what the Dajjāl will have with him better than he does." The wording in *Musnad Aḥmad* and *Muṣannaf Ibn Abī Shaybah* is, "I know what the Dajjāl will have with him better than the Dajjāl himself."

in it and drink from it, for it is cold water. And indeed, every believer will recognize the Dajjāl. He has a blind left eye over which there is a thick layer of skin. Between his eyes is written the word *kāfir*, which every literate and illiterate believer will be able to read.'"[91]

It was narrated in a similar manner by Marwān ibn Mu'āwiyah and others from Abū Mālik.

91 *Ṣaḥīḥ Muslim*, hadith no. 2934; *Musnad al-Imām Aḥmad*, Mu'assasah al-Risālah, hadith nos., 23279 and 23338; *Muṣannaf Ibn Abī Shaybah*, vol. 15, p. 133.

# 68 HADITH THIRTY-EIGHT

أ - شُعْبَةُ عَنْ عَبْدِ الْمَلِكِ بْنِ عُمَيْرٍ عَنْ رِبْعِيِّ بْنِ خِرَاشٍ عَنْ حُذَيْفَةَ عَنِ النَّبِيِّ صَلَّى اللَّهُ عَلَيْهِ وَسَلَّمَ فِي الدَّجَّالِ قَالَ مَعَهُ نَارٌ وَمَاءٌ فَنَارُهُ مَاءٌ بَارِدٌ وَمَاؤُهُ نَارٌ فَلَا تَهْلِكُوا قَالَ أَبُو مَسْعُودٍ وَأَنَا سَمِعْتُهُ مِنْ رَسُولِ اللَّهِ صَلَّى اللَّهُ عَلَيْهِ وَسَلَّمَ.

ب - مَنْصُورٌ عَنْ رِبْعِيٍّ عَنْ حُذَيْفَةَ عَنِ النَّبِيِّ صَلَّى اللَّهُ عَلَيْهِ وَسَلَّمَ قَالَ مَعَ الدَّجَّالِ نَارٌ تَحْرِقُ وَنَهْرُ مَاءٍ بَارِدٍ فَمَنْ أَرَادَ مِنْكُمْ فَلَا يَهْلَكَنَّ بِهِ فَلْيُغْمِضْ عَيْنَيْهِ وَلْيَقَعْ فِي الَّذِي يَرَى أَنَّهَا نَارٌ فَإِنَّهَا مَاءٌ بَارِدٌ.

رَوَاهُ مُعْتَمِرٌ وَزَائِدَةُ عَنْ مَنْصُورٍ نَحْوَهُ وَرَوَاهُ جَرِيرٌ عَنْ مَنْصُورٍ يُوقِفُهُ ثُمَّ رَفَعَ عَنِ ابْنِ عَبَّاسٍ وَأَبِي مَسْعُودٍ.

A) From Shu'bah from 'Abd al-Mālik ibn 'Umayr from Rib'ī ibn Khirāsh from Ḥudhayfah that the Prophet ﷺ said about the Dajjāl, "With him there is fire and water.

His fire is really cold water and his water is really fire. So do not perish."[92] Abū Mas'ūd said, "I heard it from the Messenger ﷺ."

92 68A and B were sourced in hadith 53. *Muṣannaf 'Abd al-Razzāq*, vol. 11, p. 395; *Muṣannaf Ibn Abī Shaybah*, vol. 15, p. 150.

B) From Manṣūr from Rib'ī from Ḥudhayfah that the Prophet ﷺ said, "There will be with the Dajjāl a burning fire and a river of cold water. Whoever among you sees that, let him not perish. Let him close his eyes and enter that which he sees as fire, for it is cold water."

Mu'tamir narrated it. And the addition of Manṣūr and its similar narrations were narrated by Jarīr from Manṣūr as a *mawqūf* narration. However, elsewhere it was narrated *marfū'* on the authority of Ibn 'Abbās and Abū Mas'ūd.

# 69 HADITH SIXTY-NINE

أَخْبَرَنَا مُحَمَّدُ بْنُ مُحَمَّدٍ وَحَبِيبُ بْنُ إِبْرَاهِيمَ ثَنَا مَحْمُودُ بْنُ إِسْمَاعِيلَ ثَنَا أَحْمَدُ بْنُ مَحْمُودٍ ثَنَا سُلَيْمُ بْنُ أَحْمَدَ بْنِ أَيُّوبَ ثَنَا مُحَمَّدُ بْنُ مُحَمَّدٍ التَّمَّارُ وَأَبُو خَلِيفَةَ قَالاَ ثَنَا أَبُو الْوَلِيدِ الطَّيَالِسِيُّ ثَنَا وَائِلٌ ثَنَا سِمَاكُ بْنُ حَرْبٍ عَنْ عِكْرِمَةَ عَنِ ابْنِ عَبَّاسٍ قَالَ قَالَ رَسُولُ اللهِ صَلَّى اللّٰهُ عَلَيْهِ وَسَلَّمَ الدَّجَّالُ جَعْدٌ هِجَانٌ أَقْمَرُ كَأَنَّ رَأْسَهُ غُصْنُ شَجَرَةٍ مَطْمُوسٌ عَيْنِهِ الْيُسْرَى وَالأُخْرَى كَأَنَّهَا عِنَبَةٌ طَافِيَةٌ أَشْبَهُ النَّاسِ بِهِ عَبْدُ الْعُزَّى بْنُ قَطَنٍ فَأَمَّا هَلَكَ الْهُلَّكِ فَإِنَّهُ أَعْوَرُ وَإِنَّ رَبَّكُمْ لَيْسَ بِأَعْوَرَ.

أُثْبِتُهُ عَنْ مُحَمَّدِ بْنِ أَبِي زَيْدٍ أَنَا مَحْمُودُ بْنُ إِسْمَاعِيلَ.

Muhammad ibn Muhammad and Ḥabīb ibn Ibrāhīm informed us: Maḥmūd ibn Ismāʿīl narrated to us: Aḥmad ibn Maḥmūd narrated to us: Sālim ibn Aḥmad ibn Ayyūb narrated to us: Muhammad ibn Muhammad al-Tammār and Abū Khalīfah both narrated to us saying: Abū al-Walīd al-Ṭayālisī narrated to us: Wā'il narrated to us: Simāk ibn Ḥarb narrated to us from ʿIkrimah that Ibn ʿAbbās said, "The Messenger ﷺ said, 'The Dajjāl is stocky and pale skinned. His head is as if it were the branches of trees. His left eye is blind. The other one is like a floating grape. The person who most resembles him is ʿAbd al-ʿUzzā ibn Qaṭan. Beware of perishing, for he is one-eyed and your Lord is not one-eyed."[93] It was affirmed from Muhammad ibn Zayd who said: aḥmūd ibn Ismā'īl informed us.

93 Sourced in Hadith no. 66.

# 70 HADITH SEVENTY

أَخْبَرَنَا مُحَمَّدُ بْنُ مُحَمَّدٍ وَحَبِيبُ بْنُ إِبْرَاهِيمَ ثَنَا مَحْمُودُ بْنُ إِسْمَاعِيلَ أَنَا أَحْمَدُ بْنُ مُحَمَّدٍ ثَنَا سُلَيْمُ بْنُ أَحْمَدَ بْنِ أَيُّوبَ ثَنَا إِسْحَاقُ بْنُ إِبْرَاهِيمَ الدَّبَرِيُّ عَنْ عَبْدِ الرَّزَّاقِ عَنِ الثَّوْرِيِّ عَنْ سِمَاكِ بْنِ حَرْبٍ عَنْ عِكْرِمَةَ عَنِ ابْنِ عَبَّاسٍ قَالَ قَالَ رَسُولُ اللهِ صَلَّى اللهُ عَلَيْهِ وَسَلَّمَ الدَّجَّالُ جَعْدٌ هِجَانٌ أَقْمَرُ كَأَنَّ رَأْسَهُ غُصْنُ شَجَرَةٍ مَطْمُوسٌ عَيْنِهِ الْيُسْرَى وَالأُخْرَى كَأَنَّهَا عِنَبَةٌ طَافِيَةٌ أَشْبَهُ النَّاسِ بِهِ عَبْدُ الْعُزَّى بْنُ قَطَنٍ فَأَمَّا هَلَكَ الْهُلَّكِ وَإِنَّهُ أَعْوَرُ وَإِنَّ رَبَّكُمْ لَيْسَ بِأَعْوَرَ.

أُثْبِتُهُ عَنِ الْكَرَّانِيِّ أَنَا مَحْمُودٌ مِثْلَهُ.

Muhammad ibn Muhammad and Ḥabīb ibn Ibrāhīm informed us: Maḥmūd ibn Ismāʿīl narrated to us: Aḥmad ibn Muhammad informed us: Sālim ibn Aḥmad ibn Ayyūb narrated to us: Isḥāq ibn Ibrāhīm al-Dīrī narrated to us from ʿAbd al-Razzāq from al-Thawrī from Simāk ibn Ḥarb from ʿIkrimah that Ibn ʿAbbās said, "The Messenger of Allah ﷺ said, 'The Dajjāl is stocky and pale skinned. His head is as if it is the branches of trees. His left eye is blind and the other is as if it were a floating grape. The person that most resembles him is ʿAbd al-ʿUzzā ibn Qaṭan. So be sure not to perish.

He is one-eyed and your Lord ﷻ is not one-eyed.'"[94] It was affirmed by al-Karrānī who said: Maḥmūd informed us of a similar hadith.

94 Sourced in hadith no. 66.

# 71 HADITH SEVENTY-ONE

وَبِإِسْنَادِي إِلَى حَنْبَلٍ ثَنَا أَبُو الْوَلِيدِ ثَنَا سَلْمُ بْنُ زُرَيْرٍ سَمِعْتُ أَبَا رَجَاءٍ سَمِعْتُ ابْنَ عَبَّاسٍ يَقُولُ دَعَا رَسُولُ اللهِ ﷺ ابْنَ صَائِدٍ فَقَالَ إِنِّي قَدْ خَبَأْتُ لَكَ خَبْئًا قَالَ ابْنُ صَائِدٍ دُخٌّ فَقَالَ رَسُولُ ﷺ اخْسَ.

With my chain of transmission to Ḥanbal: Abū al-Walīd narrated to us: Salam ibn Zarīr narrated to us: I heard Abū Rajā': I heard Ibn 'Abbās say, "The Messenger of Allah ﷺ called Ibn Ṣā'id and said, 'I have hidden something from you.' Ibn Ṣā'id said, '*Dukh*[95]'. The Messenger of Allah ﷺ said, 'You have failed.'"[96]

95 This word has already been discussed in the first Hadith.

96 Sourced in Hadith nos. 1 and 26.

# HADITH SEVENTY-TWO 72

أَبُو عَوَانَةَ عَنْ قَتَادَةَ عَنْ نَصْرِ بْنِ عَاصِمٍ عَنْ سُبَيْعِ بْنِ خَالِدٍ سَمِعْتُ حُذَيْفَةَ يَقُولُ قَالَ رَسُولُ اللهِ صَلَّى اللَّهُ عَلَيْهِ وَسَلَّمَ يَخْرُجُ الدَّجَّالُ مَعَهُ نَهْرُ مَاءٍ بَارِدٍ فَمَنْ وَقَعَ فِي نَهْرِهِ وَجَبَ وِزْرُهُ وَحُطَّ أَجْرُهُ وَمَنْ وَقَعَ فِي نَارِهِ وَجَبَ أَجْرُهُ وَحُطَّ وِزْرُهُ. سَمِعَهُ مِنْ خَلَفِ الْبَزَّارِ.

From Abū 'Awānah from Qatādah from Naṣr ibn 'Āṣim from Sabī' ibn Khālid: I heard Ḥudhayfah say, "The Dajjāl will emerge and with him will be a river of water. Whoever enters himself into his river obtains blame and destroys his reward. Whoever enters his fire obtains his reward and is relieved of its blame."[97]

I heard it from Khalaf al-Bazzār.

97 *Sunan Abī Dāwūd*, hadith no. 4244; *Musnad al-Imām Aḥmad*, hadith no. 23430; *Mustadrak al-Ḥākim*, vol. 4, pp. 432-433. Part of a longer hadith.

# 73 HADITH SEVENTY-THREE

يَحْيَى بْنُ آدَمَ عَنْ أَبِي بَكْرِ بْنِ عَيَّاشٍ عَنِ الأَعْمَشِ عَنْ سُلَيْمَانَ بْنِ مَيْسَرَةَ عَنْ طَارِقِ بْنِ شِهَابٍ عَنْ حُذَيْفَةَ قَالَ كُنَّا عِنْدَ النَّبِيِّ صَلَّى اللهُ عَلَيْهِ وَسَلَّمَ فَذَكَرْنَا الدَّجَّالَ فَقَالَ لَفِتْنَةُ أَحَدِكُمْ أَخْوَفُ عِنْدِي مِنْ فِتْنَةِ الدَّجَّالِ إِنَّهَا لَيْسَتْ مِنْ فِتْنَةٍ صَغِيرَةٍ وَلَا كَبِيرَةٍ إِلَّا يَصْنَعُ فِتْنَةَ الدَّجَّالِ فَمَنْ نَجَا مِنْ فِتْنَةِ مَا قَبْلَهَا نَجَا مِنْهَا وَإِنَّهُ لَا يَضُرُّ مُسْلِمًا مَكْتُوبٌ بَيْنَ عَيْنَيْهِ كَافِرٌ بِهِجَاوَةِ ك ف ر".

From Yaḥyā ibn Adam from Abū Bakr ibn ʿAyyāsh from al-Aʿmash from Sulaymān ibn Maysarah from Ṭāriq ibn Shihāb that Ḥudhayfah said, "We were in the company of the Prophet ﷺ and we mentioned the Dajjāl. He said, 'Indeed, the temptation of each of you is more worrying to me than the trial of the Dajjāl. Every temptation, great or small, will humble itself to the temptation of the Dajjāl. So, whoever is saved from that which is before it will be saved from it (the trial of the Dajjāl). And he will not be able to harm (deceive) any Muslim. Written between his two eyes, in separate letters, is (the word) *kāfir*.'"[98]

98 *Ṣaḥīḥ Ibn Ḥibbān*, Mu'assasah al-Risālah, hadith no. 6807;

# HADITH SEVENTY-FOUR

# 74

أَخْبَرَنَا مُحَمَّدُ بْنُ عَبْدِ الْبَاقِيِّ بْنِ أَحْمَدَ بْنِ سَلْمَانَ أَنَا أَبُو الْفَضْلِ أَحْمَدُ بْنُ الْحَسَنِ بْنِ خَيْرُونَ أَنَا أَبُو عَمْرٍو عُثْمَانُ بْنُ مُحَمَّدِ بْنِ يُوسُفَ الْعَلَّافُ وَأَبُو عَلِيٍّ الْحَسَنُ بْنُ أَحْمَدَ بْنِ إِبْرَاهِيمَ بْنِ شَاذَانَ قَالَا أَنَا أَبُو بَكْرٍ مُحَمَّدُ بْنُ عَبْدِ اللَّهِ بْنِ إِبْرَاهِيمَ الشَّافِعِيُّ ثَنَا إِسْحَاقُ بْنُ الْحَسَنِ بْنِ مَيْمُونَ ثَنَا عُمَرُ بْنُ حَفْصٍ ثَنَا أَبِي ثَنَا الْأَعْمَشُ عَنْ سُلَيْمِ بْنِ مَيْسَرَةَ عَنْ طَارِقِ بْنِ شِهَابٍ عَنْ حُذَيْفَةَ قَالَ قَالَ رَسُولُ اللَّهِ ﷺ وَذَكَرَ الدَّجَّالَ فَقَالَ مَكْتُوبٌ بَيْنَ عَيْنَيْهِ ك ف ر كَافِرٌ يَقْرَأُهُ كُلُّ مُسْلِمٍ.

أُثْبِتُهُ عَنِ الْحَافِظِ وَسُلَيْمَانُ قَلِيلُ الْحَدِيثِ رَوَى عَنْهُ الْأَعْمَشُ وَغَيْرُهُ وَهُوَ صُوَيْلِحٌ وَلَا شَرَّ لَهُ فِي الْكُتُبِ.

Muhammad ibn ʿAbd al-Bāqī ibn Aḥmad ibn Salmān informed us: Abū al-Faḍl Aḥmad ibn al-Ḥasan ibn Khayrūn informed us: Abū ʿAmr ʿUthmān ibn Muhammad ibn Yūsuf al-ʿAllāf and Abū ʿAlī al-Ḥasan ibn Aḥmad ibn Ibrāhīm ibn Shādhān both informed me saying: Abū Bakr Muhammad ibn ʿAbdullāh ibn Ibrāhīm al-Shāfiʿī informed us: Isḥāq ibn al-Ḥasan ibn Maymūn narrated to us: ʿUmar ibn Ḥafṣ narrated to us: al-Aʿmash narrated to us from Sulaymān ibn Maysarah from Ṭāriq ibn Shihāb that Ḥudhayfah said, "The Messenger of Allah ﷺ mentioned the Dajjāl and said, 'Written between his eyes are *kāf-fā'-rā'* – *kāfir*. Every Muslim will be able to read it.'"[99]

It was affirmed by al-Ḥāfiẓ. Sulaymān narrated only a few hadiths. He narrated from al-A'mash and others. He is a narrator whose reports are suitable as supporting evidence, and nothing bad has been reported of him in any books.

99 *Ṣaḥīḥ Muslim*, hadith no. 2933; *Ṣaḥīḥ Ibn Ḥibbān*, Mu'assasah al-Risālah, hadith no. 6807.

# HADITH SEVENTY-FIVE 75

أَخْبَرَنَا عَبْدُ الرَّزَّاقِ بْنُ إِسْمَاعِيلَ وَالْمُطَهَّرُ بْنُ عَبْدِ الْكَرِيمِ ثَنَا عَبْدُ الرَّحْمٰنِ بْنُ حَمْدِ بْنِ الْحَسَنِ ثَنَا أَحْمَدُ بْنُ الْحُسَيْنِ ثَنَا أَحْمَدُ بْنُ مُحَمَّدِ بْنِ السَّنِيِّ ثَنَا أَبُو يَعْلَى ثَنَا يَحْيَى بْنُ مَعِينٍ ثَنَا مَرْوَانُ بْنُ مُعَاوِيَةَ عَنْ مُجَالِدٍ عَنْ أَبِي الْوَدَّاكِ عَنْ أَبِي سَعِيدٍ أَنَّ رَسُولَ اللهِ ﷺ قَالَ فِي الدَّجَّالِ عَيْنُهُ عَوْرَاءُ كَخَفَاءُ لَهَا حَدَقَةٌ جَاحِظَةٌ كَأَنَّهَا نُخَاعَةٌ فِي حَائِطٍ مُجَصَّصٍ.

أُثْبِتُهُ عَنِ الْحَافِظِ.

ʿAbd al-Razzāq ibn Ismāʿīl and al-Muṭahhar ibn ʿAbd al-Karīm both informed us: ʿAbd al-Raḥmān ibn Ḥamd ibn al-Ḥasan narrated to us: Aḥmad ibn al-Ḥusayn narrated to us: Aḥmad ibn Muhammad ibn al-Sī narrated to us: Abū Yaʿlā narrated to us: Yaḥyā ibn Maʿīn narrated to us: Marwān ibn Muʿāwiyah narrated to us from Mujālid from Abū Waddāk. From Abū Saʿīd that the Messenger of Allah ﷺ said about the Dajjāl, "His eye is open like the covering of a container. His pupil will protrude as if it is phlegm on the wall of a plastered wall."[100]

I confirmed it from al-Ḥāfiẓ.

100 We did not find this hadith.

# 76 HADITH SEVENTY-SIX

وَقَالَ إِسْمَاعِيلُ بْنُ أَبِي أُوَيْسٍ حَدَّثَنِي كَثِيرُ بْنُ عَبْدِ اللهِ بْنِ عَمْرِو بْنِ عَوْفٍ عَنْ أَبِيهِ عَنْ جَدِّهِ أَنَّ رَسُولَ اللهِ صَلَّى اللَّهُ عَلَيْهِ وَسَلَّمَ قَالَ سَيُقَاتِلُونَ بَنِي الأَصْفَرِ وَيُقَاتِلُهُمْ مَنْ بَعْدَكُمْ مِنَ الْمُؤْمِنِينَ أَهْلِ الْحِجَازِ حَتَّى يَفْتَحَ اللَّهُ عَلَيْهِمْ قُسْطُنْطِينِيَّةَ وَرُومِيَّةَ بِالتَّسْبِيحِ وَالتَّكْبِيرِ فَيَنْهَدِمُ حِصْنُهَا فَيُصِيبُونَ مَالاً لَمْ يُصِيبُوا مِثْلَهُ قَطُّ حَتَّى إِنَّهُمْ يَقْتَسِمُونَ بِالأَتْرِسَةِ ثُمَّ يَصْرُخُ صَارِخٌ يَا أَهْلَ الإِسْلَامِ الْمَسِيحُ الدَّجَّالُ فِي بِلَادِكُمْ وَذَرَارِيِّكُمْ فَيَنْفُضُ النَّاسُ عَنِ الْمَالِ فَمِنْهُمُ الآخِذُ وَمِنْهُمُ التَّارِكُ الآخِذُ نَادِمٌ وَالتَّارِكُ نَادِمٌ يَقُولُونَ مَنْ هَذَا الصَّارِخُ وَلاَ يَعْلَمُونَ مَنْ هُوَ فَيَقُولُونَ ابْعَثُوا طَلِيعَةً إِلَى إِيلِيَا فَإِنْ يَكُنِ الْمَسِيحُ قَدْ خَرَجَ فَسَيَأْتُوكُمْ بِعِلْمِهِ فَيَأْتُونَ فَيَنْظُرُونَ فَلاَ يَرَوْنَ شَيْئًا وَيَرَوْنَ النَّاسَ سَاكِنِينَ فَيَقُولُونَ مَا صَرَخَ الصَّارِخُ إِلَّا لِنَبَأٍ عَظِيمٍ فَاعْتَزِمُوا ثُمَّ ارْبِضُوا فَيَعْتَزِمُونَ أَنْ نَخْرُجَ بِأَجْمَعِنَا إِلَى إِيلِيَا فَإِنْ يَكُنِ الْمَسِيحُ الدَّجَّالُ خَرَجَ نُقَاتِلُهُ حَتَّى يَحْكُمَ اللَّهُ بَيْنَنَا وَبَيْنَهُ وَإِنْ تَكُنِ الأُخْرَى فَإِنَّهَا بِلَادُكُمْ وَعَشَائِرُكُمْ إِنْ رَجَعْتُمْ إِلَيْهَا.

كَثِيرٌ رَوَى لَهُ أَبُو دَاوُدَ وَغَيْرُهُ وَهُوَ ضَعِيفٌ بِمَرَّةٍ.

Ismāʿīl ibn Abī Uways said: Kathīr ibn ʿAbdullāh ibn ʿAmr ibn ʿAwf narrated to me from his father from his grandfather that the Messenger of Allah ﷺ said, "You will soon fight the Banū al-Aṣfar[101], and those who come after you – the people of Hijaz – will fight them until they will conquer Constantinople and Rome with glorification (*tasbīḥ*) and declarations of Allah's greatness (*takbīr*). Their fortress will crumble. They will gain spoils that are unequalled in history until they divide them with shields. Then someone shouting will yell, 'O people of Islam, the Dajjāl is in your lands and among your offspring'. People will then turn away from the wealth. A few individuals will take some and others will leave without taking anything. Both those who took spoils and those who left it will regret it. They will say, 'Who is the person yelling?' They will not know who it was. They will say, 'Send a garrison to Īliyā. If it is the Dajjāl that has emerged, they will bring news of him.' So they will go, but they will not see anything. They will see people living there. And they will say, 'No one yells except for some considerable news. So, make preparations and go to your positions. We will prepare to bring all our forces to Īliyā. If it is true that the Dajjāl has emerged, we will fight him until Allah decides between us and him. If it is someone else, they are your lands and your clans to which you will have returned.'"[102] Kathīr's

101 A name for the Byzantines.

102 *Sunan Ibn Mājah*, Dār al-Risālah al-ʿĀlamiyyah, hadith no. 4094; *Musnad al-Bazzār*, hadith no. 3390.

hadiths were narrated by Abū Dāwūd and others. However, according to the agreement of the scholars he is weak to the uppermost degree.

# 77 HADITH SEVENTY-SEVEN

ابْنُ الْأَعْرَابِيِّ فِيْ مُعْجَمِهِ ثَنَا مُحَمَّدُ بْنُ عُبَيْدٍ النَّوَّاءُ ثَنَا عُبَيْدُ اللَّهِ هُوَ ابْنُ مُوْسَى ثَنَا عِيْسَى الْخَيَّاطُ عَنْ مُحَمَّدِ بْنِ يَحْيَى بْنِ حِبَّانَ سَمِعْتُ أَبَا سَعِيْدٍ الْخُدْرِيَّ يَقُوْلُ مَعَ الدَّجَّالِ امْرَأَةٌ يُقَالُ لَهَا طَيِّبَةٌ لَا تَقْدَمُ قَرْيَةً إِلَّا سَبَقَتْ إِلَيْهَا تَقُوْلُ هٰذَا الدَّجَّالُ دَخَلَ عَلَيْكُمْ فَاحْذَرُوْهُ.

From Ibn al-Aʿrābī in his *Muʿjam*: Muhammad ibn ʿUbayd al-Nawāʾ narrated to us: ʿUbayd Allāh ibn Mūsā narrated to us: ʿĪsā al-Khayyāṭ narrated to us from Muhammad ibn Yaḥyā ibn Ḥibbān: I heard Abū Saʿīd al-Khudrī say, "With the Dajjāl will be a woman who will be called La'ībah. He will not head towards any town except that she will get there first and say, 'This is the Dajjāl who has entered upon you. So, beware.'"[103]

103 This hadith was sourced in hadith 29. Narrated by Nuʿaym ibn Ḥammād in *al-Fitan*. It was also copied from that text, with reference, in *Kanz al-ʿUmmāl*, hadith no. 39691.

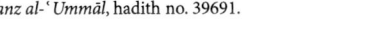

# 78 HADITH SEVENTY-EIGHT

أَخْبَرَنَا مُحَمَّدُ بْنُ عَبْدِ الْبَاقِيِّ ثَنَا أَبُو الْفَضْلِ أَحْمَدُ بْنُ الْحَسَنِ بْنِ خَيْرُونَ أَنَا أَبُو بَكْرٍ مُحَمَّدُ بْنُ عُمَرَ بْنِ الْقَاسِمِ الْيُونِينِيُّ ثَنَا أَبُو بَكْرٍ مُحَمَّدُ بْنُ عَبْدِ اللهِ بْنِ إِبْرَاهِيمَ الشَّافِعِيُّ ثَنَا مُحَمَّدُ بْنُ بِشْرِ بْنِ مَطَرٍ ثَنَا عِيسَى بْنُ سَالِمِ بْنِ عُوَيْسٍ ثَنَا عُبَيْدُ اللهِ بْنُ عَمْرٍو عَنْ أَيُّوبَ عَنْ أَبِي قِلَابَةَ قَالَ أَتَيْتُ الْمَسْجِدَ فَإِذَا رَجُلٌ قَدْ تَكَابَ عَلَيْهِ النَّاسُ وَهُمْ يَقُولُونَ صَاحِبُ رَسُولِ اللهِ ﷺ فَزَاحَمْتُ حَتَّى وَصَلْتُ إِلَيْهِ فَسَمِعْتُهُ يَقُولُ قَالَ رَسُولُ اللهِ صلى الله عليه وسلم إِنَّ مِنْ وَرَائِكُمُ الْكَذَّابَ الْمُضِلَّ وَإِنَّ رَأْسَهُ مِنْ وَرَائِهِ حُبُكٌ وَإِنَّهُ سَيَقُولُ أَنَا رَبُّكُمْ فَمَنْ قَالَ كَذَبْتَ لَسْتَ رَبَّنَا وَلَكِنَّ اللهَ رَبُّنَا عَلَيْهِ تَوَكَّلْنَا وَإِلَيْهِ أَنَبْنَا وَنَعُوذُ بِاللهِ مِنْكَ فَلاَ سَبِيلَ لَهُ عَلَيْهِ.

Muhammad ibn ʿAbd al-Bāqī informed us: Abū al-Faḍl Aḥmad ibn al-Ḥasan ibn Khayrūn narrated to us: Abū Bakr Muhammad ibn ʿUmar ibn al-Qāsim al-Yūnīnī informed us: Abū Bakr Muhammad ibn ʿAbdullāh ibn Ibrāhīm al-Shāfiʿī narrated to us: Muhammad ibn Bishr ibn Maṭar narrated to us: ʿĪsā ibn Sālim ibn ʿUways narrated to us: ʿUbayd Allāh ibn ʿAmr narrated to us from Ayyūb that Abū Qilābah said, "I went to the *masjid* and there was a man around whom people had crowded. They were saying that he was a Companion of the Messenger of Allah ﷺ. So I approached until I reached him and I heard him say, 'I heard the Messenger of Allah ﷺ say, "After you will come the misguiding arch-liar. Behind him there are wavy curls. He will say, 'I am your lord'. Whoever says, 'You have lied. You are not our Lord. Rather, Allah is our Lord. Upon Him is our reliance and to Him are we returned. We seek refuge in Allah from you' will be protected from him.""""[104]

104 This hadith was sourced in hadith no. 60. *Muṣannaf ʿAbd al-Razzāq*, hadith no. 20828.

# 79 HADITH SEVENTY-NINE

أَخْبَرَنَا مُحَمَّدُ بْنُ عَبْدِ الْبَاقِيِّ ثَنَا أَبُو الْفَضْلِ أَحْمَدُ بْنُ الْحَسَنِ بْنِ خَيْرُونَ ثَنَا مُحَمَّدُ بْنُ عُمَرَ بْنِ الْقَاسِمِ النَّرْسِيُّ ثَنَا مُحَمَّدُ بْنُ عَبْدِ اللهِ بْنِ إِبْرَاهِيمَ الشَّافِعِيُّ ثَنَا يَزِيدُ بْنُ الْهَيْثَمِ الْبَادِيُّ ثَنَا عُبَيْدُ اللهِ بْنُ عُمَرَ ثَنَا حَمَّادٌ عَنْ أَيُّوبَ عَنْ أَبِي قِلَابَةَ قَالَ دَخَلْتُ الْمَسْجِدَ فَإِذَا النَّاسُ تَكَابُوْا عَلَى رَجُلٍ مِنْ أَصْحَابِ النَّبِيِّ ﷺ فَقَالَ قَالَ النَّبِيُّ ﷺ إِنَّ بَعْدِي الْكَذَّابَ الْمُضِلَّ وَإِنَّ رَأْسَهُ مِنْ وَرَائِهِ حُبُكٌ حُبُكٌ. ثُمَّ ذَكَرَ نَحْوَهُ.

Muhammad ibn ʿAbd al-Bāqī informed us: Abū al-Faḍl Aḥmad ibn al-Ḥasan ibn Khayrūn narrated to us: Muhammad ibn ʿUmar ibn al-Qāsim al-Nursī narrated to us: Muhammad ibn ʿAbdullāh ibn Ibrāhīm al-Shāfiʿī narrated to us: Yazīd ibn al-Haytham al-Bādī narrated to us: ʿUbayd Allāh ibn ʿUmar narrated to us: Ḥammād narrated to us from Ayyūb that Abū Qilābah said, "I entered the *masjid* and people had gathered around a man from the Companions of the Prophet ﷺ. He said, 'The Prophet ﷺ said, "Indeed, after me there will come the misguiding arch-liar. Behind his head are wavy curls."'"[105]

Then he mentioned a similar hadith.

105 This hadith was sourced in hadith no. 60. *Muṣannaf ʿAbd al-Razzāq*, hadith no. 20828.

قَرَأْتُ عَلَى أَحْمَدَ بْنِ هِبَةِ اللهِ أَخْبَرَكُمُ الْمُسْلِمُ الْمَازِنِيُّ أَنَا عَبْدُ الرَّحْمَنِ بْنُ أَبِي الْحَسَنِ ثَنَا سَهْلُ بْنُ بِشْرٍ أَنَا عَلِيُّ بْنُ مُحَمَّدٍ الْفَارِسِيُّ وَأَنَا مُحَمَّدُ بْنُ أَحْمَدَ الذُّهْلِيُّ ثَنَا عُمَرُ بْنُ حَفْصٍ السَّدُوسِيُّ ثَنَا عَاصِمُ بْنُ عَلِيٍّ حَدَّثَنِي مُوسَى بْنُ عَبْدِ الْمَلِكِ بْنِ عُمَيْرٍ عَنْ أَبِيهِ عَنْ جَابِرِ بْنِ سَمُرَةَ أَنَّهُ قَالَ لِنَافِعِ بْنِ عُتْبَةَ هَلْ سَمِعْتَ رَسُولَ اللهِ ﷺ يَذْكُرُ الدَّجَّالَ بِشَيْءٍ قَالَ نَعَمْ قَدِمَ نَاسٌ مِنَ الْعَرَبِ إِلَى رَسُولِ اللَّهِ صَلَّى اللهُ عَلَيْهِ وَسَلَّمَ لِيُسَلِّمُوا عَلَيْهِمُ الصُّوفُ فَقُمْتُ فَقُلْتُ وَاللهِ لَأَحُولَنَّ بَيْنَهُمْ وَبَيْنَ رَسُولِ اللَّهِ ثُمَّ قُلْتُ فِي نَفْسِي هُوَ نَجِيُّ الْقَوْمِ قَالَ ثُمَّ أَبَتْ نَفْسِي إِلَّا أَنْ أَقُومَ إِلَيْهِ قَالَ فَسَمِعْتُهُ يَقُولُ يَغْزُونَ جَزِيرَةَ الْعَرَبِ فَيَفْتَحُهَا اللَّهُ ثُمَّ يَغْزُونَ فَارِسَ فَيَفْتَحُهَا اللَّهُ ثُمَّ يَغْزُونَ الدَّجَّالَ فَيَفْتَحُهُ اللهُ.

مُوسَى قَالَ أَبُو حَاتِمٍ الرَّازِيُّ ضَعِيفُ الْحَدِيثِ.

I recited to Aḥmad ibn Hibat Allāh: al-Muslim al-Māzinī informs you: ʿAbd al-Raḥmān ibn Abī al-Ḥasan informed us: Sahl ibn Bishr narrated to us: ʿAlī ibn Muhammad al-Fārisī informed us: And Muhammad ibn Aḥmad al-Dhihlī informed us: ʿUmar ibn Ḥafṣ al-Sadūsī narrated to us: ʿĀṣim ibn ʿAlī narrated to us: Mūsā ibn ʿAbd al-Malik ibn ʿUmayr narrated to me from his father from Jābir ibn Samurah that he said to Nāfiʿ ibn ʿUtbah, "Did you hear the Messenger of

## 80 HADITH EIGHTY

Allah ﷺ mention anything about the Dajjāl?" He responded, "Yes. Some Bedouin people went to the Messenger of Allah ﷺ to enter Islam. They had woollen clothing on. So, I got up and said, 'By Allah I will go between them and the Messenger of Allah.' Then I said within myself, 'He is the saviour of people'. So, my soul refused to do anything except stand before him. I heard him say, 'You will campaign against the Arabian peninsula and Allah will open it for you. Then, you will campaign against Persia and Allah will open it for you. Then, you will campaign against the Dajjāl and Allah will defeat him for you.'"[106]

Regarding Mūsā, Abū Ḥātim al-Rāzī said: "He is weak in hadith."

106 *Ṣaḥīḥ Muslim*, hadith no. 2900; *Mustadrak al-Ḥākim*, vol. 3, p. 431.

# HADITH EIGHTY-ONE

أَخْبَرَنَا عَبْدُ اللهِ بْنُ مُحَمَّدٍ أَنَا عَبْدُ الْقَادِرِ بْنُ مُحَمَّدٍ أَنَا الْحَسَنُ بْنُ عَلِيٍّ أَنَا أَحْمَدُ بْنُ جَعْفَرٍ نَا عَبْدُ اللهِ بْنُ نُمَيْرٍ ثَنَا إِسْمَاعِيلُ ثَنَا أَيُّوبُ عَنْ حُمَيْدِ بْنِ هِلَالٍ عَنْ بَعْضِ أَشْيَاخِهِمْ قَالَ قَالَ هِشَامُ بْنُ عَامِرٍ يَرَى لِجِيْرَانِهِ إِنَّكُمْ لَتَخْطَوْنَ إِلَى رِجَالٍ مَا كَانُوا بِأَحْضَرَ لِرَسُولِ اللَّهِ صَلَّى اللهُ عَلَيْهِ وَسَلَّمَ وَلَا أَوْعَى لِحَدِيثِهِ مِنِّي فَإِنِّي سَمِعْتُ رَسُولَ اللَّهِ صَلَّى اللهُ عَلَيْهِ وَسَلَّمَ يَقُولُ مَا بَيْنَ خَلْقِ آدَمَ عَلَيْهِ السَّلَامُ إِلَى قِيَامِ السَّاعَةِ أَمْرٌ أَكْبَرُ مِنَ الدَّجَّالِ. أهـ.

صَحِيحٌ رَوَاهُ مُسْلِمٌ عَنْ زُهَيْرِ بْنِ حَرْبٍ عَنْ أَحْمَدَ بْنِ إِسْحَاقَ الْحَضْرَمِيِّ عَنْ عَبْدِ الْعَزِيزِ بْنِ الْمُخْتَارِ عَنْ أَيُّوبَ.

رَوَاهُ ابْنُ أَبِي خَيْثَمَةَ فِي تَارِيخِهِ نَا عَفَّانُ نَا سُلَيْمَانُ بْنُ الْمُغِيرَةِ عَنْ حُمَيْدِ بْنِ هِلَالٍ قَالَ جَاءَ رِجَالٌ مِنَ إِيجِي يَتَخَطَّوْنَ هِشَامَ بْنَ عَامِرٍ إِلَى عِمْرَانَ بْنِ حُصَيْنٍ وَغَيْرِهِ فَقَالَ لَهُمْ ... وَذَكَرَ الْحَدِيثَ.

وَقَالَ عِيسَى بْنُ سَالِمٍ الشَّاشِيُّ ثَنَا عُبَيْدُ اللهِ بْنُ عَمْرٍو عَنْ أَيُّوبَ عَنْ حُمَيْدِ بْنِ هِلَالٍ عَنْ ثَلَاثَةِ رَهْطٍ مِنْ قَوْمِهِ مِنْهُمْ أَبُو قَتَادَةَ قَالَ كُنَّا نَمُرُّ عَلَى هِشَامٍ إِلَى عِمْرَانَ بْنِ حُصَيْنٍ فَقَالَ إِنَّكُمْ لَتَجَاوَزُونِي إِلَى رِجَالٍ مَا كَانُوا بِأَحْضَرَ لِرَسُولِ اللهِ ﷺ مِنِّي وَلَا بِأَعْلَمَ بِأَحَادِيثِهِ وَإِنِّي سَمِعْتُ رَسُولَ اللهِ ﷺ يَقُولُ مَا بَيْنَ خَلْقِ آدَمَ إِلَى قِيَامِ السَّاعَةِ فِتْنَةٌ أَكْبَرُ مِنْ فِتْنَةِ

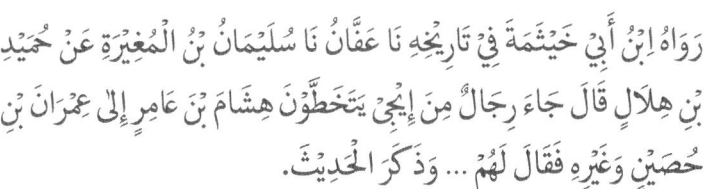

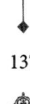

# 81 HADITH EIGHTY-ONE

الدَّجَّالِ أَكْلِ الطَّعَامِ وَمَشْيٍ فِي الْأَسْوَاقِ. فَذَكَرَهُ مُحَمَّدُ بْنُ حَاتِمٍ عَنْ عَبْدِ اللَّهِ بْنِ جَعْفَرٍ عَنْ عُبَيْدِ اللَّهِ بِهِ.

ʿAbdullāh ibn Muhammad informed us: ʿAbd al-Qādir ibn Muhammad informed us: al-Ḥasan ibn ʿAlī informed us: Aḥmad ibn Jaʿfar informed us: ʿAbdullāh ibn Numayr informed us: Ismāʿīl narrated to us: Ayyūb narrated to us from Ḥumayd ibn Hilāl that one of their sheikhs said, "Hishām ibn ʿĀmir said to his neighbour, 'You will meet some people who were not present with the Messenger of Allah ﷺ and did not memorize more of his hadiths than me. And I heard the Messenger of Allah ﷺ saying, "From the creation of Adam n to the establishing of the Hour, there is no matter greater than the Dajjāl."'"[107]

This hadith is *ṣaḥīḥ*. Muslim narrated it from Zuhayr ibn Ḥarb from Aḥmad ibn Isḥāq al-Ḥaḍramī from ʿAbd al-ʿAzīz ibn al-Mukhtār from Ayyūb.

It was also narrated by Ibn Abī Khaythamah in his *Tārīkh*: ʿAffān informed us: Sulaymān ibn al-Mughīrah informed us that Ḥumayd ibn Hilāl said, "Some men came to Ījī going from Hishām ibn ʿĀmir to ʿImrān ibn Ḥusayn and others. He said to them…" And he mentioned the rest of the hadith.

107 *Ṣaḥīḥ Muslim*, hadith no. 2946; *Muṣannaf Ibn Abī Shaybah*, vol. 15, p. 133.

# HADITH EIGHTY-ONE 81

ʿĪsā ibn Sālim al-Shāshī said: ʿUbayd Allāh ibn ʿAmr narrated to us from Ayyūb from Ḥumayd ibn Hilāl that three men from his people, among whom are Abū Qatādah, said: "We were passing by Hishām ibn ʿImrān ibn Ḥusayn. He said, 'You will pass by me to go to men who were not present with the Messenger of Allah ﷺ as much as I was and do not know as many of his hadiths as I. I heard the Messenger of Allah ﷺ say, "There is not, between the creation of Adam and the establishment of the Hour, any trial greater than the trial of the Dajjāl. He eats food and walks in the markets."'"

Muhammad ibn Ḥātim also mentioned it on the authority of ʿAbdullāh ibn Jaʿfar from ʿUbayd Allāh.

# 82 HADITH EIGHTY-TWO

قَرَأْتُ عَلَى عِيسَى بْنِ يَحْيَى الصُّوفِيِّ أَخْبَرَكُمُ الْحَسَنُ بْنُ دِينَارٍ أَنَا أَبُو طَاهِرٍ السِّلَفِيُّ أَنَا الْقَاسِمُ بْنُ الْفَضْلِ أَنَا أَبُو الْحُسَيْنِ بْنُ بِشْرَانَ ثَنَا مُحَمَّدُ بْنُ عَمْرٍو ثَنَا يَحْيَى بْنُ جَعْفَرٍ أَنَا وَهْبُ بْنُ جَرِيرٍ ثَنَا أَبِي سَمِعْتُ غَيْلَانَ بْنَ جَرِيرٍ يُحَدِّثُ عَنِ الشَّعْبِيِّ عَنْ فَاطِمَةَ بِنْتِ قَيْسٍ قَالَتْ قَدِمَ عَلَى رَسُولِ اللَّهِ صَلَّى اللَّهُ عَلَيْهِ وَسَلَّمَ تَمِيمٌ الدَّارِيُّ فَأَخْبَرَ أَنَّهُ رَكِبَ الْبَحْرَ فَتَاهَتْ سَفِينَتُهُمْ فَسَقَطُوا إِلَى جَزِيرَةٍ فَخَرَجُوا إِلَيْهَا يَلْتَمِسُونَ الْمَاءَ فَلَقِيَ إِنْسَانًا يَجُرُّ شَعْرَهُ فَقَالَ مَا أَنْتَ قَالَ أَنَا الْجَسَّاسَةُ قَالَ لَهُ أَخْبِرْنَا فَقَالَ لَا أُخْبِرُكُمْ وَلَكِنْ عَلَيْكُمْ بِهَذِهِ الْخَرِبَةِ فَدَخَلْنَاهَا فَإِذَا مُقَيَّدٌ فَقَالَ مَا أَنْتُمْ قُلْنَا نَاسٌ مِنَ الْعَرَبِ قَالَ مَا فَعَلَ هَذَا النَّبِيُّ الَّذِي خَرَجَ فِيكُمْ قُلْنَا آمَنَ بِهِ النَّاسُ وَاتَّبَعُوهُ وَصَدَّقُوهُ قَالَ ذَاكَ خَيْرٌ لَهُمْ أَلَا تُخْبِرُونِي عَنْ عَيْنِ زُغَرٍ مَا فَعَلَتْ فَأَخْبَرْنَاهُ عَنْهَا فَوَثَبَ وَثْبَةً كَادَ يَخْرُجُ مِنْ وَرَاءِ الْجِدَارِ ثُمَّ قَالَ مَا فَعَلَ نَخْلُ بَيْسَانَ هَلْ أُطْعِمَ بَعْدُ فَأَخْبَرْنَاهُ أَنَّهُ قَدْ أُطْعِمَ فَوَثَبَ مِثْلَهَا ثُمَّ قَالَ أَمَا لَوْ أُذِنَ لِي بِالْخُرُوجِ لَوَطِئْتُ الْبِلَادَ كُلَّهَا غَيْرَ طَيْبَةَ قَالَتْ فَخَرَجَ رَسُولُ اللَّهِ صَلَّى اللَّهُ عَلَيْهِ وَسَلَّمَ فَحَدَّثَ النَّاسَ وَقَالَ هَذِهِ طَيْبَةُ وَذَاكَ الدَّجَّالُ.

أَخْرَجَهُ مُسْلِمٌ عَنْ أَحْمَدَ بْنِ عُثْمَانَ النَّوْفَلِيِّ عَنْ وَهْبِ بْنِ جَرِيرٍ نَحْوَهُ وَبَاقِي طُرُقِ حَدِيثِ فَاطِمَةَ سَيَأْتِي.

I recited to ʿĪsā ibn Yaḥyā al-Ṣūfī: al-Ḥasan ibn Dīnār informs you: Abū Ṭāhir al-Silafī informed us: al-Qāsim ibn al-Faḍl informed us: Abū al-Ḥusayn ibn Bishrān informed us: Muhammad ibn ʿAmr narrated to us: Yaḥyā ibn Jaʿfar narrated to us: Wahb ibn Jarīr narrated to us: I heard Ghaylān ibn Jarīr narrating from al-Shaʿbī that Fāṭimah bint Qays said, "Tamīm al-Dārī went to the Messenger of Allah ﷺ. He informed the Messenger of Allah ﷺ that he had travelled by sea. Their boat approached the shore of an island and they descended and went towards it seeking water. They met a man that was very hairy. They said, 'Who are you?' He said, 'I am the spy.' They said, 'Give us some news.' He (the spy) said, 'I will not inform you. However, you must enter those ruins.' So they entered it and there was someone chained up. He said, 'Who are you?' We said, 'Some people from the Arabs.' He said, 'What has the Prophet that emerged among you done?' They said, 'Some people believed in him, followed him, and confirmed his truthfulness.' He said, 'Will you inform me of the spring of Zughar? What has it done?' They informed him about it, and he leapt with joy so ecstatically that he nearly came out from behind the wall. Then he said, 'How about the date orchards of Beisan? Have they begun to give fruits again?' We informed him that they had begun to give fruits. He jumped similarly to the first time. Then he said, 'Indeed, if I were given permission to emerge, I would enter every land except Ṭaybah.' So the Messenger of Allah ﷺ came out and spoke to the people. He said, 'This is Ṭaybah, and that is the Dajjāl.'"[108] The rest of the chains of transmission of the hadith of Fāṭimah (bint Qays) will come.



108 *Ṣaḥīḥ Muslim*, hadith no. 2942; *Sunan Abī Dāwūd*, Mu'assasah al-Risālah, hadith no. 4326; *Sunan Ibn Mājah*, Dār al-Risālah al-'Ālamiyyah, hadith no. 4084.

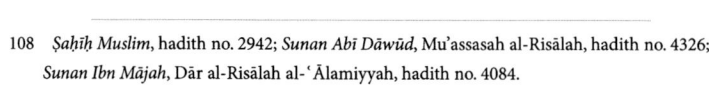

اَلطَّحَاوِيُّ ثَنَا يَزِيدُ بْنُ سِنَانَ نَا سَعِيدُ بْنُ سُفْيَانَ الْجَحْدَرِيُّ نَا ابْنُ عَوْنٍ عَنْ مُجَاهِدٍ قَالَ كُنَّا فِي الْبَحْرِ سَنَةَ سِتِّينَ عَلَيْنَا جُنَادَةُ أَبُو أُمَيَّةَ فَخَطَبَنَا ذَاتَ يَوْمٍ فَقَالَ أَتَيْنَا رَجُلًا مِنْ أَصْحَابِ النَّبِيِّ صَلَّى اللَّهُ عَلَيْهِ وَسَلَّمَ فَقُلْنَا حَدِّثْنَا مَا سَمِعْتَ مِنْ رَسُولِ اللهِ ﷺ فَقَالَ قَامَ فِينَا رَسُولُ اللهِ ذَاتَ يَوْمٍ فَقَالَ أُنْذِرُكُمُ الْمَسِيحَ أُنْذِرُكُمُ الْمَسِيحَ إِنَّهُ رَجُلٌ مَمْسُوحٌ أَظُنُّهُ قَالَ الْيُسْرَى يَمْكُثُ فِي الْأَرْضِ أَرْبَعِينَ صَبَاحًا مَعَهُ جِبَالُ خُبْزٍ وَأَنْهَارُ مَاءٍ يَبْلُغُ سُلْطَانُهُ كُلَّ مَنْهَلٍ لَا يَأْتِي أَرْبَعَةَ مَسَاجِدَ الْمَسْجِدَ الْحَرَامَ وَالْأَقْصَى وَمَسْجِدَ الطُّورِ وَمَسْجِدِي غَيْرَ أَنَّ مَا كَانَ مِنْ ذَلِكَ فَاعْلَمُوا أَنَّ اللهَ لَيْسَ بِأَعْوَرَ قَالَهَا ثَلَاثًا.

سَعِيدٌ رَوَاهُ يَزِيدُ بْنُ هَارُونَ عَنِ ابْنِ عَوْنٍ وَشَيْبَةَ وَرَوَى نَحْوَهُ قَيْسُ بْنُ سَعْدٍ عَنْ مُجَاهِدٍ.

From al-Ṭaḥāwī: Yazīd ibn Sinān narrated to us: Saʿīd ibn Sufyān al-Jaḥdarī informed us: Ibn ʿAwn informed us that Mujāhid said, "We were in the sea in the year seventy-six under the command of Junādah ibn Abī Umayyah. One day, he addressed us, saying, 'We came to a man from the Companions of the Prophet ﷺ, and we said to him, "Narrate to us something you heard from the Messenger of Allah ﷺ." He said, "The Messenger of Allah ﷺ stood up in front of us

# 83 HADITH EIGHTY-THREE

one day and said, 'I warn you of al-Masīḥ. I warn you of al-Masīḥ. He is a man who is blind' – I believe he said in his left eye. 'He will remain on the Earth for forty days. With him is a mountain of rice and rivers of water. His rule will reach every place, but he will not approach four *masjids*: al-Masjid al-Ḥarām (in Makkah), al-Aqṣā' (in Jerusalem), Masjid al-Ṭūr, and my (the Prophet's ﷺ) *masjid*. Those who are in any other should know that Allah is not one-eyed.' He repeated it three times.'""[109]

It was also narrated by Yazīd ibn Hārūn from Ibn 'Awn and Shaybah. And Qays ibn Sa'd narrated something similar from Mujāhid.

109 *Kanz al-'Ummāl*, hadith no. 39699, narrating from al-Baghawī; *Musnad al-Imām Aḥmad*, Mu'assasah al-Risālah, hadith no. 23090.

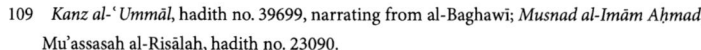

# HADITH EIGHTY-FOUR 84

أَحْمَدُ بْنُ أَيُّوبَ ثَنَا عَلِيُّ بْنُ عَبْدِ الْعَزِيزِ ثَنَا أَبُو نُعَيْمٍ ح وَثَنَا عُمَرُ بْنُ حَفْصٍ السَّدُوسِيُّ ثَنَا عَاصِمُ بْنُ عَلِيٍّ قَالَا ثَنَا حَشْرَجُ بْنُ نُبَاتَةَ ثَنَا سَعِيدُ بْنُ جُمْهَانَ عَنْ سَفِينَةَ قَالَ خَطَبَنَا رَسُولُ اللهِ صَلَّى اللهُ عَلَيْهِ وَسَلَّمَ فَقَالَ إِنَّهُ لَمْ يَكُنْ نَبِيٌّ إِلَّا قَدْ حَذَّرَ أُمَّتَهُ الدَّجَّالَ هُوَ أَعْوَرُ عَيْنُهُ الْيُسْرَى بِعَيْنِهِ الْيُمْنَى ظَفَرَةٌ غَلِيظَةٌ بَيْنَ عَيْنَيْهِ مَكْتُوبٌ كَافِرٌ يَخْرُجُ مَعَهُ وَادِيَانِ أَحَدُهُمَا جَنَّةٌ وَالْآخَرُ نَارٌ فَجَنَّتُهُ نَارٌ وَنَارُهُ جَنَّةٌ مَعَهُ مَلَكَانِ مِنَ الْمَلَائِكَةِ يَشْهَدَانِ مِنَ الْأَنْبِيَاءِ أَحَدُهُمَا عَنْ يَمِينِهِ وَالْآخَرُ عَنْ شِمَالِهِ وَذَلِكَ فِتْنَةُ النَّاسِ فَيَقُولُ أَلَسْتُ بِرَبِّكُمْ أُحْيِي وَأُمِيتُ فَيَقُولُ أَحَدُ الْمَلَكَيْنِ كَذَبْتَ فَمَا سَمِعَهُ أَحَدٌ مِنَ النَّاسِ إِلَّا صَاحِبُهُ فَيَقُولُ لَهُ صَاحِبُهُ صَدَقْتَ وَسَمِعَهُ النَّاسُ فَيَحْسَبُونَ أَنَّهُ صَدَّقَ الدَّجَّالَ وَذَلِكَ فِتْنَةٌ ثُمَّ يَسِيرُ حَتَّى يَأْتِيَ الْمَدِينَةَ وَلَا يُؤْذَنُ لَهُ فِيهَا فَيَقُولُ هَذِهِ قَرْيَةُ ذَاكَ الرَّجُلِ ثُمَّ يَسِيرُ حَتَّى يَأْتِيَ الشَّامَ فَيُهْلِكُهُ اللهُ عِنْدَ عَقَبَةِ الْفِيقِ.

رَوَاهُ أَبُو دَاوُدَ الطَّيَالِسِيُّ عَنِ الْحَشْرَجِ بْنِ نُبَاتَةَ كَذَلِكَ قُلْتُ وَوَقَعَ لَنَا فِي كِتَابِ حَنْبَلٍ رَوَاهُ عَنْ عَاصِمِ بْنِ عَلِيٍّ مِثْلَهُ وَرَوَاهُ الْإِمَامُ أَحْمَدُ فِي مُسْنَدِهِ ثَنَا أَبُو النَّضْرِ ثَنَا حَشْرَجُ فَذَكَرَهُ.

From Aḥmad ibn Ayyūb: ʿAlī ibn ʿAbd al-ʿAzīz narrated to us: Abū Nuʿaym narrated to us.

# 84 HADITH EIGHTY-FOUR

In another chain: ʿUmar ibn Ḥafṣ al-Dawsī narrated to us: ʿĀṣim ibn ʿAlī narrated to us.

Both said: Ḥashraj ibn Nubātah narrated to us: Saʿīd al-Jaḥdarī narrated to us that Safīnah said, "The Messenger of Allah ﷺ addressed us, saying, 'No Prophet has come except that he warned his people about the Dajjāl. His left eye is defective, and his right eye has a thick layer of skin over it. Between his two eyes is written (the word) *kāfir*. He will emerge and with him will be two valleys. One of them is a garden and the other is a fire. His garden is fire and his fire is a garden. He will be accompanied by two Angels resembling two Prophets. One of them will be on his right and the other will be on his left. That is a trial for people. He will say, "Am I not your Lord, as I give life and I cause death?" One of the Angels will say, "You have lied." No human being will hear what he has said, save his companion. The companion will say, "You have told the truth." People will hear him and will believe that he has confirmed the truthfulness of the Dajjāl. That is a trial. Then, he will travel until he reaches Madinah. He will not be permitted to enter. So, he will say, "This is a town and that is a man." Then he will travel until he reaches Shām and Allah ﷻ will cause him to perish close to the mountain pass of Fīq.'"[110]

110 Al-Ṭabarānī, *Al-Muʿjam al-Kabīr*, vol. 7, p. 84; *Musnad al-Imām Aḥmad*, Muʾassasah al-Risālah, hadith no. 21929.

Abū Dāwūd al-Ṭayālisī narrated it similarly from al-Ḥashraj ibn Nubātah.

I (al-Maqdisī) say: We also found it in the book of Ḥanbal. He narrated it from ʿĀṣim ibn ʿAlī in a similar manner. Imam Aḥmad also narrated it in his *Musnad* with the chain of transmission: Abū al-Naḍar narrated to us: Ḥashraj narrated to us. Then he mentioned the same hadith.

# 85 HADITH EIGHTY-FIVE

يَعْقُوبُ الْفَسَوِيُّ نَا يَحْيَى بْنُ بُكَيْرٍ حَدَّثَنَا خُنَيْسُ بْنُ عَامِرِ بْنِ يَحْيَى الْمُعَافِرِيُّ عَنْ أَبِي قُبَيْلٍ عَنْ جُنَادَةَ بْنِ أَبِي أُمَيَّةَ أَنَّ قَوْمًا دَخَلُوا عَلَى مُعَاذِ بْنِ جَبَلٍ وَهُوَ مَرِيضٌ فَقَالُوا لَهُ حَدَّثْنَا حَدِيثًا سَمِعْتَهُ مِنْ رَسُولِ اللهِ ﷺ لَمْ تَنْسِبْهُ وَلَمْ يَشْتَبِهْ عَلَيْكَ فَقَالَ أَجْلِسُونِي فَأَخَذَ بَعْضُ الْقَوْمِ بِيَدِهِ وَجَلَسَ بَعْضُهُمْ خَلْفَهُ فَقَالَ سَمِعْتُ رَسُولَ اللَّهِ صَلَّى اللَّهُ عَلَيْهِ وَسَلَّمَ يَقُولُ مَا مِنْ نَبِيٍّ إِلَّا وَقَدْ حَذَّرَ أُمَّتَهُ الدَّجَّالَ وَأَنَا أُحَذِّرُكُمْ أَمْرَ الدَّجَّالِ إِنَّهُ أَعْوَرُ وَإِنَّ رَبِّي لَيْسَ بِأَعْوَرَ مَكْتُوبٌ بَيْنَ عَيْنَيْهِ كَافِرٌ يَقْرَأُهُ الْكَاتِبُ وَغَيْرُ الْكَاتِبِ مَعَهُ جَنَّةٌ وَنَارٌ فَنَارُهُ جَنَّةٌ وَجَنَّتُهُ نَارٌ.

إِسْنَادُهُ جَيِّدٌ تَفَرَّدَ بِهِ خُنَيْسٌ وَمَا عَلِمْتُ فِي خُنَيْسٍ جَرْحَةً.

From Yaʿqūb al-Fasawī: Yaḥyā ibn Bukayr informed us: Khunays ibn ʿĀmir ibn Yaḥyā al-Muʿāfirī narrated to us from Abū Qabīl from Junādah ibn Abī Umayyah that some people entered upon Muʿādh ibn Jabal while he was sick. They said to him, "Narrate to us a hadith that you heard from the Messenger of Allah ﷺ, which you have not forgotten and about which you have not become confused." He said, "Sit me up." So, some people took him by the hand and some people sat behind him. He said, "I heard the Messenger of Allah ﷺ say, 'No Prophet has come except that he warned his people of the Dajjāl. And I warn you of the affair of the Dajjāl. He is one-eyed. My Lord (Mighty and Majestic is He) is not one-eyed. Written between his eyes is (the word) *kāfir*. It will be legible to the literate and the illiterate alike. With him is a garden and a fire. His fire is a garden and his garden is a fire.'"[111]

Its chain of transmission is good. Only Khunays narrated it. However, I do not know any criticism of him.

111 Al-Ṭabarānī, *Al-Muʿjam al-Kabīr*, vol. 20, p. 61; *Musnad al-Bazzār*, vol. 4, p. 137. It also has two supporting narrations in *Ṣaḥīḥ Muslim*: hadith nos. 2933 and 2934.

# 86 HADITH EIGHTY-SIX

عَبْدُ الرَّزَّاقِ قَالَ أَخْبَرَنَا مَعْمَرٌ عَنْ أَيُّوبَ عَنْ أَبِي قِلَابَةَ عَنْ هِشَامِ بْنِ عَامِرٍ قَالَ قَالَ رَسُولُ اللَّهِ صَلَّى اللهُ عَلَيْهِ وَسَلَّمَ إِنَّ رَأْسَ الدَّجَّالِ مِنْ وَرَائِهِ حُبُكٌ حُبُكٌ فَمَنْ قَالَ أَنْتَ رَبِّيْ فَقَدِ افْتُتِنَ وَمَنْ قَالَ كَذَبْتَ رَبِّيَ اللَّهُ وَعَلَيْهِ تَوَكَّلْتُ وَإِلَيْهِ أُنِيبُ فَلَا يَضُرُّهُ أَوْ قَالَ فَلَا فِتْنَةَ عَلَيْهِ.

From ʿAbd al-Razzāq: Maʿmar informed us from Abū Ayyūb from Abū Qilābah that Hishām ibn ʿĀmir said, "The Messenger of Allah ﷺ said, 'The head of the Dajjāl has wavy curls behind it. If someone says, "You are my lord", he will have been seduced. Whoever says, "You have lied. My Lord is Allah. Upon Him is my reliance" will not be harmed by him.' Or, he said, 'He will not be seduced by him.'"[112]



112 This hadith was sourced in hadith no. 60. *Muṣannaf ʿAbd al-Razzāq*, hadith no. 20828.

# HADITH EIGHTY-SEVEN 87

وَأَخْبَرَنَا مَعْمَرٌ عَنِ ابْنِ طَاوُسٍ عَنْ أَبِيْهِ عَنْ كَعْبٍ قَالَ يَخْرُجُ الدَّجَّالُ مِنَ الْعِرَاقِ.

Maʿmar informed us from Ibn Ṭāwūs from his father that Kaʿb said, "The Dajjāl will emerge from Iraq."[113]



113 *Muṣannaf ʿAbd al-Razzāq*, hadith no. 21755.

# 88 HADITH EIGHTY-EIGHT

أَخْبَرَنَا مُحَمَّدُ بْنُ مُحَمَّدٍ وَحُبَيْبُ بْنُ إِبْرَاهِيمَ ثَنَا مَحْمُودُ بْنُ إِسْمَاعِيلَ ثَنَا أَحْمَدُ بْنُ مُحَمَّدِ بْنِ الْحُسَيْنِ ثَنَا سُلَيْمَانُ بْنُ أَحْمَدَ بْنِ أَيُّوبَ ثَنَا مُحَمَّدُ بْنُ عَبْدُوسَ بْنِ كَامِلٍ السَّرَاجُ ثَنَا الْحَسَنُ بْنُ الصَّبَّاحِ الْبَزَّارُ ثَنَا رَوْحُ بْنُ عُبَادَةَ ثَنَا سَعِيدُ بْنُ أَبِي عَرُوبَةَ عَنْ قَتَادَةَ عَنِ الْحَسَنِ عَنْ سَمُرَةَ بْنِ جُنْدُبٍ قَالَ قَالَ رَسُولُ اللهِ ﷺ الدَّجَّالُ خَارِجٌ وَهُوَ أَعْوَرُ عَيْنِ الشِّمَالِ عَلَيْهَا ظَفَرَةٌ غَلِيظَةٌ وَإِنَّهُ يُبْرِئُ الْأَكْمَهَ وَالْأَبْرَصَ وَيُحْيِي الْمَوْتَىٰ وَيَقُولُ لِلنَّاسِ أَنَا رَبُّكُمْ فَمَنْ قَالَ أَنْتَ رَبِّي فَقَدْ فُتِنَ وَمَنْ قَالَ رَبِّيَ اللَّهُ حَتَّىٰ يَمُوتَ عَلَىٰ ذَٰلِكَ فَقَدْ عُصِمَ مِنْ فِتْنَةِ الدَّجَّالِ وَلَا فِتْنَةَ عَلَيْهِ فَيَلْبَثُ فِي الْأَرْضِ مَا شَاءَ اللَّهُ ثُمَّ يَجِيءُ عِيسَى ابْنُ مَرْيَمَ مِنْ قِبَلِ الْمَغْرِبِ مُصَدِّقًا بِمُحَمَّدٍ ﷺ فَيَقْتُلُ الدَّجَّالَ وَإِنَّمَا هُوَ قِيَامُ السَّاعَةِ.

أُثْبِتُهُ عَنِ الْكَرَّانِيِّ أَنَا مَحْمُودٌ رَوَاهُ أَحْمَدُ فِي سَنَدِهِ عَنْ رَوْحٍ وَعَبْدُ الْوَهَّابِ بْنُ عَطَاءٍ عَنْ سَعِيدٍ.

Muhammad ibn Muhammad and Ḥabīb ibn Ibrāhīm both informed us: Maḥmūd ibn Ismāʿīl narrated to us: Aḥmad ibn Muhammad ibn al-Ḥusayn narrated to us: Sulaymān ibn Aḥmad ibn Ayyūb narrated to us: Muhammad ibn ʿAbdūs ibn Kāmil al-Sirāj narrated to us: al-Ḥasan ibn al-Ṣabbāḥ al-Bazzār narrated to us: Rawḥ ibn ʿUbādah narrated to us:

Sa'īd ibn Abī 'Arūbah narrated to us from Qatādah from al-Ḥasan that Samurah ibn Jundub said, "The Messenger of Allah ﷺ said, 'The Dajjāl will certainly emerge. He is one-eyed. His left eye will have a thick layer of skin over it. He will heal the people born blind and the lepers. He will give life to the dead. Then he will say to the people, "I am your lord." Whoever says, "You are my lord" has been seduced. Whoever says, "My Lord is Allah" until he dies upon that will have been protected from the trial of the Dajjāl. No temptation will befall him. He will remain on the Earth as long as Allah wills. Then, 'Īsā ibn Maryam will come from the West confirming the truth of Muhammad ﷺ. He will kill the Dajjāl. He is only the establishment of the Hour.'"[114]

I also confirmed this hadith from al-Karrānī, who narrated it from Maḥmūd. And Aḥmad narrated it in his *Musnad* from Rawḥ and 'Abd al-Wahhāb ibn 'Aṭā' from Sa'īd.

114 *Musnad al-Imām Aḥmad*, Mu'assasah al-Risālah, hadith no. 20151; al-Ṭabarānī, *al-Mu'jam al-Kabīr*, vol. 7, p. 221 and vol. 7, p. 65; *Musnad al-Bazzār*, vol. 4, p. 143.

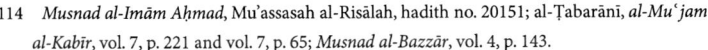

# 89 HADITH EIGHTY-NINE

أَخْبَرَنَا مُحَمَّدُ بْنُ مُحَمَّدٍ وَحُبَيْبُ بْنُ إِبْرَاهِيمَ ثَنَا مَحْمُودُ بْنُ إِسْمَاعِيلَ ثَنَا أَحْمَدُ بْنُ مُحَمَّدٍ ثَنَا سَلَمُ بْنُ أَحْمَدَ ثَنَا مُحَمَّدُ بْنُ عَبْدِ اللهِ بْنِ بَكْرٍ السِّرَاجُ الْعَسْكَرِيُّ ثَنَا سُلَيْمُ بْنُ عُمَرَ بْنِ خَالِدٍ الرَّقِّيُّ حَدَّثَنِي أَبِي عَنِ الْخَلِيلِ بْنِ مُرَّةَ ح وَثَنَا عَبْدُ اللهِ بْنُ أَحْمَدَ بْنِ حَنْبَلٍ ثَنَا سَلَمَةُ بْنُ شَبِيبٍ ثَنَا يَزِيدُ بْنُ أَبِي حَكِيمٍ عَنْ إِبْرَاهِيمَ بْنِ طَهْمَانَ عَنِ الْحَجَّاجِ بْنِ الْحَجَّاجِ جَمِيعًا عَنْ قَتَادَةَ عَنِ الْحَسَنِ عَنْ سَمُرَةَ قَالَ قَالَ رَسُولُ اللهِ ﷺ إِنَّ الدَّجَّالَ خَارِجٌ وَإِنَّهُ أَعْوَرُ عَيْنِ الشِّمَالِ فِيهَا ظَفَرَةٌ غَلِيظَةٌ وَإِنَّهُ يُبْرِئُ الْأَكْمَهَ وَالْأَبْرَصَ وَيُحْيِي الْمَوْتَىٰ وَيَقُولُ لِلنَّاسِ أَنَا رَبُّكُمْ فَمَنْ قَالَ أَنْتَ رَبِّي فَقَدِ افْتُرِيَ وَمَنْ قَالَ رَبِّيَ اللَّهُ حَتَّىٰ يَمُوتَ عَلَىٰ ذٰلِكَ فَقَدْ عُصِمَ مِنْ فِتْنَةِ الدَّجَّالِ.

وَاللَّفْظُ لِخَلِيلِ بْنِ مُرَّةَ. اهـ.

أَنْبَأَنِيهِ ابْنُ الْبُخَارِيِّ عَنِ الْكَرَّانِيِّ أَنَا مَحْمُودٌ.

A) Muhammad ibn Muhammad and Ḥabīb ibn Ibrāhīm informed us: Maḥmūd ibn Ismā'īl narrated to us: Aḥmad ibn Muhammad narrated to us: Salam ibn Aḥmad narrated to us: Muhammad ibn 'Abdullāh ibn Bakr al-Sirāj al-'Askarī narrated to us: Sālim ibn 'Umar ibn Khālid al-Raqī narrated to us: My father narrated to me from al-Khalīl ibn Murrah. And 'Abdullāh ibn Aḥmad ibn Ḥanbal narrated to us: Salamah ibn Shabīb narrated to us: Yazīd ibn Abī Ḥakīm narrated to us: from Ibrāhīm ibn Ṭahmān from al-Ḥajjāj ibn al-Ḥajjāj – all from Qatādah from al-Ḥasan that Samurah said, "The Messenger of Allah ﷺ said, 'The Dajjāl will certainly emerge. He is one-eyed. His left eye will have a thick covering of skin over it. He will cure the people born blind and the leper, as well as give life to the dead. He will then say to people, "I am your lord." Whoever says, "You are my lord" will have lied. Whoever says, "My Lord is Allah" until he dies upon that will have been saved from the trial of the Dajjāl.'"[115]

The wording is from al-Khalīl ibn Murrah. Ibn al-Bukhārī also related it to me from al-Karrānī saying, "Maḥmūd informed us of it."

B) And it is related from Ḥawṭ al-ʿAbdī that ʿAbdullāh ibn Masʿūd ﷺ said, "The ear of the donkey of the Dajjāl will give shade to seventy thousand."

However, Ḥawṭ is unknown. Abū Mūsā mentioned him among the Companions, so his status became known.

115 *Musnad al-Imām Aḥmad*, Mu'assasah al-Risālah, hadith no. 20151; al-Ṭabarānī, *al-Muʿjam al-Kabīr*, vol. 7, p. 221 and vol. 7, p. 65; *Musnad al-Bazzār*, vol. 4, p. 143.

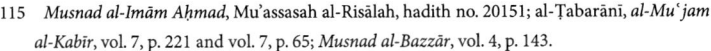

# 90 HADITH NINETY

أَخْبَرَنَا سِنْقَرُ نَا عَبْدُ اللَّطِيفِ أَنَا عَبْدُ الْحَقِّ أَنَا عَلِيُّ بْنُ الْعَلَّافِ أَنَا عَلِيُّ بْنُ الْحِمَامِيُّ أَنَا ابْنُ قَانِعٍ أَنَا إِسْمَاعِيلُ بْنُ إِبْرَاهِيمَ الْقَطْرَانِيُّ بِالْكُوفَةِ نَا عَبْدُ الْحَمِيدِ بْنُ صَالِحٍ ثَنَا مُحَمَّدُ بْنُ أَبَانَ عَنْ يَزِيدَ بْنِ جَابِرٍ عَنْ بِشْرِ بْنِ عُبَيْدِ اللهِ عَنْ أَبِي إِدْرِيسَ عَنْ نَهِيكِ بْنِ صُرَيْمٍ عَنِ النَّبِيِّ ﷺ قَالَ تُقَاتِلُونَ الْكُفَّارَ حَتَّى تُقَاتِلَ بَقِيَّةٌ مِنْكُمُ الدَّجَّالَ بِالْأُرْدُنِ هُمْ غَرْبِيَّهُ وَأَنْتُمْ شَرْقِيَّةٌ. رَوَاهُ إِبْرَاهِيمُ بْنُ سُلَيْمَانَ وَسَعِيدُ بْنُ سَالِمٍ عَنْ مُحَمَّدِ بْنِ أَبَانَ قَالَ [إِنْ] كَانَ الْجُعْفِيُّ فَهُوَ ضَعِيفٌ.

Sinqar informed us: 'Abd al-Laṭīf informed us: 'Abd al-Ḥaqq informed us: 'Alī ibn 'Allāf informed us: 'Alī ibn al-Hammāmī informed us: Ibn Qāni' informed us: Ismā'īl ibn Ibrāhīm al-Qaṭrānī informed us in Kufah: 'Abd al-Ḥamīd ibn Ṣāliḥ informed us: Muhammad ibn Abān narrated to us from Yazīd ibn Jābir from Bishr ibn 'Ubayd Allāh from Abū Idrīs from Nahīk ibn Ṣuraym that the Prophet ﷺ said, "You will fight the disbelievers until the remainder of you fight the Dajjāl in Jordan. They are westerners and you are easterners."[116] It was narrated by Ibrāhīm ibn Sulaymān and Sa'īd ibn Sālim from Muhammad ibn Abān. He said, "If (Muhammad ibn Abān) is al-Ju'fī, he is a weak narrator."

116 We did not find the source of this hadith.

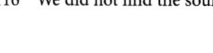

# HADITH NINETY-ONE 91

أَخْبَرَنَا عَبْدُ اللهِ بْنُ مُحَمَّدٍ ثَنَا عَبْدُ الْقَادِرِ بْنُ مُحَمَّدٍ أَنَا الْحَسَنُ بْنُ عَلِيٍّ ثَنَا أَحْمَدُ بْنُ جَعْفَرٍ نَا عَبْدُ اللهِ حَدَّثَنِي أَبِي ثَنَا رَوْحٌ ثَنَا سَعِيدٌ ثَنَا سَعِيدٌ وَعَبْدُ الْوَهَّابِ ثَنَا سَعِيدٌ عَنْ قَتَادَةَ عَنِ الْحَسَنِ عَنْ سَمُرَةَ بْنِ جُنْدُبٍ أَنَّ النَّبِيَّ ﷺ يَقُولُ إِنَّ الدَّجَّالَ خَارِجٌ وَهُوَ أَعْوَرُ عَيْنِ الشِّمَالِ عَلَيْهَا ظَفَرَةٌ غَلِيظَةٌ وَإِنَّهُ يُبْرِئُ الْأَكْمَهَ وَالْأَبْرَصَ وَيُحْيِي الْمَوْتَى وَيَقُولُ لِلنَّاسِ أَنَا رَبُّكُمْ فَمَنْ قَالَ أَنْتَ رَبِّي فَقَدْ فُتِنَ وَمَنْ قَالَ رَبِّيَ اللَّهُ حَتَّى يَمُوتَ فَقَدْ عُصِمَ مِنْ فِتْنَةٍ فَلَا فِتْنَةَ عَلَيْهِ وَلَا عَذَابَ فَيَلْبَثُ فِي الْأَرْضِ مَا شَاءَ اللَّهُ ثُمَّ يَجِيءُ عِيسَى بْنُ مَرْيَمَ عَلَيْهِمَا السَّلَامُ مِنْ قِبَلِ الْمَغْرِبِ مُصَدِّقًا لِمُحَمَّدٍ ﷺ وَعَلَى مِلَّتِهِ فَيَقْتُلُ الدَّجَّالَ ثُمَّ إِنَّمَا هُوَ قِيَامُ السَّاعَةِ.

ʿAbdullāh ibn Muhammad informed us: ʿAbd al-Qādir ibn Muhammad narrated to us: al-Ḥasan ibn ʿAlī informed us: Aḥmad ibn Jaʿfar narrated to us: ʿAbdullāh informed us: My father ﵀ narrated to me: Rawḥ narrated to us: Saʿīd and ʿAbd al-Wahhāb narrated to us: Saʿīd narrated to us from Qatādah from al-Ḥasan from Samurah ibn Jundub that the Prophet ﷺ used to say, "The Dajjāl will certainly emerge. He is one-eyed. His left eye has a thick layer of skin over it. He will cure the people born blind and the lepers, as well as give life to the dead. He will say to people, 'I am your lord.' Whoever says, 'You are my lord' will have been seduced. Whoever says, 'My Lord is Allah' until he dies will have been protected from his trial. So, there will be neither temptation for him nor any punishment. He will remain on the Earth as long as Allah ﷻ wills. Then, ʿĪsā ibn Maryam ﷺ will come from the West confirming the truth of Muhammad ﷺ and following his religion. He will kill the Dajjāl. Then, all that will remain is the establishment of the Hour."[117]

117 *Musnad al-Imām Aḥmad*, Mu'assasah al-Risālah, hadith no. 20151; al-Ṭabarānī, *al-Muʿjam al-Kabīr*, vol. 7, p. 221 and vol. 7, p. 65; *Musnad al-Bazzār*, vol. 4, p. 143.

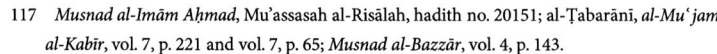

# HADITH NINETY-TWO 92

سُلَيمَانُ بْنُ بِلاَلٍ أَخبَرَنِي يَحيَى بْنُ سَعِيدٍ أَخبَرَنِي مُحَمَّدُ بْنُ يَحيَى بْنِ حِبَّانَ عَنْ دَاوُدَ بْنِ أَبِي دَاوُدَ قَالَ قَالَ لِي عَبْدُ اللهِ بْنُ سَلاَمٍ إِنْ سَمِعتَ بِالدَّجَّالِ قَدْ خَرَجَ وَأَنْتَ عَلَى وَدِيَّةٍ تَغرِسُهَا فَلاَ تَعجَلْ أَنْ تُصلِحَهَا فَإِنَّ لِلنَّاسِ بَعْدَ ذَلِكَ عَيشًا.

From Sulaymān ibn Bilāl: Yaḥyā ibn Sa'īd informed me: Muhammad ibn Yaḥyā ibn Ḥibbān informed me that Dāwūd ibn Abī Dāwūd said, "'Abdullāh ibn Salām ﷺ said to me, 'If you hear that the Dajjāl has emerged and you are planting a sapling, do not abandon erecting it. For people will live after his *fitnah*.'"[118]

118 Al-Bukhārī, *al-Adab al-Mufrad*, vol. 1, p. 480.

# 93 HADITH NINETY-THREE

أَخْبَرَنَا أَبُو زُرْعَةَ طَاهِرُ بْنُ مُحَمَّدِ بْنِ طَاهِرٍ الْمَقْدِسِيُّ بِبَغْدَادَ ثَنَا أَبُو مَنْصُورٍ مُحَمَّدُ بْنُ الْحُسَيْنِ بْنِ أَحْمَدَ بْنِ الْهَيْثَمِ الْمُعَوِصِيُّ إِجَازَةً إِنْ لَمْ يَكُنْ سِمَاعًا ثَنَا أَبُو طَلْحَةَ الْقَاسِمُ بْنُ أَبِي الْمُنْذِرِ الْخَطِيبُ ثَنَا أَبُو الْحَسَنِ عَلِيُّ بْنُ إِبْرَاهِيمَ بْنِ سَلَمَةَ الْقَطَّانُ ثَنَا أَبُو عَبْدِ اللهِ مُحَمَّدُ بْنُ يَزِيدَ بْنِ مَاجَه الْقَزْوِينِيُّ ثَنَا مُحَمَّدُ بْنُ عَبْدِ اللهِ بْنِ نُمَيْرٍ وَعَلِيُّ بْنُ مُحَمَّدٍ قَالَا حَدَّثَنَا أَبُو مُعَاوِيَةَ ثَنَا الأَعْمَشُ عَنْ شَقِيقٍ عَنْ حُذَيْفَةَ قَالَ قَالَ رَسُولُ اللهِ صَلَّى اللهُ عَلَيْهِ وَسَلَّمَ الدَّجَّالُ أَعْوَرُ عَيْنِ الشِّمَالِ الْيُسْرَى جُفَالُ الشَّعَرِ مَعَهُ جَنَّةٌ وَنَارٌ فَنَارُهُ جَنَّةٌ وَجَنَّتُهُ نَارٌ. أهـ.

أَنَا بِهِ سِنْقَرُ أَنَا الْمُوَفَّقُ أَنَا أَبُو زُرْعَةَ صَحِيحٌ رَوَاهُ مُسْلِمٌ عَنْ مُحَمَّدِ بْنِ عَبْدِ اللهِ بْنِ نُمَيْرٍ وَأَبِي كُرَيْبٍ وَإِسْحَاقَ بْنِ رَاهَوَيْه عَنْ أَبِي مُعَاوِيَةَ.

Abū Zurʿah Ṭāhir ibn Muhammad ibn Ṭāhir al-Maqdisī informed us in Baghdad: Abū Manṣūr Muhammad ibn al-Ḥusayn ibn Aḥmad ibn al-Haytham al-Muqawwimī narrated to us by way of *ijāzah* though we had not heard it directly from him: Abū Ṭalḥah al-Qāsim ibn Abī Mundhir al-Khaṭīb narrated to us: Abū al-Ḥasan ʿAlī ibn Ibrāhīm ibn Salamah al-Qaṭṭān narrated to us: Abū ʿAbdillāh Muhammad ibn Yazīd ibn Mājah al-Qazwīnī narrated to us: Muhammad ibn ʿAbdullāh ibn Numayr and ʿAlī ibn Muhammad both narrated to us, saying: Abū Mu'āwiyah narrated to us: Al-A'mash narrated to us from Shaqīq that Ḥudhayfah said, "The Messenger of Allah ﷺ said, 'The Dajjāl is blind in his left eye and has wooly hair. With him is a garden and a fire. His fire is really a garden and his garden is really a fire.'"[119]

Sinfar informed us of it saying: al-Muwaffaq informed us: Abū Zur'ah informed us.

It is an authentic hadith. Muslim narrated it from Muhammad ibn 'Abdullāh ibn Numayr and Abī Kurayb and Isḥāq ibn Rāhawayh from Abū Mu'āwiyah.

119 *Ṣaḥīḥ Muslim*, hadith no. 2934, *Sunan Ibn Mājah*, Dār al-Risālah al-'Ālamiyyah, hadith no. 4071; *Musnad al-Imām Aḥmad*, Mu'assasah al-Risālah, hadith no. 23250.

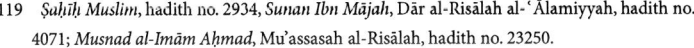

# 94 HADITH NINETY-FOUR

بَقِيٌّ ثَنَا يَحْيَ الْحِمَانِيُّ نَا حَشْرَجُ بْنُ نُبَاتَةَ حَدَّثَنِي حُسَيْنُ الْجُهَنِيُّ عَنْ حُذَيْفَةَ قُلْتُ يَا رَسُولَ اللَّهِ أَيَكُونُ بَعْدَ هَذَا الْخَيْرِ شَرٌّ كَمَا كَانَ قَبْلَهُ قَالَ نَعَمْ قُلْتُ فَبِمَ نَعْتَصِمُ قَالَ بِالسَّيْفِ قُلْتُ ثُمَّ مَاذَا قَالَ هُدْنَةٌ عَلَى دَخَنٍ قُلْتُ ثُمَّ مَاذَا قَالَ ثُمَّ يَنْشَأُ دُعَاةُ الضَّلَالَةِ وَإِنَّ لِلَّهِ فِي الْأَرْضِ خَلِيفَةٌ فَإِنْ ضَرَبَ ظَهْرَكَ وَأَخَذَ مَالَكَ فَكُنْ مَعَهُ ثُمَّ يَخْرُجُ أَعْوَرُ الدَّجَّالُ وَمَعَهُ نَهْرٌ وَنَارٌ فَمَنْ وَقَعَ فِي نَهْرِهِ وَجَبَ وِزْرُهُ وَحُبِطَ أَجْرُهُ وَمَنْ وَقَعَ فِي نَارِهِ وَجَبَ أَجْرُهُ وَحُبِطَ وِزْرُهُ. قُلْتُ حَشْرَجُ صَدُوقٌ مِنْ طَبَقَةِ حَمَّادِ بْنِ سَلَمَةَ.

From Baqī: Yaḥyā ibn al-Hamānī narrated to us: Ḥashraj ibn Nubāṭah informed us: Ḥusayn al-Juhanī narrated to me from Ḥudhayfah, "I said to the Messenger of Allah ﷺ, 'Will there be, after this good, evil as was before?' He replied, 'Yes.' I said, 'How should we protect ourselves?' He replied, 'With the sword.' I said, 'Then what?' He said, 'Then there will be good with some murkiness.' I said, 'Then what?' He said, 'Then, preachers of misguidance shall arise, and Allah will have a *khalīfah* in the Earth. If he strikes your back and takes your wealth, remain with him. Then, the one-eyed Dajjāl will emerge. With him are a river and a fire. Whoever enters his river takes on its blame and destroys its reward. Whoever enters his fire obtains his reward and casts off his blame.'"[120] I (al-Maqdisī) say: Ḥashraj is an honest narrator from the generation of Ḥammād ibn Salamah.

120 *Sunan Abū Dāwūd*, Dār al-Risālah al-ʿĀlamiyyah, hadith no. 4244; *Musnad al-Imām Aḥmad*, Mu'assasah al-Risālah, hadith no. 23430. A similar hadith was narrated from Ḥudhayfah in *Ṣaḥīḥ al-Bukhārī*, hadith no. 3606 and 7084; *Ṣaḥīḥ Muslim*, hadith no. 1848 and *Sunan Ibn Mājah*, Dār al-Risālah al-ʿĀlamiyyah, hadith no. 3979.

# 95 HADITH NINETY-FIVE

أَخْبَرَنَا عَبْدُ اللهِ بْنُ مُحَمَّدٍ ثَنَا عَبْدُ الْقَادِرِ بْنُ مُحَمَّدٍ ثَنَا الْحَسَنُ بْنُ عَلِيٍّ ثَنَا أَحْمَدُ بْنُ جَعْفَرٍ الْقَطِيعِيُّ ثَنَا عَبْدُ اللهِ بْنُ أَحْمَدَ بْنِ حَنْبَلٍ حَدَّثَنِي أَبِي ثَنَا يَزِيدُ بْنُ هَارُونَ ثَنَا ابْنُ أَبِي ذِئْبٍ عَنْ مُحَمَّدِ بْنِ عَمْرِو بْنِ عَطَاءٍ عَنْ ذَكْوَانَ عَنْ عَائِشَةَ قَالَتْ جَاءَتْ يَهُودِيَّةٌ فَاسْتَطْعَمَتْ فَقَالَتْ أَطْعِمُونِي أَعَاذَكُمُ اللهُ مِنْ فِتْنَةِ الدَّجَّالِ وَمِنْ فِتْنَةِ عَذَابِ الْقَبْرِ قَالَتْ فَلَمْ أَزَلْ أَحْبِسُهَا حَتَّى جَاءَ رَسُولُ اللهِ صَلَّى اللهُ عَلَيْهِ وَسَلَّمَ فَرَفَعَ يَدَيْهِ مَدًّا يَسْتَعِيذُ بِاللهِ مِنْ فِتْنَةِ الدَّجَّالِ وَمِنْ فِتْنَةِ عَذَابِ الْقَبْرِ فَقُلْتُ يَا رَسُولَ اللهِ مَا تَقُولُ هَذِهِ الْيَهُودِيَّةُ قَالَ وَمَا تَقُولُ قُلْتُ تَقُولُ أَعَاذَكُمُ اللهُ مِنْ فِتْنَةِ الدَّجَّالِ وَمِنْ فِتْنَةِ عَذَابِ الْقَبْرِ قَالَتْ عَائِشَةُ فَقَامَ رَسُولُ اللهِ صَلَّى اللهُ عَلَيْهِ وَسَلَّمَ فَرَفَعَ يَدَهُ مَدًّا يَسْتَعِيذُ بِاللهِ مِنْ فِتْنَةِ الدَّجَّالِ وَمِنْ فِتْنَةِ عَذَابِ الْقَبْرِ فَقَالَ أَمَّا فِتْنَةُ الدَّجَّالِ فَإِنَّهُ لَمْ يَكُنْ نَبِيٌّ إِلَّا قَدْ حَذَّرَ أُمَّتَهُ وَسَأُحَذِّرُكُمُوهُ تَحْذِيرًا لَمْ يُحَذِّرْهُ أُمَّتَهُ إِنَّهُ أَعْوَرُ وَاللهُ لَيْسَ بِأَعْوَرَ مَكْتُوبٌ بَيْنَ عَيْنَيْهِ كَافِرٌ يَقْرَؤُهُ كُلُّ مُؤْمِنٍ.

فَأَمَّا فِتْنَةُ الْقَبْرِ فَبِي تُفْتَنُونَ وَعَنِّي تُسْأَلُونَ فَإِذَا كَانَ الرَّجُلُ الصَّالِحُ أُجْلِسَ فِي قَبْرِهِ غَيْرَ فَزِعٍ وَلَا مَشْعُوفٍ ثُمَّ يُقَالُ لَهُ فِيمَا كُنْتَ فَيَقُولُ فِي الْإِسْلَامِ فَيُقَالُ مَا هَذَا الرَّجُلُ الَّذِي كَانَ فِيكُمْ فَيَقُولُ مُحَمَّدٌ رَسُولُ اللهِ جَاءَنَا بِالْبَيِّنَاتِ مِنْ عِنْدِ اللهِ جَلَّ وَعَزَّ فَصَدَّقْنَاهُ فَيُفْرَجُ لَهُ فُرْجَةٌ قِبَلَ

النَّارِ فَيَنْظُرُ إِلَيْهَا يَحْطِمُ بَعْضُهَا بَعْضًا فَيُقَالُ لَهُ انْظُرْ إِلَىٰ مَا وَقَاكَ اللّٰهُ عَزَّ وَجَلَّ ثُمَّ يُفْرَجُ لَهُ فُرْجَةٌ إِلَى الْجَنَّةِ فَيَنْظُرُ إِلَىٰ زَهْرَتِهَا وَمَا فِيهَا فَيُقَالُ لَهُ هٰذَا مَقْعَدُكَ مِنْهَا عَلَى الْيَقِينِ كُنْتَ وَعَلَيْهِ مِتَّ وَعَلَيْهِ تُبْعَثُ إِنْ شَاءَ اللّٰهُ وَإِذَا كَانَ الرَّجُلُ السُّوءُ أُجْلِسَ فِي قَبْرِهِ فَزِعًا مَسْعُوفًا فَيُقَالُ لَهُ فِيمَ كُنْتَ فَيَقُولُ لَا أَدْرِي فَيُقَالُ مَا هَذَا الرَّجُلُ الَّذِي كَانَ فِيكُمْ فَيَقُولُ سَمِعْتُ النَّاسَ يَقُولُونَ قَوْلًا فَقُلْتُ كَمَا قَالُوا فَتُفْرَجُ لَهُ فُرْجَةٌ قِبَلَ الْجَنَّةِ فَيَنْظُرُ إِلَىٰ زَهْرَتِهَا وَإِلَىٰ مَا فِيهَا فَيُقَالُ انْظُرْ إِلَىٰ مَا صَرَّفَ اللّٰهُ عَنْكَ ثُمَّ يُفْرَجُ لَهُ فُرْجَةٌ قِبَلَ النَّارِ فَيَنْظُرُ إِلَيْهَا يَحْطِمُ بَعْضُهَا بَعْضًا وَيُقَالُ هَذَا مَقْعَدُكَ مِنْ قِبَلِكَ عَلَى الشَّكِّ وَعَلَيْهِ مِتَّ وَعَلَيْهِ تُبْعَثُ إِنْ شَاءَ اللّٰهُ ثُمَّ يُعَذَّبُ.

ʿAbdullāh ibn Muhammad informed us: ʿAbd al-Qādir ibn Muhammad narrated to us: al-Ḥasan ibn ʿAlī narrated to us: Aḥmad ibn Jaʿfar al-Qaṭīʿī narrated to us: ʿAbdullāh ibn Aḥmad ibn Ḥanbal narrated to us: My father narrated to me: Yazīd ibn Hārūn narrated to us: Ibn Abī Dhi'b narrated to us from Muhammad ibn ʿAmr ibn ʿAṭā' from Dhakwān that ʿĀ'ishah i said, "A Jewish woman came and requested food. She said, 'Feed me, may Allah protect you from the trial of the Dajjāl and the trial of the punishment of the grave.' I kept her with me until the Messenger of Allah ﷺ came. I said to him, 'O Messenger of Allah, what is it that this Jewish woman is saying?' He said, 'What is she saying?'

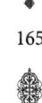

# 95 HADITH NINETY-FIVE

I said, 'She says, "May Allah protect you from the trial of the Dajjāl and from the trial of the punishment of the grave."' The Messenger of Allah ﷺ then stood up, raised and spread open his two hands, and sought refuge in Allah from the trial of the Dajjāl and from the trial of the punishment of the grave. Then he ﷺ said, 'As for the trial of the Dajjāl, no Prophet has come except that he warned his people of him. And I will warn you in a way that no Prophet (before) had warned his people. He is one-eyed. And Allah ﷻ is not one-eyed. Between his two eyes is written (the word) *kāfir*. Every believer will be able to read it. As for the trial of the grave, you will be tried through me and asked about me. If a man is pious, he will be sat up in his grave without intimidation or abuse. Then it will be said to him, "In what (situation) were you?" He will reply, "In Islam." It will be said, "Who is this man that was among you?" He will reply, "Muhammad, the Messenger of Allah ﷺ. He came with clear signs from Allah ﷻ. And we confirmed his truthfulness." An opening will then be made for him towards the Fire. He will look at it, with parts of it engulfing its other parts. It will be said to him, "Look towards that from which Allah ﷻ has saved you." Then an opening will be made for him towards Paradise. He will look at its radiance and what is in it. And it will be said to him, "This is your place in it." It will then be said, "You were upon certainty. You died upon it. And to it you will be resurrected if Allah so wills." "'If it is an evil man, he will be sat up in his grave with intimidation and force. It will be said to him, "In what (situation) were you?" He will say, "I do not know." It will be said, "Who is this man that was among you?" He will say, "I heard people saying something, so I said what they said." An opening will then be made for him towards Paradise. He will look at its radiance and what is in it. It will be said to him, "Look at what Allah ﷻ has diverted from you." Then an opening will be made for him towards the Fire. He will look towards it, with parts of it engulfing its other parts. It will be said to him, "This is your abode in it. You lived upon doubt, you died upon it, and upon it you will be resurrected if Allah so wills." Then he will be punished.'"[121]

121 *Musnad al-Imām Aḥmad*, Mu'assasah al-Risālah, hadith no. 25089.

# 96 HADITH NINETY-SIX

قَالَ مُحَمَّدُ بْنُ عَمْرٍو فَحَدَّثَنِي سَعِيدُ بْنُ مُعَاذٍ عَنْ أَبِي هُرَيْرَةَ عَنِ النَّبِيِّ صَلَّى اللَّهُ عَلَيْهِ وَسَلَّمَ قَالَ إِنَّ الْمَيِّتَ تَحْضُرُهُ الْمَلاَئِكَةُ فَإِذَا كَانَ الرَّجُلُ الصَّالِحُ قَالُوا اخْرُجِي أَيَّتُهَا النَّفْسُ الطَّيِّبَةُ كَانَتْ فِي الْجَسَدِ الطَّيِّبِ وَاخْرُجِي حَمِيدَةً وَأَبْشِرِي بِرَوْحٍ وَرَيْحَانٍ وَلاَ يَزَالُ يُقَالُ لَهَا ذٰلِكَ حَتَّى يُنْتَهَى بِهَا إِلَى السَّمَاءِ الَّتِي فِيهَا اللَّهُ تَعَالَى فَإِذَا كَانَ الرَّجُلُ السُّوءُ قَالُوا اخْرُجِي أَيَّتُهَا النَّفْسُ الْخَبِيثَةُ كَانَتْ فِي الْجَسَدِ الْخَبِيثِ اخْرُجِي مِنْهُ ذَمِيمَةً وَأَبْشِرِي بِحَمِيمٍ وَغَسَّاقٍ وَآخَرَ مِنْ شَكْلِهِ أَزْوَاجٍ فَلاَ يَزَالُ يُقَالُ لَهَا ذٰلِكَ حَتَّى تَخْرُجَ ثُمَّ يُعْرَجَ بِهَا إِلَى السَّمَاءِ فَيُسْتَفْتَحُ لَهَا فَيُقَالُ مَنْ هَذَا فَيُقَالُ فُلاَنٌ فَيُقَالُ لاَ مَرْحَبًا بِالنَّفْسِ الْخَبِيثَةِ الَّتِي كَانَتْ فِي الْجَسَدِ الْخَبِيثِ ارْجِعِي ذَمِيمَةً فَإِنَّهُ لاَ تُفْتَحُ لَكِ أَبْوَابُ السَّمَاءِ فَتُرْسَلُ مِنَ السَّمَاءِ ثُمَّ يَصِيرُ إِلَى الْقَبْرِ فَيُجْلَسُ الرَّجُلُ الصَّالِحُ فَيُقَالُ لَهُ وَيَرِدُ مِثْلَ مَا فِي حَدِيثِ عَائِشَةَ سَوَاءً وَيُجْلَسُ الرَّجُلُ السُّوءُ فَيُقَالُ لَهُ وَيَرِدُ مِثْلَ مَا فِي حَدِيثِ عَائِشَةَ سَوَاءً.

Muhammad ibn ʿAmr said: Saʿīd ibn Yasār narrated to me from Abū Hurayrah that the Prophet ﷺ said, "The dying person will be visited by Angels. If he is a pious man, they will say, 'Come out, O pure soul that dwelled in a pure chest. Come out being praiseworthy and receive glad tidings of rest and a pleasant fragrance.' They will continue to say that until it exits. Then they will rise with it to the Heavens and request they be opened for him. It will be said, 'Who is this?' It will be said, 'So and so.' It will be said, 'Welcome to the pure soul that dwelled in a pure chest. Enter being praiseworthy and receive glad tidings of rest, pleasant fragrances, and a Lord that is not angry.' They will continue to say that until he arrives at the heaven in which there is (the presence of) Allah ﷻ. "If the dying person is an evil man, they will say, 'Come out, O impure soul that dwelled in an impure chest. Come out from it blameworthy and receive the news of boiling water, pus, and other similar kinds of punishment.' They will continue to say that until it exits. Then, it will be raised to the Heavens and they will request it to be opened. It will be said, 'Who is this?' They will say, 'So and so.' It will be said, 'You are not welcome, O impure soul that dwelled in an impure chest. Return blameworthy, for the gates of Heaven will not be open for you.' So, he will be lowered from Heaven and placed in the grave. "The pious man will thereafter be sat up and it will be said to him '...'" (the narrator then related the matter similar to how it was related in the hadith of 'Ā'ishah). And the impious man will be sat up and it will be said to him '...'" (the narrator then related the matter similar to how it was related in the hadith of 'Ā'ishah).[122]

122 *Musnad al-Imām Aḥmad,* Mu'assasah al-Risālah, hadith no. 25090.

# 97 HADITH NINETY-SEVEN

هُدْبَةُ بْنُ خَالِدٍ ثَنَا أَبَانُ ثَنَا يَحْيَى بْنُ أَبِي كَثِيرٍ حَدَّثَنِي الْحَضْرَمِيُّ بْنُ لَاحِقٍ أَنَّ أَبَا صَالِحٍ السَّمَانُ حَدَّثَهُ عَنْ عَائِشَةَ أَنَّ النَّبِيَّ ﷺ دَخَلَ عَلَيْهَا وَهِيَ تَبْكِي فَقَالَ مَا يُبْكِيكِ قَالَتْ ذَكَرْتُ الدَّجَّالَ فَبَكَيْتُ قَالَ فَلَا تَبْكِ فَإِنَّهُ إِنْ يَخْرُجْ وَأَنَا حَيٌّ أَكْفِيكُمُوهُ وَإِنْ مِتُّ فَإِنَّ رَبِّي لَيْسَ بِأَعْوَرَ.

رَوَاهُ عَبْدُ اللهِ بْنُ أَحْمَدَ فِي السُّنَّةِ عَنْ هُدْبَةَ.

From Hudbah ibn Khālid: Abān narrated to us: Yaḥyā ibn Abī Kathīr narrated to us: al-Ḥaḍramī ibn Lāḥiq narrated to me: Abū Ṣāliḥ al-Sammān informed us that it was narrated to him about ʿĀʾishah that the Prophet ﷺ entered upon her while she was crying. He said, "What is making you cry?" I said, "I remembered the Dajjāl so I began to cry." He said, "Do not cry. For if he emerges while I am alive, I will suffice you all against him. And if I will have passed away, my Lord is not one-eyed."[123]

It was narrated by ʿAbdullāh ibn Aḥmad in *al-Sunnah* on the authority of Hudbah.



123 *Musnad al-Imām Aḥmad*, Muʾassasah al-Risālah, hadith no. 24467; *Muṣannaf Ibn Abī Shaybah*, vol. 15, p. 134; *Ṣaḥīḥ Ibn Ḥibbān*, Muʾassasah al-Risālah, hadith no. 6822.

# HADITH NINETY-EIGHT 98

أَخْبَرَنَا عَبْدُ اللهِ بْنُ مُحَمَّدٍ ثَنَا أَبُو طَالِبٍ الْيُوسُفِيُّ ثَنَا أَبُو عَلِيٍّ التَّمِيمِيُّ ثَنَا أَبُو بَكْرٍ الْقَطِيعِيُّ ثَنَا عَبْدُ اللهِ حَدَّثَنِي أَبِي ثَنَا يَحْيَى بْنُ سَعِيدٍ عَنْ عُيَيْنَةَ حَدَّثَنِي أَبِي عَنْ أَبِي بَكْرَةَ قَالَ قَالَ رَسُولُ اللهِ ﷺ الدَّجَّالُ أَعْوَرُ بِعَيْنِ الشِّمَالِ بَيْنَ عَيْنَيْهِ مَكْتُوبٌ كَافِرٌ يَقْرَأُهُ الْأُمِّيُّ وَالْكَاتِبُ.

'Abdullāh ibn Muhammad informed us: Abū Ṭālib al-Yūsufī narrated to us: Abū 'Alī al-Tamīmī narrated to us: Abū Bakr al-Qaṭī'ī narrated to us: 'Abdullāh narrated to us: My father narrated to me: Yaḥyā ibn Sa'īd narrated to us from 'Uyaynah: My father narrated to me that Abū Bakrah said, "The Messenger of Allah ﷺ said, 'The Dajjāl is blind of the left eye[124]. Between his eyes is written (the word) *kāfir*, which every illiterate or literate person will be able to read.'"[125]

124 There is an apparent contradiction between some hadiths that mention that the defective eye is his left eye and some that mention his right eye as being the defective eye. Each one is authentic. However, Qāḍī 'Iyāḍ offered a solution to this apparent contradiction, based on the fact that the majority of the narrations that mention the right eye use the word طافية, while the ones that mention the left eye use the word طافئة. The former indicates a lazy eye or one that bulges while the latter indicates an eye that is discolored and blind. The Qāḍī said, "So that we may join between the different narrations of all whose chains of transmission are authentic, we would say that it is the right eye. And it is neither putrid nor bulging. Rather it is dull and blind. The one that is like a glittering star – or like phlegm – is none other than the left eye" (al-Nawawī, Sharḥ *Ṣaḥīḥ Muslim*, vol. 2, p. 235).

125 *Musnad al-Imām Aḥmad*, Mu'assasah al-Risālah, hadith no. 20401.

# 99 HADITH NINETY-NINE

أَخْبَرَنَا حَبِيبُ بْنُ إِبْرَاهِيمَ وَمُحَمَّدُ بْنُ مُحَمَّدٍ ثَنَا مَحْمُودُ بْنُ إِسْمَاعِيلَ ثَنَا أَحْمَدُ بْنُ مُحَمَّدِ بْنِ الْحُسَيْنِ ثَنَا سُلَيْمُ بْنُ أَحْمَدَ بْنِ أَيُّوبَ الطَّبَرَانِيُّ ثَنَا مُحَمَّدُ بْنُ رُزَيْقِ بْنِ جَامِعٍ الْمِصْرِيُّ نَا عَمْرُو بْنُ سَوَادٍ السَّرْحِيُّ ثَنَا ابْنُ وَهْبٍ أَخْبَرَنِي يُونُسُ بْنُ يَزِيدَ عَنْ عَطَاءٍ الْخُرَاسَانِيِّ عَنْ يَحْيَى بْنِ أَبِي عَمْرٍو الشَّيْبَانِيِّ عَنْ عَمْرٍو الْحَضْرَمِيِّ مِنْ أَهْلِ حِمْصَ عَنْ أَبِي أُمَامَةَ الْبَاهِلِيِّ قَالَ خَطَبَنَا رَسُولُ اللهِ صَلَّى اللهُ عَلَيْهِ وَسَلَّمَ يَوْمًا وَكَانَ أَكْثَرُ خُطْبَتِهِ ذِكْرَ الدَّجَّالِ يُحَذِّرُنَا عَنْهُ حَتَّى فَرَغَ مِنْ خُطْبَتِهِ وَكَانَ فِيمَا قَالَ لَنَا يَوْمَئِذٍ إِنَّ اللهَ عَزَّ وَجَلَّ لَمْ يَبْعَثْ نَبِيًّا إِلَّا حَذَّرَهُ أُمَّتَهُ وَإِنِّي آخِرُ الْأَنْبِيَاءِ وَأَنْتُمْ آخِرُ الْأُمَمِ وَهُوَ خَارِجٌ فِيكُمْ لَا مَحَالَةَ فَإِنْ يَخْرُجْ وَأَنَا بَيْنَ أَظْهُرِكُمْ فَأَنَا حَجِيجُ كُلِّ مُسْلِمٍ وَإِنْ يَخْرُجْ فِيكُمْ بَعْدِي فَكُلُّ امْرِئٍ حَجِيجُ نَفْسِهِ وَاللهُ خَلِيفَتِي عَلَى كُلِّ مُسْلِمٍ وَإِنَّهُ يَخْرُجُ مِنْ خَلَّهٍ بَيْنَ الْعِرَاقِ وَالشَّامِ عَاثَ يَمِينًا وَشِمَالًا يَا عِبَادَ اللهِ اثْبُتُوا فَإِنَّهُ يَبْدَأُ بِقَوْلِ أَنَا نَبِيٌّ وَلَا نَبِيَّ بَعْدِي وَإِنَّهُ مَكْتُوبٌ بَيْنَ عَيْنَيْهِ كَافِرٌ يَقْرَأُهُ كُلُّ مُؤْمِنٍ فَلْيَتْفُلْ فِي وَجْهِهِ وَلْيَقْرَأْ بِفَوَاتِحِ سُورَةِ الْكَهْفِ. وَإِنَّهُ يُسَلَّطُ عَلَى نَفْسٍ مِنْ حَادِمَ فَيَقْتُلُهَا ثُمَّ يُحْيِيهَا وَإِنَّهُ لَا يَعْدُو ذَلِكَ وَلَا يُسَلَّطُ عَلَى نَفْسٍ غَيْرِهَا وَإِنَّ مِنْ فِتْنَتِهِ أَنَّ مَعَهُ جَنَّةً وَنَارًا فَنَارُهُ جَنَّةٌ وَجَنَّتُهُ نَارٌ فَمَنِ ابْتُلِيَ بِنَارِهِ فَلْيُغْمِضْ عَيْنَيْهِ وَلْيَسْتَعِنْ بِاللهِ تَكُونُ بَرْدًا وَسَلَامًا كَمَا كَانَتِ النَّارُ بَرْدًا وَسَلَامًا عَلَى إِبْرَاهِيمَ وَإِنَّ أَيَّامَهُ أَرْبَعُونَ يَوْمًا يَوْمًا كَسَنَةٍ وَيَوْمًا كَشَهْرٍ وَيَوْمًا كَجُمُعَةٍ وَيَوْمًا كَالْأَيَّامِ وَآخِرُ أَيَّامِهِ

# HADITH NINETY-NINE 99

كَالسَّرَابِ يُصْبِحُ الرَّجُلُ عِنْدَ بَابِ الْمَدِيْنَةِ فَيُمْسِيْ قَبْلَ أَنْ يَبْلُغَ بَابَهَا الْآخَرَ قَالَ فَكَيْفَ نُصَلِّيْ يَا رَسُوْلَ اللهِ فِيْ تِلْكَ الْأَيَّامِ الْقِصَارِ قَالَ تُقْدَرُوْنَ فِيْهَا كَمَا تُقْدَرُوْنَ الْأَيَّامَ الطِّوَالَ.

Ḥabīb ibn Ibrāhīm and Muhammad ibn Muhammad both informed us: Maḥmūd ibn Ismā'īl narrated to us: Aḥmad ibn Muhammad ibn al-Ḥusayn narrated to us: Sulaymān ibn Aḥmad ibn Ayyūb al-Ṭabarānī narrated to us: Muhammad ibn Ruzayq ibn Jāmi' al-Miṣrī narrated to us: 'Amr ibn Sawād al-Sarḥī informed us: Ibn Wahb narrated to us: Yūnus ibn Yazīd informed me from 'Aṭā' al-Khurāsānī from Yaḥyā ibn Abī 'Amr al-Shaybānī from 'Amr al-Ḥaḍramī – of the people of Homs – that Abū Umāmah al-Bāhilī said, "The Messenger of Allah ﷺ addressed us one day. The majority of his sermon was about the Dajjāl and warning us of him until we became frightened by his sermon. From that which he said to us on that day was, 'Indeed Allah ﷻ did not send any Prophet except that he warned his people of him. And I am the last of the Prophets and you are the last of the nations. He will undoubtedly emerge among you. If he emerges and I am among you, I will be the arbiter of every Muslim. If he emerges among you after me, each man must arbitrate for himself. And Allah is my *khalīfah* over every Muslim. He will emerge from one of the roads between Iraq and Syria. He will wreak havoc right and left. O servants of Allah, be firm! For he will begin by saying, "I am a Prophet." And there is no Prophet after me. Between his eyes is written (the word) *kāfir*. Every believer will be able to read it. So, spit in his face and recite Sūrah al-Kahf. He will attack a person that inflames him. He will kill him and then revive him. He will not do anything beyond that. And he will not attack any soul other than that one. From his trial is that he will have with him a garden and a fire. His fire is really a garden and his garden is really a fire. So, whoever is tested with his fire, let him close his eyes and seek help from Allah. It will become cool and safe just like the fire became cool and safe for Ibrāhīm. His days number forty: one day like a year, one day like a month, one day like a week, and one day like normal days. The rest of his days will be like the passing of a cloud. A man may start that day at one gate of Madinah and enter the night before reaching its other gate.' Some people said, 'How should we pray, O Messenger of Allah, during those short days?' He said, 'You should estimate like you estimate during the long days.'"[126]

126 Different versions of this hadith have been narrated in *Sunan Ibn Mājah*, Dār al-Risālah al-'Ālamiyyah, hadith no. 4077, *Ṣaḥīḥ Muslim*, hadith no. 2937 and others.

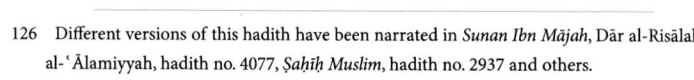

# HADITH ONE HUNDRED 100

أَخْبَرَنَا مُحَمَّدُ بْنُ مُحَمَّدٍ وَحَبِيبُ بْنُ إِبْرَاهِيمَ ثَنَا مَحْمُودُ بْنُ إِسْمَاعِيلَ أَنَا أَحْمَدُ بْنُ مُحَمَّدٍ ثَنَا سُلَيْمَانُ بْنُ أَحْمَدَ بْنِ أَيُّوبَ ثَنَا يَحْيَى بْنُ عَبْدِ الْبَاقِي الْأَدْنِيُّ ثَنَا ابْنُ عُمَيْرِ بْنِ النَّحَّاسِ ثَنَا ضَمْرَةُ عَنْ يَحْيَى بْنِ أَبِي عَمْرٍو الشَّيْبَانِيِّ عَنْ عَمْرِو بْنِ عَبْدِ اللهِ الْحَضْرَمِيِّ عَنْ أَبِي أُمَامَةَ الْبَاهِلِيِّ قَالَ خَطَبَنَا رَسُولُ اللهِ ﷺ فَذَكَرَ مِثْلَهُ.

Muhammad ibn Muhammad and Ḥabīb ibn Ibrāhīm informed us: Maḥmūd ibn Ismāʿīl narrated to us: Aḥmad ibn Muhammad informed us: Sulaymān ibn Aḥmad ibn Ayyūb narrated to us: Yaḥyā ibn ʿAbd al-Bāqī al-Adnā narrated to us: Ibn ʿUmayr ibn al-Nūḥas narrated to us: Ḍamrah narrated to us from Yaḥyā ibn Abī ʿAmr al-Shaybānī from ʿAmr ibn ʿAbdullāh al-Ḥaḍramī that Abū Umāmah al-Bāhilī said, "The Messenger of Allah ﷺ addressed us…" He then mentioned the same hadith as above.[127]



127 See previous footnote.

# 101 HADITH ONE HUNDRED ONE

أَخْبَرَنَا مُحَمَّدُ بْنُ مُحَمَّدٍ وَحَبِيبُ بْنُ إِبْرَاهِيمَ ثَنَا مَحْمُودُ بْنُ إِسْمَاعِيلَ ثَنَا أَحْمَدُ بْنُ مُحَمَّدٍ ثَنَا سُلَيْمَانُ بْنُ أَحْمَدَ بْنِ أَيُّوبَ ثَنَا جَعْفَرُ بْنُ أَحْمَدَ الشَّامِيُّ ثَنَا أَبُو كُرَيْبٍ ثَنَا فِرْدَوْسُ بْنُ الْأَشْعَرِيِّ عَنْ مَسْعُودِ بْنِ سُلَيْمَانَ عَنْ حَبِيبِ بْنِ أَبِي ثَابِتٍ عَنْ مُجَاهِدٍ عَنْ عَبْدِ اللَّهِ بْنِ عَمْرٍو عَنْ رَسُولِ اللَّهِ صَلَّى اللَّهُ عَلَيْهِ وَسَلَّمَ أَنَّهُ قَالَ فِي الدَّجَّالِ مَا شُبِّهَ مِنْهُ فَإِنَّ اللَّهَ لَيْسَ بِأَعْوَرَ يَخْرُجُ فَيَكُونُ فِي الْأَرْضِ أَرْبَعِينَ صَبَاحًا يَرِدُ مِنْهَا كُلَّ مَنْهَلٍ إِلَّا الْكَعْبَةَ وَبَيْتَ الْمَقْدِسِ وَالْمَدِينَةَ الشَّهْرُ كَالْجُمُعَةِ وَالْجُمُعَةُ كَالْيَوْمِ وَمَعَهُ جَنَّةٌ وَنَارٌ فَنَارُهُ جَنَّةٌ وَجَنَّتُهُ نَارٌ مَعَهُ جَبَلٌ مِنْ خُبْزٍ وَنَهْرٌ مِنْ مَاءٍ يَدْعُو بِرَجُلٍ لَا يُسَلِّطُهُ اللَّهُ إِلَّا عَلَيْهِ فَيَقُولُ مَا تَقُولُ فِيهِ فَيَقُولُ أَنْتَ عَدُوُّ اللَّهِ وَأَنْتَ الدَّجَّالُ الْكَذَّابُ فَيَدْعُو بِمِنْشَارٍ فَيَضَعُهُ حَذْوَ رَأْسِهِ فَيَشُقُّهُ حَتَّى يَقَعَ الْأَرْضَ ثُمَّ يُحْيِيهِ فَيَقُولُ لَهُ مَا تَقُولُ فِيهِ فَيَقُولُ وَاللَّهِ مَا كُنْتُ أَشَدَّ نُصْرَةٍ مِنِّي فِيكَ الْآنَ أَنْتَ عَدُوُّ اللَّهِ الدَّجَّالُ الَّذِي أَخْبَرَنَا عَنْكَ رَسُولُ اللَّهِ صَلَّى اللَّهُ عَلَيْهِ وَسَلَّمَ قَالَ فَيَهْوِي إِلَيْهِ بِسَيْفِهِ فَلَا يَسْتَطِيعُهُ فَيَقُولُ أَخِّرُوهُ عَنِّي. رَوَاهُ الطَّبَرَانِيُّ كَذَلِكَ وَهُوَ حَدِيثٌ غَرِيبٌ. أَخْبَرَنَاهُ أَحْمَدُ بْنُ سَلَامَةَ وَغَيْرُهُ عَنْ مُحَمَّدِ بْنِ أَبِي زَيْدٍ الْكَرَّانِيِّ أَنَا أَحْمَدُ ثَنَا مَحْمُودُ بْنُ إِسْمَاعِيلَ فَذَكَرَهُ. وَقَرَأْتُهُ عَلَى سُلَيْمَانَ بْنِ قُدَامَةَ أَنَا مُحَمَّدُ بْنُ عَبْدِ الْوَاحِدِ أَنَا مُحَمَّدُ بْنُ أَحْمَدَ الصَّيْدَلَانِيُّ أَنَا فَاطِمَةُ بِنْتُ عَبْدِ اللَّهِ أَنَا ابْنُ رِيذَةَ أَنَا سُلَيْمَانُ فَذَكَرَهُ.

# HADITH ONE HUNDRED ONE 101

Muhammad ibn Muhammad and Ḥabīb ibn Ibrāhīm informed us: Maḥmūd ibn Ismāʿīl narrated to us: Aḥmad ibn Muhammad narrated to us: Sulaymān ibn Aḥmad ibn Ayyūb narrated to us: Jaʿfar ibn Aḥmad al-Shāmī narrated to us: Abū Kurayb narrated to us: Firdaws ibn al-Ashʿarī narrated to us from Masʿūd ibn Sulaymān from Ḥabīb ibn Abī Thābit from Mujāhid from ʿAbdullāh ibn ʿAmr that the Messenger of Allah ﷺ said regarding the Dajjāl, "Do not be discouraged by him, for Allah ﷻ is not one-eyed. He will emerge and will remain on the Earth for forty days. He will enter every piece of land except the Kaʿbah, Jerusalem, and Madinah. A month will be like a week and a week like a day. He will have with him a garden and a fire. His fire is really a garden and his garden is really a fire. He will have a mountain of rice and a river of water. He will call a man. Allah will not allow him to attack anyone besides him. He will say, 'What do you say about me?' He will say, 'You are the enemy of Allah, the arch-liar, and the Dajjāl.' He will call for a large cutting blade, place it in the middle of his head and split him until he reaches the ground. Then, he will bring him back to life and say to him, 'What do you say about me (now)?' The man will reply, 'By Allah, I have not had more insight about you than I do now. You are the enemy of Allah, the Dajjāl about whom the Messenger of Allah ﷺ informed us.' He will attempt to strike him with his sword but will be unable. So, he will say, 'Distance him from me.'"[128] It was narrated this way by al-Ṭabarānī. It is a *gharīb* hadith. Aḥmad ibn Salamah and others informed us of it from Muhammad ibn Abī Zayd al-Karrānī: Aḥmad informed us: Maḥmūd ibn Ismā'īl narrated to us. Then he mentioned the hadith.

I also recited it to Sulaymān ibn Qudāmah: Muhammad ibn 'Abd al-Wāḥid informed us: Muhammad ibn Aḥmad al-Ṣaydalānī informed us: Fāṭimah bint 'Abdullāh informed us: Ibn Rabdhah informed us: Sulaymān al-Ṭabarānī informed us. Then he mentioned the hadith.



128 Al-Ṭabarānī, *al-Mu'jam al-Kabīr*, vol. 16, p. 215.

# 102 HADITH ONE HUNDRED TWO

أَخْبَرَنَا الْمُسْلِمُ بْنُ مُحَمَّدٍ الْقَيْسِيُّ كِتَابَةً عَنْ أَبِي طَاهِرٍ الْحَشْوِيِّ وَغَيْرِهِ عَنْ أَبِي عَلِيٍّ الْحَدَّادِ أَنَّ أَحْمَدَ بْنَ جَعْفَرٍ الْفَقِيهَ أَخْبَرَهُمْ أَنَا أَحْمَدُ بْنُ إِبْرَاهِيمَ الْقَصَّارُ أَنَا أَبُو أَحْمَدَ الْعَسَّالُ فِي كِتَابِ الْمَعْرِفَةِ لَهُ ثَنَا مُحَمَّدُ بْنُ أَيُّوبَ ثَنَا أَحْمَدُ بْنُ عِيسَى الْمِصْرِيُّ نَا ابْنُ وَهْبٍ أَخْبَرَنِي مَخْرَمَةُ بْنُ بُكَيْرٍ عَنْ أَبِيهِ عَنْ عُرْوَةَ قَالَ قَالَتْ أُمُّ سَلَمَةَ ذَكَرْتُ الْمَسِيحَ الدَّجَّالَ لَيْلَةً فَلَمْ يَأْتِنِي النَّوْمُ فَلَمَّا أَصْبَحْتُ دَخَلْتُ عَلَى رَسُولِ اللَّهِ صَلَّى اللَّهُ عَلَيْهِ وَسَلَّمَ فَأَخْبَرْتُهُ فَقَالَ لِي لَا تَفْعَلِي فَإِنَّهُ إِنْ يَخْرُجْ وَأَنَا فِيكُمْ يَكْفِيكُمُ اللَّهُ وَإِنْ يَخْرُجْ بَعْدَ أَنْ أَمُوتَ يَكْفِيكُمُ اللَّهُ بِالصَّالِحِينَ ثُمَّ قَامَ فَذَكَرَ الدَّجَّالَ فَقَالَ مَا مِنْ نَبِيٍّ إِلَّا قَدْ حَذَّرَ أُمَّتَهُ يَعْنِي مِنْهُ وَإِنِّي أُحَذِّرُكُمُوهُ إِنَّهُ أَعْوَرُ وَاللَّهُ لَيْسَ بِأَعْوَرَ.

هَذَا حَدِيثٌ جَيِّدُ الْإِسْنَادِ ضَيِّقُ الْمَخْرَجِ لَا يُعْرَفُ إِلَّا مِنْ هَذَا الْوَجْهِ.

Muslim ibn Muhammad al-Qaysī informed us in writing from Abū Ṭāhir al-Ḥashawī and others from Abī ʿAlī al-Ḥaddād that Aḥmad ibn Jaʿfar al-Faqīh informed them: Aḥmad ibn Ibrāhīm al-Qaṣṣār informed us: Abū Aḥmad al-ʿAssāl informed us in *Kitāb al-Maʿrifah*: Sulaymān ibn Ayyūb narrated to us: Aḥmad ibn Muhammad ibn Nāfiʿ al-Ṭaḥḥān al-Miṣrī narrated to us: Ibn Wahb informed us: Makhramah ibn Bukayr informed me from his father that ʿUrwah said, "Umm Salamah said, 'Al-Masīḥ al-Dajjāl was mentioned one night so I could not sleep. When morning came, I entered

# 102 HADITH ONE HUNDRED TWO

upon the Messenger of Allah ﷺ and informed him. He said to me, "Do not do that. For if he emerges and I am among you, Allah will suffice you by me. If he emerges after I die, Allah will suffice you by the pious." Then he mentioned the Dajjāl and said, "No Prophet came except that he warned his people about him. And I am warning you about him. He is one-eyed and Allah is not one-eyed."""[129]



129 Al-Ṭabarānī, *al-Mu'jam al-Kabīr*, vol. 23, p. 268.

# HADITH ONE HUNDRED THREE 103

أَخْبَرَنَا إِسْمَاعِيلُ بْنُ عَبْدِ الرَّحْمٰنِ بْنِ الْفَرَّاءِ أَنَا الْإِمَامُ أَبُو مُحَمَّدِ بْنِ قُدَامَةَ الْمَقْدِسِيُّ قَالَ أَخْبَرَنَا مُحَمَّدُ بْنُ عَبْدِ الْبَاقِي بْنِ أَحْمَدَ بْنِ سَلْمَانَ أَنَا أَبُو الْفَضْلِ أَحْمَدُ بْنُ الْحَسَنِ بْنِ خَيْرُوْنَ ح وَثَنَا يَحْيَى بْنُ ثَابِتٍ ثَنَا أَبِي قَالَا ثَنَا الْبَرْقَانِيُّ قَالَ قَرَأْتُ عَلَى أَبِي الْحَسَنِ مُحَمَّدِ بْنِ مَحْمُودِ بْنِ عَبْدِ اللَّهِ بْنِ عُبَيْدِ اللَّهِ الْمَحْمُودِيِّ بِمَرْوٍ حَدَّثَكُمْ أَبُو عَبْدِ اللَّهِ عَبْدُ الرَّحْمٰنِ بْنُ عَبْدِ اللَّهِ بْنِ أَبِي مَسْعُودٍ الْمَعْرُوْفُ بِالسَّاسَجَرْدِيِّ فِيْ مَدِيْنَةِ الدَّاخِلَةِ بِمَرْوٍ سَنَةَ خَمْسٍ وَّتِسْعِيْنَ وَمِائَتَيْنِ ثَنَا عَبْدَانُ عَبْدُ اللَّهِ بْنُ عُثْمَانَ بْنِ جَبَلَةَ بْنِ أَبِي رَوَّادٍ الْعَتَكِيُّ ثَنَا أَبُو حَمْزَةَ عَنْ قَيْسِ بْنِ وَهْبٍ الْهَمْدَانِيِّ عَنْ أَبِي الْوَدَّاكِ عَنْ أَبِي سَعِيْدٍ الْخُدْرِيِّ قَالَ قَالَ رَسُوْلُ اللَّهِ صَلَّى اللَّهُ عَلَيْهِ وَسَلَّمَ يَخْرُجُ الدَّجَّالُ فَيَتَوَجَّهُ قِبَلَهُ رَجُلٌ مِنَ الْمُسْلِمِيْنَ فَيَلْقَاهُ مَسَالِحُ الدَّجَّالِ فَيَقُوْلُوْنَ أَيْنَ تُرِيْدُ فَيَقُوْلُ إِلَى هٰذَا الَّذِيْ خَرَجَ فَيَقُوْلُوْنَ أَمَا تُؤْمِنُ بِرَبِّنَا فَيَقُوْلُ مَا بِرَبِّنَا خَفَاءٌ فَيَقُوْلُ اقْتُلُوْهُ فَيَقُوْلُ بَعْضُهُمْ لِبَعْضٍ أَلَيْسَ قَدْ نَهَاكُمْ رَبُّكُمْ أَنْ تَقْتُلُوْا أَحَدًا دُوْنَهُ فَيَنْطَلِقُوْنَ بِهِ إِلَى الدَّجَّالِ فَإِذَا رَآهُ الْمُؤْمِنُ قَالَ يَا أَيُّهَا النَّاسُ هٰذَا الدَّجَّالُ الَّذِيْ ذَكَرَهُ رَسُوْلُ اللَّهِ صَلَّى اللَّهُ عَلَيْهِ وَسَلَّمَ يَقُوْلُ الدَّجَّالُ خُذُوْهُ وَشَجُّوْهُ فَيُوَسِّعُ ظَهْرَهُ وَبَطْنَهُ ضَرْبًا وَيَقُوْلُ أَمَا تُؤْمِنُ بِيْ فَيَقُوْلُ أَنْتَ الْمَسِيْحُ الْكَذَّابُ فَيُؤْمَرُ بِهِ فَيُنْشَرُ بِالْمِنْشَارِ مِنْ مَفْرِقِ رَأْسِهِ حَتّٰى يُفَرَّقَ بَيْنَ رِجْلَيْهِ ثُمَّ يَمْشِي الدَّجَّالُ بَيْنَ الْقِطْعَتَيْنِ ثُمَّ يَقُوْلُ لَهُ قُمْ فَيَسْتَوِيْ قَائِمًا فَيَقُوْلُ لَهُ أَتُؤْمِنُ بِيْ فَيَقُوْلُ مَا ازْدَدْتُ فِيكَ

# 103 HADITH ONE HUNDRED THREE

إِلَّا بَصِيرَةً ثُمَّ يَقُولُ يَا أَيُّهَا النَّاسُ إِنَّهُ لَا يَفْعَلُ بَعْدِي بِأَحَدٍ مِنَ النَّاسِ مَا فَعَلَ بِي فَيَأْخُذُهُ الدَّجَّالُ لِيَذْبَحَهُ فَيَتَحَوَّلُ مَا بَيْنَ رَقَبَتِهِ إِلَى تَرْقُوَتِهِ نُحَاسًا فَلَا يَسْتَطِيعُ إِلَيْهِ سَبِيلًا فَيَأْخُذُ بِيَدَيْهِ وَرِجْلَيْهِ فَيَقْذِفُ بِهِ فَيَحْسَبُ النَّاسُ أَنَّمَا يَقْذِفُ إِلَى النَّارِ وَإِنَّمَا أُلْقِيَ فِي الْجَنَّةِ فَقَالَ رَسُولُ اللَّهِ صَلَّى اللَّهُ عَلَيْهِ وَسَلَّمَ هُوَ أَعْظَمُ النَّاسِ شَهَادَةً عِنْدَ رَبِّ الْعَالَمِينَ.

Ismāʿīl ibn ʿAbd al-Raḥmān ibn al-Farrāʾ informed us: Imam Abū Muhammad ibn Qudāmah al-Maqdisī informed us, saying: Muhammad ibn ʿAbd al-Bāqī ibn Aḥmad ibn Salmān informed us: Abū al-Faḍl Aḥmad ibn al-Ḥasan ibn Khayrūn informed us. And Yaḥyā ibn Thābit narrated to us: My father narrated to us, saying: al-Burqānī narrated to us, saying: I recited to Abū al-Ḥasan Muhammad ibn Maḥmūd ibn ʿAbdullāh ibn ʿUbayd Allāh al-Maḥmūdī in Merv: Abū ʿAbdillāh ʿAbd al-Raḥmān ibn ʿAbdullāh ibn Abī Masʿūd – famously known as al-Sāsajardī – narrates to you in the inner city of Merv in the year 295: ʿAbdān ʿAbdullāh ibn ʿUthmān ibn Jabalah ibn Abī Ruwwād al-ʿAtakī narrated to us: Abū Ḥamzah narrated to us from Qays ibn Wahb al-Hamdānī from Abū al-Waddāk that Abū Saʿīd al-Khudrī said, "The Messenger of Allah ﷺ said, 'The Dajjāl will emerge. Then a man from the Muslims will set out towards him. The Dajjāl's bodyguards will intercept him and say, "Where are you going?" He will say, "Towards the one who has emerged."

They will say, "Do you not believe in our lord?" He will say, "Our Lord is not hidden." They will say, "Kill him." However, one of them will say to the other, "Has your lord not forbidden you to kill anyone without (consulting) him?" So, they will go to the Dajjāl. When the believer sees him, he will say, "O people, this is the Dajjāl which the Messenger of Allah ﷺ mentioned." The Dajjāl will say, "Seize him and lay him flat." He will then be beaten on his back and his stomach. He (the Dajjāl) will say (again), "Do you not believe in me?" The man will say, "You are the lying Masīḥ." He will then order for him to be sawn from the top of his head to his groin area. Then, the Dajjāl will walk between the two pieces and will say to him, "Stand up straight." He will say to him, "Do you believe in me?" The man will reply, "I have only been increased in insight regarding you. O people, he will not do to anyone else among mankind what he has done to me." The Dajjāl will then seize him and attempt to slaughter him, but the entire area of his neck will become bronze. So, he will not be able to harm him. Subsequently, he will grab his two hands and two feet and throw him. The people will believe that he will have been cast into the Fire when in reality he will have been cast into Paradise.' Then the Messenger of Allah ﷺ said, 'He is the greatest of people in martyrdom in the estimation of the Lord of the worlds.'"[130]

130 *Ṣaḥīḥ Muslim*, hadith no. 938; Ibn Mandah, *al-Īmān*, hadith no. 937; *Musnad Abū Yaʿlā*, vol. 2,

# 104 HADITH ONE HUNDRED FOUR

أَخْبَرَنَا أَحْمَدُ بْنُ هِبَةُ اللهِ بِقِرَاءَتِي عَنِ ابْنِ رَوْحٍ أَنَّ تَمِيمَ بْنَ أَبِي سَعِيدٍ أَخْبَرَهُ أَنَا أَبُو سَعِيدٍ النَّجْرَذُ سَنَةَ تِسْعٍ وَّأَرْبَعِينَ وَأَرْبَعِمَائَةٍ نَا ابْنُ جَهْرَانَ أَنَا أَبُو يَعْلَى ثَنَا سُفْيَانُ بْنُ وَكِيعِ بْنِ الْجَرَّاحِ حَدَّثَنِي أَبِي عَنْ جَدِّي عَنْ قَيْسِ بْنِ وَهْبٍ عَنِ ابْنِ الْوَدَّاكِ عَنْ أَبِي سَعِيدٍ قَالَ رَسُولُ اللهِ ﷺ يَخْرُجُ الدَّجَّالُ فَيَتَوَجَّهُ قِبَلَهُ رَجُلٌ مِنَ الْمُسْلِمِينَ فَيَلْقَاهُ مَسَالِحُ الدَّجَّالِ فَيَقُولُونَ أَيْنَ تُرِيدُ أَيْنَ تَعْمَدُ فَيَقُولُ أَعْمَدُ إِلَى هٰذَا الَّذِي خَرَجَ. وَسَاقَ الْحَدِيثَ كَمَا تَرَاهُ.

وَأَخْبَرَنَا أَبُو الْمَعَالِي الْأَبَرْقُوهِيُّ أَنَا أَبُو سَهْلٍ الْبَيْرَمَوِيُّ حُضُورًا أَنْبَا شَهْرَدَارُ بْنُ شَيْرَوَيْهِ أَنَا أَحْمَدُ بْنُ عُمَرَ الْبَيِّعُ أَنَا حُمَيْدُ بْنُ الْمَأْمُونِ أَنَا أَحْمَدُ بْنُ عَبْدِ الرَّحْمٰنِ الْحَافِظُ ثَنَا مُحَمَّدُ بْنُ مَحْمُودٍ الْفَقِيهُ مِثْلَهُ.

صَحِيحٌ رَوَاهُ مُسْلِمٌ عَنْ مُحَمَّدِ بْنِ عَبْدِ اللهِ بْنِ قُهْزَاذَ عَنْ عَبْدَانَ وَرَوَاهُ شُرَيْكٌ عَنْ قَيْسِ بْنِ وَهْبٍ.

Aḥmad ibn Hibat Allāh informed us through my recitation from Ibn Rawḥ that Tamīm ibn Abī Saʿīd informed him: Abū Saʿīd al-Najradh informed us in the year 449: Ibn Jahrān

p. 534.

informed us: Abū Ya'lā informed us: Sufyān ibn Wakī' ibn al-Jarrāḥ narrated to us: My father narrated to me from my grandfather from Qays ibn Wahb from Ibn al-Waddāk from Abū Sa'īd: The Messenger of Allah ﷺ said, "The Dajjāl will emerge and a man from the Muslims will go towards him. The guards of the Dajjāl will intercept him and say, 'Where are you intending to go?' He will say, 'I intend to go to that one who has emerged.'" Then he mentioned the rest of the hadith, as stated in the previous narration.[131]

Abū al-Ma'ālī al-Abarqūhī informed us: Abū Sahl al-Bīramwī informed me while I was present: Shahr Dār ibn Shīrawayh related to us: Aḥmad ibn 'Umar al-Bay' informed us: Ḥumayd ibn al-Ma'mūn informed us: Aḥmad ibn 'Abd al-Raḥmān al-Ḥāfiẓ informed us: Muhammad ibn Maḥmūd al-Faqīh narrated to us a hadith similar to this.

It is an authentic hadith which was narrated by Muslim from Muhammad ibn 'Abdullāh al-Qahzāz from 'Abdān. Sharīk also narrated it from Qays ibn Wahb.



131 *Musnad Abū Ya'lā al-Mawṣilī*, vol. 2, p. 534.

# 105 HADITH ONE HUNDRED FIVE

عَبْدُ الرَّحْمٰنِ بْنُ يَزِيدَ بْنِ جَابِرٍ حَدَّثَنِي يَحْيَ بْنُ جَابِرٍ الطَّائِيُّ قَاضِي حِمْص حَدَّثَنِي عَبْدُ الرَّحْمٰنِ بْنُ حَنْدَرِيق حَدَّثَنِي أَبِي أَنَّهُ سَمِعَ النَّوَّاسَ بْنَ سَمْعَانَ الْكِلَابِيَّ يَقُولُ ذَكَرَ رَسُولُ اللهِ صَلَّى اللهُ عَلَيْهِ وَسَلَّمَ الدَّجَّالَ ذَاتَ غَدَاةٍ فَخَفَّضَ فِيهِ وَرَفَّعَ حَتّٰى ظَنَنَّا أَنَّهُ فِي طَائِفَةِ النَّخْلِ فَلَمَّا رُحْنَا إِلَي رَسُولِ اللهِ ﷺ عَرَفَ ذَلِكَ فِينَا فَقَالَ مَا شَأْنُكُمْ فَقُلْنَا يَا رَسُولَ اللهِ ذَكَرْتَ الدَّجَّالَ الْغَدَاةَ فَخَفَّضْتَ فِيهِ وَرَفَّعْتَ حَتّٰى ظَنَنَّا أَنَّهُ فِي طَائِفَةِ النَّخْلِ فَقَالَ غَيْرُ الدَّجَّالِ أَخْوَفُنِي عَلَيْكُمْ إِنْ يَخْرُجْ وَأَنَا فِيكُمْ فَأُحَجِّجُهُ دُونَكُمْ وَإِنْ يَخْرُجْ وَلَسْتُ فِيكُمْ فَامْرُؤٌ حَجِيجُ نَفْسِهِ وَاللهُ خَلِيفَتِي عَلٰى كُلِّ مُسْلِمٍ إِنَّهُ شَابٌّ قَطَطٌ عَيْنُهُ طَافِيَةٌ كَأَنِّي أُشَبِّهُ بِعَبْدِ الْعُزَّى بْنِ قَطَنٍ فَمَنْ رَآهُ مِنْكُمْ فَلْيَقْرَأْ فَوَاتِحَ سُورَةِ الْكَهْفِ إِنَّهُ يَخْرُجُ مِنْ خَلَّةٍ بَيْنَ الْعِرَاقِ وَالشَّامِ فَعَاثَ يَمِينًا وَعَاثَ شِمَالًا يَا عِبَادَ اللهِ اثْبُتُوا.

قُلْنَا يَا رَسُولَ اللهِ مَا لَبْثُهُ فِي الْأَرْضِ قَالَ أَرْبَعُونَ يَوْمًا يَوْمٌ كَسَنَةٍ وَيَوْمٌ كَشَهْرٍ وَيَوْمٌ كَجُمُعَةٍ وَسَائِرُ أَيَّامِهِ كَأَيَّامِكُمْ هٰذِهِ قُلْنَا فَذَلِكَ الْيَوْمُ كَسَنَةٍ أَيَكْفِينَا فِيهِ صَلَاةُ يَوْمٍ قَالَ اقْدُرُوا لَهُ قَدْرَهُ قُلْنَا فَمَا إِسْرَاعُهُ فِي الْأَرْضِ قَالَ كَالْغَيْثِ اسْتَدْبَرَتْهُ الرِّيحُ فَيَأْتِي الْقَوْمَ فَيَدْعُوهُمْ فَيُؤْمِنُونَ بِهِ وَيَسْتَجِيبُونَ لَهُ فَيَأْمُرُ السَّمَاءَ أَنْ تُمْطِرَ وَالْأَرْضَ أَنْ تُنْبِتَ فَتَرُوحُ عَلَيْهِمْ سَارِحَتُهُمْ أَطْوَلَ مَا كَانَتْ. وَزَادَ ابْنُ لَهِيعَةَ ضُرُوعًا وَأَمَدَّهُ خَوَاصِرَ ثُمَّ يَأْتِي

الْقَوْمَ فَيَدْعُوهُمْ فَيَرُدُّونَ عَلَيْهِ قَوْلَهُ فَيَنْصَرِفُ عَنْهُمْ فَيَتْبَعُهُ أَمْوَالُهُمْ فَيُصْبِحُونَ مُمْحِلِينَ مَا بِأَيْدِيهِمْ شَيْءٌ وَيَمُرُّ بِالْخَرِبَةِ فَيَقُولُ لَهَا أَخْرِجِي كُنُوزَكِ فَيَنْطَلِقُ يَتْبَعُهُ كُنُوزُهَا كَيَعَاسِيبِ النَّحْلِ ثُمَّ يَدْعُو رَجُلًا مُمْتَلِئًا شَبَابًا فَيَضْرِبُهُ بِالسَّيْفِ يَقْطَعُهُ جَزْلَتَيْنِ رَمْيَةَ الْغَرَضِ ثُمَّ يَدْعُوهُ فَيُقْبِلُ وَيَتَهَلَّلُ وَجْهُهُ.

فَبَيْنَمَا هُمْ كَذَلِكَ إِذْ بَعَثَ اللَّهُ الْمَسِيحَ بْنَ مَرْيَمَ فَيَنْزِلُ عِنْدَ الْمَنَارَةِ الْبَيْضَاءِ شَرْقِيَّ دِمَشْقَ بَيْنَ مِنْ وَذَلْسَرَ وَاضِعًا كَفَّيْهِ عَلَى أَجْنِحَةِ مَلَكَيْنِ فَإِذَا طَأْطَأَ رَأْسَهُ قَطَرَ وَإِذَا رَفَعَهُ تَحَدَّرَ مِنْهُ جُمَانٌ كَاللُّؤْلُؤِ وَلَا يَحِلُّ لِكَافِرٍ أَنْ يَجِدَ رِيحَ نَفَسِهِ إِلَّا مَاتَ وَنَفَسُهُ يَنْتَهِي حَيْثُ يَنْتَهِي طَرْفُهُ فَيَطْلُبُهُ حَتَّى يُدْرِكَهُ عِنْدَ بَابِ لُدٍّ فَيَقْتُلُهُ ثُمَّ يَأْتِي نَبِيُّ اللَّهِ عِيسَى ابْنُ مَرْيَمَ عَلَيْهِ السَّلَامُ قَوْمًا عَصَمَهُمُ اللَّهُ مِنْهُ فَيَمْسَحُ عَنْ وُجُوهِهِمْ وَيُحَدِّثُهُمْ بِدَرَجَاتِهِمْ فِي الْجَنَّةِ.

فَبَيْنَمَا هُمْ كَذَلِكَ إِذْ أَوْحَى اللَّهُ يَا عِيسَى إِنِّي قَدْ أَخْرَجْتُ عِبَادًا لِي لَا يَدَانِ لِأَحَدٍ بِقِتَالِهِمْ فَحَرِّزْ عِبَادِي إِلَى جَبَلِ الطُّورِ وَيَبْعَثُ اللَّهُ يَأْجُوجَ وَمَأْجُوجَ وَهُمْ كَمَا قَالَ اللَّهُ ﴿مِنْ كُلِّ حَدَبٍ يَنْسِلُونَ﴾. فَيَمُرُّ أَوَائِلُهُمْ عَلَى بُحَيْرَةِ طَبَرِيَّةَ فَيَشْرَبُونَ مَا فِيهَا فَيَمُرُّ آخِرُهُمْ فَيَقُولُونَ لَقَدْ كَانَ بِهَذِهِ مَرَّةً مَاءٌ

# 105 HADITH ONE HUNDRED FIVE

وَيُحصَرُ نَبِيُّ اللهِ عِيسَى وَأَصْحَابُهُ حَتَّى يَكُونَ رَأْسُ الثَّوْرِ لِأَحَدِهِمْ خَيْرًا مِنْ مِئَةِ دِينَارٍ لِأَحَدِكُمُ الْيَوْمَ فَيَرْغَبُ عِيسَى إِلَى اللهِ فَيُرْسِلُ عَلَيْهِمُ النَّغَفَ فِيْ رِقَابِهِمْ فَيُصْبِحُوْنَ فَرْسَى كَمَوْتِ نَفْسٍ وَاحِدَةٍ وَيَهْبِطُ عِيسَى وَأَصْحَابُهُ فَلَا يَجِدُوْنَ فِيْ الْأَرْضِ مَوْضِعَ شَجَرَةٍ إِلَّا مَلَأَهُ زَهَمُهُمْ وَنَتْنُهُمْ وَدِمَاؤُهُمْ فَيَرْغَبُ نَبِيُّ اللهِ وَأَصْحَابُهُ إِلَى اللهِ فَيُرْسِلُ اللهُ عَلَيْهِمْ طَيْرًا كَأَعْنَاقِ الْبُخْتِ فَتَحْمِلُهُمْ فَتَطْرَحُهُمْ حَيْثُ شَاءَ اللهُ ثُمَّ يُرْسِلُ اللهُ تَعَالَى مَطَرًا لَا يَكُنُّ مِنْهُ بَيْتُ مَدَرٍ وَلَا وَبَرٍ فَيَغْسِلُ الْأَرْضَ حَتَّى يَتْرُكَهَا كَالزَّلَفَةِ ثُمَّ يُقَالُ لِلْأَرْضِ أَنْبِتِي ثَمَرَتَكِ وَرُدِّي بَرَكَتَكِ فَيَوْمَئِذٍ تَأْكُلُ الْعِصَابَةُ مِنَ الرُّمَّانَةِ فَتُشْبِعُهُمْ وَيَسْتَظِلُّوْنَ بِقِحْفِهَا الرُّسُلُ حَتَّى أَنَّ اللِّقْحَةَ مِنَ الْإِبِلِ تَكْفِي الْفِئَامَ مِنَ النَّاسِ وَاللِّقْحَةَ مِنَ الْبَقَرِ تَكْفِي الْقَبِيلَةَ مِنَ النَّاسِ وَاللِّقْحَةَ مِنَ الْغَنَمِ تَكْفِي الْفَخِذَ مِنَ النَّاسِ.

فَبَيْنَمَا هُمْ كَذَلِكَ إِذْ بَعَثَ اللهُ رِيحًا طَيِّبَةً تَحْتَ آبَاطِهِمْ فَتَقْبِضُ رُوحَ كُلِّ مُسْلِمٍ وَيَبْقَى سَائِرُ النَّاسِ يَتَهَارَجُوْنَ كَمَا تَتَهَارَجُ الْحُمُرُ فَعَلَيْهِمْ تَقُومُ السَّاعَةُ..

أَخْرَجَهُ مُسْلِمٌ وَزَادَ فِيهِ بْنُ حُجْرٍ وَغَيْرُهُ عَنِ الْوَلِيدِ بْنِ مُسْلِمٍ نَا عَبْدُ الرَّحْمٰنِ بْنُ يَزِيدَ بْنِ جَابِرٍ فِيْ ذِكْرِ يَأْجُوجَ وَمَأْجُوجَ ثُمَّ يَسِيرُوْنَ حَتَّى

يَنْتَهُوْنَ إِلَى جَبَلِ بَيْتِ الْمَقْدِسِ فَيَقُوْلُوْنَ قَدْ قَتَلْنَا مَنْ فِيْ الْأَرْضِ فَلْنَقْتُلْ مَنْ فِيْ السَّمَاءِ فَيَرْمُوْنَ بِنَشَابِهِمْ إِلَى السَّمَاءِ فَيَرُدُّ اللهِ عَلَيْهِمْ نَشَابَهُمْ مَخْضُوْبَةً دَمًا.

وَأَخْبَرَتْنَاهُ سِتُّ الْأَهْلِ بِنْتُ عَلْوَانَ أَنَا الْبَهَاءُ عَبْدُ الرَّحْمٰنِ أَنَا عَبْدُ الْحَقِّ أَنَا اِبْنُ خَشِيْشٍ أَنَا أَبُوْ عَلِيٍّ الْبَزَّازُ أَنَا أَبُوْ عَمْرٍو الدَّقِيْقِيُّ ثَنَا حَنْبَلٌ ثَنَا الْهَيْثَمُ بْنُ خَارِجَةَ الْمَرْوَرُّوْذِيُّ ثَنَا عَبْدُ اللهِ بْنُ عَبْدِ الرَّحْمٰنِ بْنِ يَزِيْدَ بْنِ جَابِرٍ سَمِعْتُ أَبِيْ يُحَدِّثُ عَنْ يَحْيَ بْنِ جَابِرٍ فَذَكَرَ الْحَدِيْثَ بِطُوْلِهِ نَحْوًا مِنْهُ.

From ʿAbd al-Raḥmān ibn Yazīd ibn Jābir: Yaḥyā ibn Jābir al-Ṭāʾī the judge of Homs, narrated to me: ʿAbd al-Raḥmān ibn Ḥandarīq narrated to me: My father narrated to me that he heard al-Nawwās ibn Samʿān al-Kilābī say, "The Messenger of Allah ﷺ mentioned the Dajjāl one morning. He was lowering and raising his voice until we believed that he was in the area of the date palm trees. When we went to the Messenger of Allah ﷺ, he noticed that in us. So, he said, 'What is the matter with you?' We said, 'O Messenger of Allah, you mentioned the Dajjāl this morning and you were lowering and raising your voice until we believed that he was in the area of the date palm trees.' He said, 'It is something other than the Dajjāl that worries me about you. If he emerges and I am among you, I will contend with him on your behalf. If he emerges and I am not among you, then a man must contend for himself. And Allah is my *khalīfah* over every Muslim. He is a young, curly-headed man. His eye bulges. It is as if he resembles 'Abd al-'Uzzā ibn Qaṭan to me. If any one of you sees him, let him read the opening of Sūrah al-Kahf. He will emerge from one of the roads between Iraq and Syria. And he will wreak havoc right and left. O servants of Allah, be firm.' We said, 'O Messenger of Allah, how long will he remain on the Earth?' He said, 'Forty days: one day like a year, one like a month, one like a week, and the rest of his days like normal days.' We said, 'On the day that is like a year, will the prayers of one day suffice us?' He said, 'Rather, estimate their timings.' We said, 'How fast will he move on the Earth?' He said, 'Like the rain clouds pushed by the wind. He will come to one people and call them. They will believe in him and answer his call. So, he will command the sky to rain and the Earth will sprout forth many plants. Their livestock will return to them more plentiful than before (Ibn Lahī'ah added, 'fattened with their waists enlarged').

"'Then, he will come to another people and call them. However, they will reject him. So, he will turn away from them and their possessions will leave them and they will wake up bankrupt, having nothing in their hands. He will pass by a ruin and say to it, "Bring out your treasures." Its treasures will emerge and follow him like bees to their queen. Then, he will call a man brimming with youth. He will strike him with his sword and cut him into two pieces, placing them at a distance from each other, similar to the archer and his target. Then, he will call him and he will come with his face brimming with laughter. While they are in that condition, Allah will send al-Masīḥ ibn Maryam. He will descend near the white minaret in the Eastern part of Damascus, wearing two yellow garments and placing his two palms on the wings of two Angels. When he lowers his head it will drip. And when he raises it, drops like pearls will scatter from it. No disbeliever will be allowed to smell the scent of his breath except that he will die. His breath will reach as far as his eyes can see. He will seek him (the Dajjāl) out until he catches him at the Gate of Ludd. He will kill him. Then, the Prophet of Allah, 'Īsā ibn Maryam n will approach a people whom Allah had protected. He will anoint their faces and inform them of their ranks in Paradise. While they are in that situation, Allah will inspire him, "O 'Īsā, I have caused to emerge some servants of Mine that no one can stand to fight. So, take shelter with My servants in Mount Ṭūr." Allah will then send forth Ya'jūj and Ma'jūj. They will, as Allah says, descend from every slope[132]. The first of them will pass by Lake Tiberias (Sea of Galilee). They will drink from it and the last of them will pass by it and say, "This used to be water."

"'They will besiege the Prophet of Allah 'Īsā and his companions until the head of an ox will, on that day, be more desirable for one of them than one hundred dinars to one of you today. 'Īsā will then plead with Allah and He will send a worm against them that will affect their necks. They will all die at once as a single soul. 'Īsā and his companions will then descend but they will not find any place the size of a tree except that it will be filled with their stench, corpses, and blood. So, the Prophet of Allah and his companions will beseech Allah. Allah ﷻ will then send a flock of birds with necks like camels. They will carry them off and cast them wherever Allah wills. Then Allah ﷻ will send rain, and no house made of mud or clay will be left standing. The entire Earth will be cleansed until it gleams like glass. Then, it will be said to the Earth, "Bring out your fruit and give forth your blessing." That day, an entire clan will eat from a single pomegranate. It will fill their stomachs and they will shade themselves in its shell. They will be blessed with leisure to the extent that the udder of a she-camel will give enough milk

132 *Al-Anbiyā'*, 96.

for a number of mouths, the udder of the cow will suffice a tribe, and the udder of a sheep will suffice a clan. While they are in that situation, Allah will send a blessed wind which will affect their axillae. It will take the spirit of every Muslim and only the worst of mankind will remain. They will have sexual relations openly just as donkeys do. It is upon these people that the Hour will be established.'"[133]

Muslim narrated it. Ibn Ḥajar and others made additions from al-Walīd ibn Muslim: ʿAbd al-Raḥmān ibn Yazīd ibn Jābir informed us in mention of Ya'jūj and Ma'jūj: "Then, they will travel until they come to the mountain in Jerusalem. They will say, 'We have killed those in the Earth. Let us kill those in Heaven. They will shoot their arrows towards the sky. And Allah will return it to them seemingly stained with blood."

Sitt al-Ahl bint ʿAlwān informed us of it, saying: Abū ʿAmr al-Daqīqī informed us: Ḥanbal narrated to us: al-Haytham ibn Khārijah al-Marwarūdhī narrated to us: ʿAbdullāh ibn ʿAbd al-Raḥmān ibn Yazīd ibn Jābir narrated to us: I heard my father narrating from Yaḥyā ibn Jābir. Then he mentioned the hadith in its entirety with similar wording as above.

133 *Ṣaḥīḥ Muslim*, hadith no. 2937; *Sunan Abī Dāwūd*, Dār al-Risālah al-ʿĀlamiyyah, hadith no. 4321; *Sunan al-Tirmidhī*, Mu'assasah al-Risālah, hadith no. 2390.

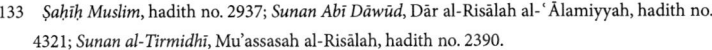

# 106 HADITH ONE HUNDRED SIX

الرُّوْيَانِيُّ فِي مُسْنَدِهِ ثَنَا عَبْدُ اللهِ بْنُ هَارُوْنَ الْفَرَوِيُّ حَدَّثَنِي قُدَامَةُ بْنُ مُحَمَّدٍ الْخَشْرَمِيُّ عَنْ أَبِيْهِ عَنْ بُكَيْرِ بْنِ عَبْدِ اللهِ الْأَشَجِّ عَنِ ابْنِ شِهَابٍ قَالَ أَنَسُ بْنُ مَالِكٍ حَدَّثَنِي رَسُوْلُ اللهِ ﷺ أَنَّهُ أُسْرِيَ بِهِ قَبْلَ أَنْ يَخْرُجَ إِلَى الْمَدِيْنَةِ بِسَنَةٍ فَقَالَ يَا أَنَسُ إِنَّا مَعَاشَرَ الْأَنْبِيَاءِ لَا نَتَوَضَّأُ لِلصَّلَاةِ تَنَامُ أَعْيُنُنَا وَلَا تَنَامُ قُلُوْبُنَا تُنَاجِي رَبَّنَا بَيْنَا أَنَا عَلَى ذٰلِكَ جَاءَنِي جِبْرِيْلُ وَإِسْرَافِيْلُ بِالْبُرَاقِ قُلْتُ يَا رَسُوْلَ اللهِ صِفْهَا لِي قَالَ رَأْسُهَا مِنْ لُؤْلُؤَةٍ بَيْضَاءَ وَرِكَابُهَا مِنْ زَبَرْجُدَةٍ خَضْرَاءَ وَهُوَ مِنْ يَاقُوْتِهِ حَمْرَاءَ أَجْنَابُهَا مَا بَيْنَ السَّمَاوَاتِ ثُمَّ طَوَيْتُ إِلَى الْأَرْضِ فَاسْتَدَقَّ جِبْرِيْلُ السَّمَاءَ الدُّنْيَا فَقِيْلَ مَنْ مَّعَكَ قَالَ مَنْ مَعَكَ قَالَ مُحَمَّدٌ خَاتَمُ النَّبِيِّيْنَ قَالُوْا مَرْحَبًا بِالنَّبِيِّ الْمُبَارَكِ الْمَيْمُوْنِ. إِلَى أَنْ قَالَ ثُمَّ ذَهَبُوْا بِي إِلَى السَّمَاءِ الثَّالِثَةِ فَإِذَا بِأَبِي آدَمَ فِيْهَا وَمُوْسٰى وَعِيْسٰى وَإِبْرَاهِيْمَ فَقَالَ آدَمُ أَجِدُهُ مَكْتُوْبًا فِي يَمِيْنِي مُبَارَكٌ مَيْمُوْنٌ وَإِذَا أَنَا بِمُوْسٰى أَشْعَرُ أَهْلَبُ جَعْدٌ كَأَنَّ رَأْسَهُ تَقْطُرُ وَرَأَيْتُ عِيْسٰى حَدِيْدَ الْبَصَرِ ذَا بَطَنٍ أَشْبَهُ النَّاسِ بِهِ عُرْوَةُ بْنُ مَسْعُوْدٍ الثَّقَفِيُّ وَرَأَيْتُ إِبْرَاهِيْمَ أَشْبَهُ النَّاسِ بِهِ أَنَا وَرَأَيْتُ الْأَعْوَرَ الدَّجَّالَ كَأَنَّ عَيْنَهُ عِنَبَةٌ طَافِيَةٌ أَشْبَهُ النَّاسِ بِهِ عَبْدُ الْعُزَّى بْنُ قَطَنٍ. ثُمَّ ذُهِبَ بِي إِلَى بَيْتِ الْمَقْدِسِ فَأَمَّمْتُ النَّبِيِّيْنَ كُلَّهُمْ صَلَّيْتُ بِهِمُ الْمَصْبَحَ وَالظُّهْرَ وَالْعَصْرَ وَالْعِشَاءَ وَالْعَتَمَةَ ثُمَّ رُجِعْتُ إِلَى السَّمَاءِ فَسَأَلْتُ رَبِّيْ فَأَعْطَانِي مَا رَضِيْتُ بِهِ ثُمَّ هُبِطْتُ إِلَى الْأَرْضِ مَعِي جِبْرِيْلُ فَلَمَّا صَلَّيْتُ الصُّبْحَ

# HADITH ONE HUNDRED SIX 106

خَطَبْتُ النَّاسَ عَلَى الْمِنْبَرِ ثُمَّ قُلْتُ يَا مَعْشَرَ قُرَيْشٍ إِنِّيْ أُسْرِيَ بِي اللَّيْلَةَ وَذَكَرَ الْحَدِيْثَ بِطُوْلِهِ. هٰكَذَا حَدِيْثٌ مَوْضُوْعٌ رَوَاهُ أَبُوْ مُوْسَى الْمَدِيْنِيُّ فِيْ الطِّوَالَاتِ وَقَالَ هٰذَا حَدِيْثٌ غَرِيْبُ الْإِسْنَادِ شَاذُّ الْمَتْنِ مَعَ شُهْرَةِ رُوَاتِهِ خَالَفَ فِيْ عَامَّةِ أَلْفَاظِهِ الرِّوَايَاتَ الْمَشْهُوْرَةَ.

قُلْتُ مِنْ شُهْرَةِ رُوَاتِهِ أَقْدَمْتُ عَلَى أَنَّهُ مَوْضُوْعٌ وَالْخَشْرَمِيُّ قَدْ رَوَى لَهُ النَّسَائِيُّ وَضَعَّفَهُ ابْنُ حِبَّانَ وَأَبُوْهُ نَكِرَةٌ لَا تُعْرَفُ كَأَنَّهُ خَلَطَةٌ بِكَلَامِ الطُّرُقِيَّةِ.

From al-Rūyānī in his *Musnad*: ʿAbdullāh ibn Hārūn al-Farawī narrated to us: Qudāmah ibn Muhammad al-Khashramī narrated to me from his father from Bukayr ibn ʿAbdullāh al-Ashajj from Ibn Shihāb that Anas ibn Mālik said, "The Messenger of Allah ﷺ related to me that he was made to travel on his journey one year before he left for Madinah. He said, 'O Anas, we Prophets do not perform ablution for prayer. Our eyes sleep, but our hearts do not sleep. They commune with our Lord. While I was in that state, Jibrīl and Isrāfīl came with the Burāq.' I said, 'O Messenger of Allah, describe it to me.' He said, 'Its head is like a white pearl. Its stirrups are of green emeralds. It is from red rubies. Its flanks fill that which is between the

Heavens and the Earth. Then, I traversed the Earth quickly and Jibrīl knocked on the sky of the Earth. It was said, "Who is with you?" He said, "Muhammad, the Seal of the Prophets." They said, "Welcome to the blessed, protected Prophet…'" Until he said, 'Then, they sent me to the third Heaven. There I met my father Adam. In it are Mūsā, 'Īsā, and Ibrāhīm. Adam said, "I find him written on my right hand, blessed and protected." Then I met Mūsā. He was dark-skinned with kinky hair, as if his head were pearls. I saw 'Īsā with a piercing sight and a belly. The person that resembles him most is 'Urwah ibn Mas'ūd al-Thaqafī. I also saw Ibrāhīm. The person that resembles him most is I. I also saw the one-eyed Dajjāl. It was as if his eye was a bulging grape. The person that resembles him most is 'Abd al-'Uzzā ibn Qaṭan. Then, I was taken to Jerusalem and I led all the Prophets in prayer. I led them in the dawn prayer, as well as Ẓuhr, 'Asr, Maghrib, and 'Ishā. Then, I returned to the Heavens and I asked my Lord and He gave me that which satisfied me. Then, I descended to the Earth along with Jibrīl. When I prayed the dawn prayer, I addressed people from the minbar. And then I said, "O Quraysh. I was taken last night on a journey…'" and he mentioned the hadith in its entirety."

This hadith is fabricated. Abū Mūsā al-Madīnī narrated it in *al-Muṭawwalāt*. He said, "This hadith's chain of